CONTENTS

Editor's Welcome 2

Choosing the Design That's Right for You 3

10 Most Popular Features of a Good Home Design 4

Cost-Saving Tips for Building a Home in the 90's 5

The "Source 1" Plan Package — Complete Construction Blueprints 12

What You Need to Know Before You Order 14

Ordering Blueprints 15

Country-Style Home Plans Collection 7

    Photo Gallery — Outstanding Country Homes in Living Color 7

    One-Stories from 1,400 to 2,000 Square Feet 17

    One-Stories from 2,000 to 5,000 Square Feet 59

    New Releases: One-Stories C-1

    New Releases: Two-Stories C-12

    Two-Stories from 1,000 to 2,000 Square Feet 113

    Two-Stories from 2,000 to 4,500 Square Feet 145

EDITOR'S WELCOME

Welcome to Home Designs for Country-Style Living, Volume One. This entire book is devoted to showcasing home plans with that "country" look and feel that is so highly prized by so many families in today's society — whether they live in urban, suburban or rural settings.

To create this book, we studied more than 4,000 home plans from 35 of America's leading residential designers. We also carefully reviewed plan sales statistics from the past five years to select only the most popular country-style homes, so you are assured of seeing proven plans that have stood the test of time and are likely to continue to be popular in the coming decades.

The major portion of this book is made up of such proven plans. However, there is also an exciting section of 32 fresh, innovative designs that promise to be popular country-style homes in the near future.

As you page through Home Designs for Country-Style Living, Volume One, you'll see over 200 eye-catching designs, ranging in size from about 1,000 to nearly 5,000 square feet, both one- and two-stories.

Whether you live in the city, suburbs or a new development along the eastern, western or southern coastlines, in the spectacular mountains that make up the great Appalachians, Rockies, Cascades, and Sierra Nevadas, or among the hills, rivers and valleys of the great Midwestern plains — wherever you live, and whatever your lifestyle, you're bound to find your dream home in this book.

At HomeStyles "SOURCE 1" Designers' Network, we not only design home plans, we build dreams. For 45 years (since 1946), we've supplied more than 175,000 home plans to professional builders, home owners, and do-it-yourselfers. All have shared the common goal of building their dream home. The tremendous variety of designs represented in this book allows you to choose the home that best suits your lifestyle, budget, and building site.

Keep in mind that the most important part of a home design is the floor plan — the layout and flow of the rooms. If the floor plan excites you, minor changes are easily made by qualified professionals. Also, exterior styling and appearance can be easily modified. Wood siding can be changed to shakes or even to stucco, for example.

Window and trim styles can also be changed. The only limits to creative customizing are your own taste and ingenuity.

As you let your dreams run wild, you'll discover one of the most exciting aspects about this book is the tremendous savings that our home plans give to you. Custom designs cost thousands of dollars, usually 5% to 15% of the cost of construction. The design costs for a $100,000 home, for example, can range from $5,000 to $15,000.

A "SOURCE 1" plan costs only $190 to $420 depending on the size of the home and the number of sets of blueprints that you order. When you order a "SOURCE 1" plan, you save the money you need to truly build your dream — to add a deck, swimming pool, beautiful kitchen, elegant master bedroom, luxurious bathroom, or other extras.

You can be assured of the quality of "SOURCE 1" plans. All of the blueprints are designed by licensed architects or members of the AIBD (American Institute of Building Designers). Each plan is designed to meet the nationally recognized building codes in effect, at the time and place that they were drawn.

Please note that all "SOURCE 1" plans are designed to meet the specifications of seismic zones I or II. Because the United States has such temendous variety in geography and climate, each county and municipality will have its own codes, ordinances, zoning requirements, and building regulations.

Therefore, depending on where you live, your plan may need to be modified to comply with your local building requirements — snow loads, energy codes, seismic zones, etc. If you need information or have questions regarding your specific requirements, call your local contractor, municipal building department, lumber yard, the AIBD (1-800-366-2423), or the National Association of Home Builders (NAHB) (1-800-368-5242).

Building a home is truly the American dream. This book includes articles on how to select the right home design, offers money-saving tips on cutting construction costs, and most importantly, contains over 200 new, up-to-date and best-selling home designs.

"SOURCE 1" doesn't just design homes, we build dreams! We hope that this book brings you one step closer to building yours.

CHOOSING THE DESIGN THAT'S RIGHT FOR YOU

For most of us, our home is the largest investment we will ever make. As a result, the style and type of home that we build is largely an economic decision. But of equal importance are issues of lifestyle, personal taste, and self-expression. Inevitably, our home is both our castle and our captor. We invest in it with the incomes that we earn from our weekday labor, and on the weekends, we invest in it with our saws, hammers, paintbrushes, and lawn tools. Our homes are truly an all-consuming labor of love.

Recognizing that love is in the eyes of the beholder, the following is a helpful guide to follow as you search for your dream home.

BUDGET

As a general rule, building a home costs between $60 and $100 per square foot of living space. However, as with most rules, the exceptions are greater than the rule. The greatest variables are land costs, labor and material costs, and individual tastes and style. The best bet is to contact your local builders association, lumberyard, or contractor.

Once you have an idea of what you can afford, determine any changes that you foresee in your income over the next five to ten years. For many, the future holds a greater income and therefore the possibility of a larger house. For others — young parents considering part-time work or empty-nesters soon to retire, the future may hold a reduction in income. Keep these considerations in mind as you evaluate your home plan needs.

LIFESTYLE

Just as your income may change, so too may your lifestyle. Select a plan that is flexible, versatile and adaptable. Young families may need a design that allows for expansion or flexibility in the floor plan. A 10' x 10' nursery may be adequate for a young child but will be terribly cramped for a teenager. On the other hand, a nursery today may become a den tomorrow.

For empty-nesters, there are other considerations. Children leave but they also return with friends, spouses, and grandchildren. The flexibility of the home design is a major consideration in dealing with these changes.

Your final lifestyle consideration is "aging." As we get older stairs become more difficult, doors are harder to open, and kitchens and bathrooms become more difficult to manage (especially in a wheelchair). If you plan on aging with your home, be sure to design your home so that it ages with you. Wider hallways, reinforced bathrooms for handgrips and railings, and gradual slopes in stairways are easy and less expensive to install at the time of construction. Renovating your home for wheelchair accessibility or handicapped living can be extremely costly down the line.

"Does the kitchen have a nook or breakfast bar?"

"Do we want a 'Great Room'?"

"Is there expansion space — bonus room, unfinished basement or attic?"

"How will it fit on our lot?"

"As we get older, will we want our home to be handicap accessible?"

"Is there enough storage space?"

"Can we add on later — a sunroom, deck or porch?"

"Do we want the master bedroom close to the kids or as far away as possible?"

"Can we afford it?"

"Where do I want the utility room — off the garage, near the kitchen or bedrooms, or in the basement?"

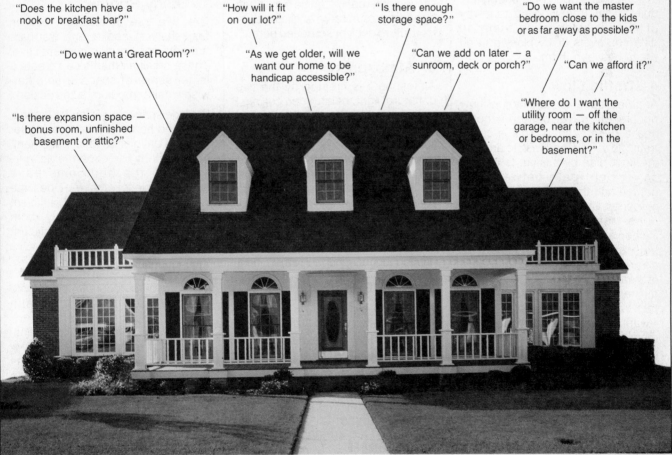

Plan E-3000

10 Most Popular Elements of a Good Home Design

1. Eye-Catching Exterior

Your house is a form of self-expression. Whether simple or subdued, stately or elegant, the exterior creates the first impression of your home. Does the exterior appearance of the home suit your tastes? If not, will changing the exterior materials or the color help?

2. Entryway Warmth

An inviting entryway sets the tone and atmosphere of your home. Does the entry have ample closet storage? Are the entrances covered or sheltered from rain or snow?

3. Zoning

There are three major zones in each home: working zones — kitchen, utility room, garage, bathrooms, and entryways; living zones — the living room, dining room, nook, family room, and/or Great Room; quiet zones — master bedroom, secondary bedrooms, library, den, and study.

As you look at your home plan, keep in mind that a good plan buffers the quiet zones from working zones by physically separating them on different levels or by placing living areas between them.

4. Traffic Flow

Another issue to consider is how people will travel between rooms and between zones. This is called traffic flow. You may wish to analyze the floor plan by asking: Is there a convenient path between the garage and the kitchen for carrying groceries and other supplies? How does traffic pass between the kitchen and other eating areas? Are bathrooms easily accessible to bedrooms and the family and recreation areas? Do I want the master bedroom close to or separate from the other bedrooms? Do I want the utility area in the basement, near the kitchen or near the bedrooms?

5. Openness, Flexibility, and Versatility

Look for a design that is open and airy and has rooms with multiple uses to change with your family's

Plan P-6563

needs. For example, the "Great Room" concept has become increasingly popular. In this idea, the kitchen, breakfast room, and family room work together as one large area yet function as separate spaces with their own identities. Also, ask yourself, can a nursery or spare bedroom be converted into a study, library, or parlour? Could the kitchen or Great Room be expanded by adding a sun room or sliding door for a future deck or screened porch?

6. Atmosphere

Atmosphere is created by the use of natural light, heightened ceilings, skylights, clerestory windows, and creative use of built-in artificial lights. Heightened ceilings create a greater sense of space and volume without increasing the actual dimensions of the room. A ceiling can also change the entire atmosphere of a room — vaulted and cathedral ceilings provide a contemporary "feel," trayed ceilings are more formal and elegant, and beamed ceilings create a casual and homey atmosphere.

7. Master Suites and Luxurious Master Bathrooms

A spacious, refreshing, and relaxing private bedroom retreat is highly popular. Walk-in closets, dual vanities, skylights, a separate shower and tub are added luxuries in high demand.

8. Kitchens

The kitchen has become a social center often incorporated with a breakfast nook and Great Room. A large, open kitchen with plenty of counter space, an island or peninsula counter, and a breakfast bar are highly desirable features.

9. Storage, Built-ins, and Utility Rooms

Creative use of alcoves, built-in bookshelves, nooks, and wet bars are both popular and cost effective. These small elements can create a larger sense of space in an otherwise small or medium-sized design.

Storage spaces are in high demand. Does the home you are looking for have an unfinished attic, basement, bonus room, or expandable garage? Do the bedrooms have adequate closet space? Does the kitchen have a pantry and sufficient cupboards? Does the utility room have extra storage and sufficient space?

10. Inside/Outside

To bring the outdoors in, new home designs are incorporating sun rooms, solariums, and greenhouses, as well as decks, patios, and porches. Creative window shapes and energy-efficient glass doors allow your home design to capture the beauty and freshness of the outdoors. If your home does not have a backyard deck or patio, could these be added without major expense?

See 116, 120

OST-SAVING TIPS FOR BUILDING A HOME IN THE 90's

With construction costs and land values on the rise, record numbers of home builders are looking for money-saving ideas to build an affordable "dream home." Real estate, design costs, building materials, and contracting are the four areas that offer the greatest savings potential for new home buyers.

REAL ESTATE TIPS

The cost of land will vary depending on its location, whether or not it is developed or undeveloped, and whether the site poses any problems such as a difficult terrain, complicated configuration, or local zoning requirements.

1. When evaluating the land you wish to buy, keep in mind that undeveloped land is generally cheaper than developed land. It also has greater potential for appreciation as the surrounding area develops.

2. Despite potential problems, a difficult site can be a blessing in disguise. Although additional expenses may be required to excavate or provide access, the savings on the lot can be greater than the extra construction costs. Also, buying a problem site may enable you to live in a community you could not otherwise afford.

NOTE: Although unimproved and problem sites are cheaper, the costs of road access, electricity, water, and sewage must be carefully evaluated.

Plan P-7659

DESIGN TIPS

Once you have your lot, you must select a design that fits both your site and your lifestyle.

Identify your family's current and future needs and income. As a general rule, it is much safer to select a design that is within your budget and is flexible for future expansion. When selecting your "dream" design, keep in mind the following items:

1. Select a design that fits your site — one that will minimize excavation and grading.

2. There can be tremendous savings using predesigned blueprints from "SOURCE 1" or other reputable stock blueprint companies. Architects' fees for custom drawn blueprints will range from 5% to 15% of the cost of building your home. Design costs for a $100,000 home, for example, can range from $5,000 to $15,000. However, complete construction blueprints are available from most stock design companies for $165-$395.

3. A rectangular design with simple roof lines is significantly less expensive than a home with numerous angles, nooks and crannies. Also, building up is significantly less expensive than building out. (A two-story home is less expensive than a one-story home with the same living space).

4. Look for a design that is open, flexible, and versatile allowing rooms to change as your family grows. Built-in furniture is a cost effective way of utilizing small spaces. It gives a sense of greater volume in a small home. Look for a home with unfinished space such as an unfinished basement or attic.

5. Decks, patios, screened in porches, greenhouses, and sun rooms add tremendously to the comfort and pleasure that you'll have in living in your home. They also translate to increased value for resale!

6. Design your home for energy efficiency. 2x6 construction of the walls may be more expensive

Plan R-1028

5

Plan H-930

in the short run, but these minimal costs will be paid back in energy savings.

Site your house correctly. A southern exposure in colder climates and a northern exposure in warmer climates will have a surprising effect on your fuel bills.

MATERIAL TIPS

The materials used to build your home are the most expensive costs of construction. Don't compromise on materials to save money! Savings can be made in using pre-manufactured materials and standard sizes.

1. Limit custom work! As attractive as elaborate detailing can be, the cost is often exorbitant. Look for mass produced detailing wherever possible.

2. Areas such as the kitchen and the bathroom are often very expensive to build due to the number of appliances, cabinets and features. Your builder and local supplier can design the kitchen and bathroom to take advantage of pre-designed cabinetry and counters.

CONTRACTING TIPS

Cutting construction costs (i.e. labor and materials) requires experience, time, and organizational skills.

As a home builder you have four options:

1. A construction company;

2. A general contractor (carpenter/builder);

3. Act as your own general contractor;

4. Build your own home.

In all of these cases, the contractor is responsible for coordinating the work of all "trades" — electricians, plumbers, painters, builders, etc., securing permits, handling finances and ensuring quality. There are advantages and disadvantages to each option:

1. A general construction company may offer some cost savings because your project will be consolidated with a number of other concurrent projects and there may be labor savings with sub-contractors. However, your house is one of many and you will not have much personal contact with your builder.

2. The general contractor can provide more personalized attention than a construction company. However, you will have to spend more time reviewing and comparing competitive bids and possibly specifying materials. A general contractor usually works on a "cost-plus" basis — the costs of materials and sub-contractors' charges plus the contract fee. This can either be a fixed cost or a percentage of the cost.

3. Acting as your own general contractor significantly reduces costs but also significantly increases the time and responsibility you must commit to the project. In this role, you have the responsibility of hiring, supervising, securing permits, and getting materials. This requires knowledge of local building codes and means working with construction specialists. Although the savings are significant, you must weigh the extensive commitment and time involved against having the work done by a professional.

4. The most cost efficient approach is to act as your own contractor and builder. In this case you eliminate all the costs except for materials. This option can be rewarding but requires a tremendous commitment of time — first in educating yourself, and then in doing it.

Plan E-2208

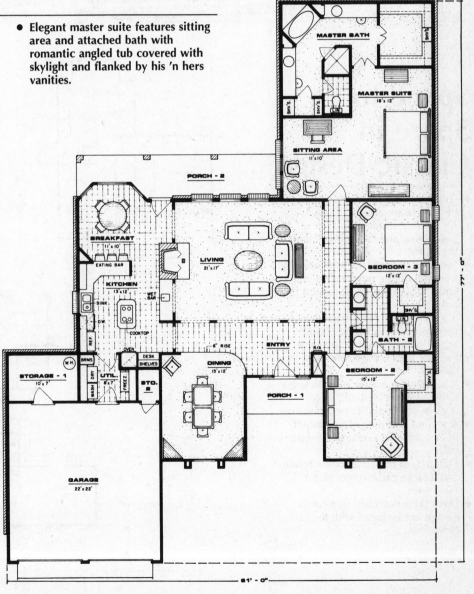

"Adult Retreat" in Master Bedroom Suite

- Exciting living room is virtually open on three sides.
- Wet bar lies between living area and large kitchen, which offers an eating bar and island cooktop.

- Elegant master suite features sitting area and attached bath with romantic angled tub covered with skylight and flanked by his 'n hers vanities.

Plan E-2106

Bedrooms: 3	Baths: 2

Space:

Total living area:	2,177 sq. ft.
Basement:	approx. 2,177 sq. ft.
Garage and storage:	570 sq. ft.
Porches:	211 sq. ft.

Exterior Wall Framing:	2x4

Foundation options:
Standard basement.
Crawlspace.
Slab.
(Foundation & framing conversion diagram available — see order form.)

Blueprint Price Code:	C

Space to Spare in Classic Design

- Grace and space are the hallmarks of this classic design.
- An inviting veranda presents a welcoming and comfortable look to the world.
- Inside, a roomy foyer is flanked by a formal dining room on the left and a large study or library on the right.
- A generously sized kitchen is surrounded by a spacious family room, sunny breakfast area and hallway with a door to a back porch.
- A sumptuous master suite includes a majestic private bath, large walk-in closet and cozy sitting area.
- A second bedroom offers pocket-door access to a second downstairs bath.
- Upstairs, note two more bedrooms and a large game room, plus a third bath.
- Plans for a detached two-car garage are included with the blueprints.

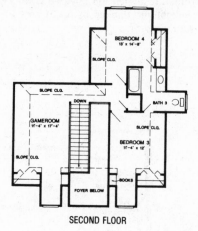

SECOND FLOOR

Plan L-308-FC	
Bedrooms: 4	**Baths:** 3

Space:	
Upper floor:	2,519 sq. ft.
Main floor:	787 sq. ft.
Total living area:	3,306 sq. ft.
Exterior Wall Framing:	2x4

Ceiling Heights:	
Upper floor:	9'
Main floor:	9'

Foundation options:
Slab only.
(Foundation & framing conversion diagram available — see order form.)

Blueprint Price Code: E

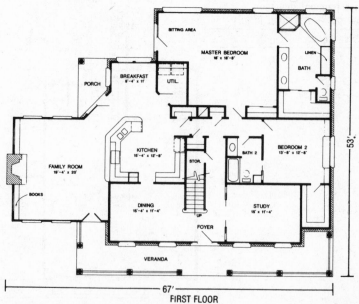

FIRST FLOOR

Plan L-308-FC

Luxury Home with Outdoor Orientation

- Courtyards, patios and a sun room orient this multi-level home to the outdoors.
- Interior design is carefully zoned for informal family living and formal entertaining.
- Expansive kitchen includes large island and plenty of counter space, and a sunny nook adjoins the kitchen.
- Soaring entry area leads visitors to the vaulted living room with fireplace, or to the more casual family room.
- An optional fourth bedroom off the foyer would make an ideal home office.
- Upstairs master suite includes luxury bath and big walk-in closet.
- Daylight basement version adds nearly 1,500 more square feet of space.

Plans P-7659-3A & P-7659-3D

Bedrooms: 3-4	Baths: 3
Space:	
Upper floor:	1,050 sq. ft.
Main floor:	1,498 sq. ft.
Total living area:	**2,548 sq. ft.**
Basement:	1,490 sq. ft.
Garage:	583 sq. ft.
Exterior Wall Framing:	2x4

Foundation options:
Daylight basement, Plan P-7659-3D.
Crawlspace, Plan P-7659-3A.
(Foundation & framing conversion diagram available — see order form.)

Blueprint Price Code:	D

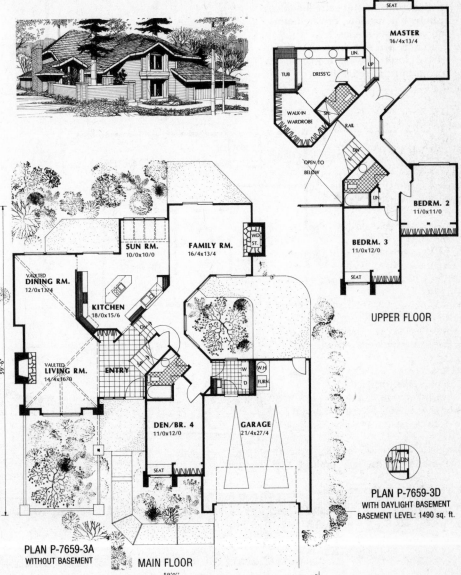

UPPER FLOOR

PLAN P-7659-3D
WITH DAYLIGHT BASEMENT
BASEMENT LEVEL: 1490 sq. ft.

PLAN P-7659-3A
WITHOUT BASEMENT

MAIN FLOOR

Plans P-7659-3A & -3D

Wrap-Around Veranda Lends Homey, Welcoming Look

- Traditional farmhouse designs such as this never seem to lose their popularity.
- The large, welcoming veranda conjures up images of sipping lemonade with family and friends on mild summer evenings.
- A big living room includes a fireplace and three large windows.
- The breakfast nook is flooded with natural light from the bay window, and adjoins the family room.
- A convenient utility room and half-bath are located in the garage entry area.
- The luxurious master suite includes a sunny bay window, private bath and large walk-in closet.
- Bedrooms two and three also offer roomy closets and share a large, compartmentalized bath.

UPPER FLOOR

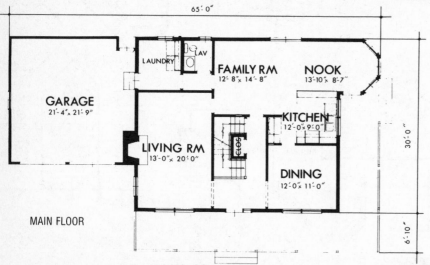

MAIN FLOOR

Plans H-1414-1 & -1A

Bedrooms: 3	**Baths:** 2½

Space:	
Upper floor:	1,103 sq. ft.
Main floor:	1,138 sq. ft.
Total living area:	**2,241 sq. ft.**
Basement:	1,138 sq. ft.
Garage:	464 sq. ft.

Exterior Wall Framing:	2x6

Foundation options:
Standard basement (H-1414-1).
Crawlspace (H-1414-1A).
(Foundation & framing conversion diagram available — see order form.)

Blueprint Price Code:	C

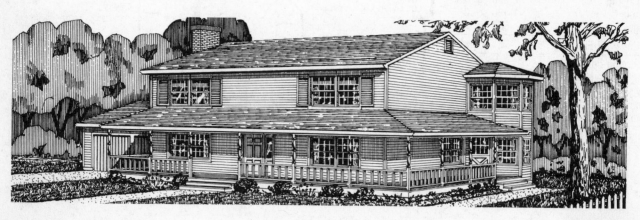

TO ORDER THIS BLUEPRINT, CALL TOLL-FREE 1-800-547-5570
(Prices and details on pp. 12-15.)

Plans H-1414-1 & -1A

Small Home
Big On Style

- This elegant design borrows from classic French architecture.
- The fine exterior detailing includes the raised-brick corners (quoins), a Palladian window, leaded glass door and corbeled brick chimney.
- Inside, the floor plan is designed to incorporate features rarely found in a home of this modest size.
- Note the 'morning room' which adjoins the roomy kitchen and protrudes into the back yard.
- A formal dining room and grand living room are separated by a roomy foyer.
- The master suite is impressive, with a superb private bath and large closet.

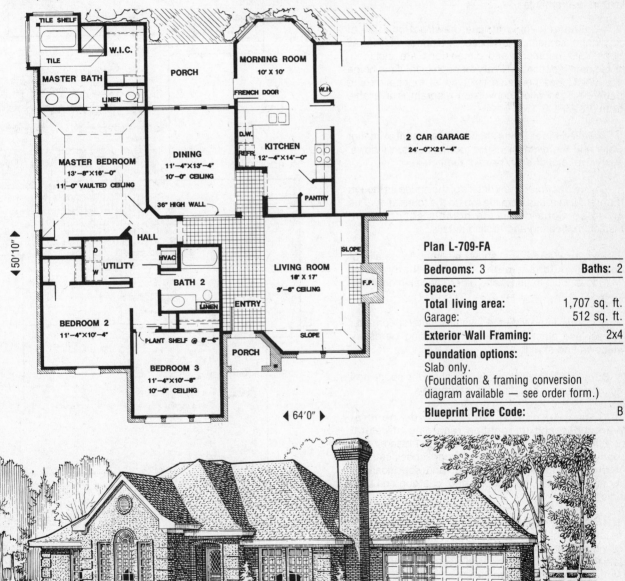

Plan L-709-FA

Bedrooms: 3	Baths: 2
Space:	
Total living area:	1,707 sq. ft.
Garage:	512 sq. ft.
Exterior Wall Framing:	2x4
Foundation options: Slab only. (Foundation & framing conversion diagram available — see order form.)	
Blueprint Price Code:	B

HomeStyles
SOURCE 1
DESIGNERS NETWORK

Plan L-709-FA

*TO ORDER THIS BLUEPRINT,
CALL TOLL-FREE 1-800-547-5570*
(Prices and details on pp. 12-15.) 11

WHAT OUR PLANS INCLUDE

"SOURCE 1" construction blueprints are detailed, clear and concise. All blueprints are designed by licensed architects or members of the A.I.B.D. (American Institute of Building Designers), and each plan is designed to meet the nationally recognized building codes (either the Uniform Building Code, Standard Building Code or Basic Building Code) at the time and place they were drawn.

Although blueprints will vary depending on the size and complexity of the home and on the individual designer's style, each set will include the following elements:

1. **Exterior Elevations** show the front, rear, and the sides of the house including exterior materials, details, and measurements.

2. **Foundation Plans** include drawings for a full or daylight basement, crawlspace, or slab foundation. All necessary notations and dimensions are included. (Foundation options will vary for each plan. If the home you want does not have the type of foundation you desire, a foundation conversion diagram is available from "SOURCE 1".)

3. **Detailed Floor Plans** show the placement of interior walls and the dimensions for rooms, doors, windows, stairways, etc. of each level of the house.

4. **Cross Sections** show details of the house as though it were cut in slices from the roof to the foundation. The cross sections detail the home's construction, insulation, flooring and roofing details.

5. **Interior Elevations** show the specific details of cabinets (kitchen, bathroom, and utility room) fireplaces, built-in units, and other special interior features.

6. **Roof Plans** provide the layout of rafters, dormers, gables, and other roof elements including clerestory windows and skylights.

7. **Schematic Electrical Layouts** show the suggested location for switches, fixtures, and outlets.

8. **General Specifications** provide general instructions and information regarding structural specifications, excavating and grading, masonry and concrete work, carpentry and wood specifications, thermal and moisture protection, and specifications about drywall, tile, flooring, glazing, caulking and sealants.

NOTE: Due to regional variations, local availability of materials, local codes, methods of installation, and individual preferences, it is impossible to include much detail on heating, plumbing, and electrical work on your plans. The duct work, venting, and other details will vary depending on the type of heating and cooling system (forced air, hot water, electric, solar) and the type of energy (gas, oil, electricity, solar) that you use. These details and specifications are easily obtained from your builder, contractor, and/or local suppliers.

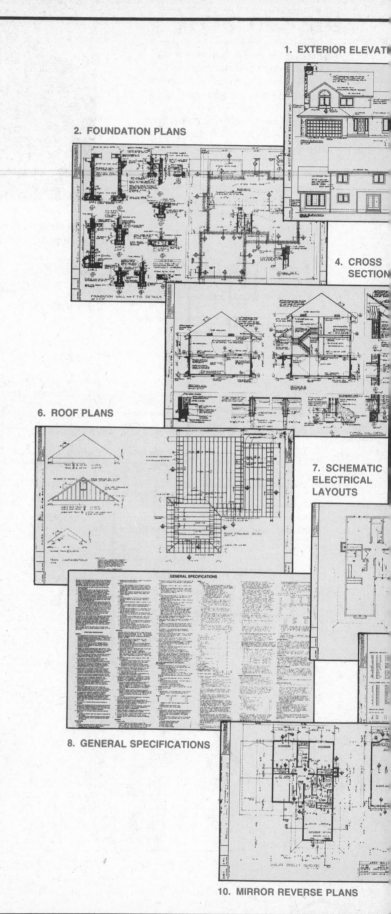

1. EXTERIOR ELEVATI

2. FOUNDATION PLANS

4. CROSS SECTION

6. ROOF PLANS

7. SCHEMATIC ELECTRICAL LAYOUTS

8. GENERAL SPECIFICATIONS

10. MIRROR REVERSE PLANS

CONSTRUCTION BLUEPRINTS TO BUILD YOUR HOME

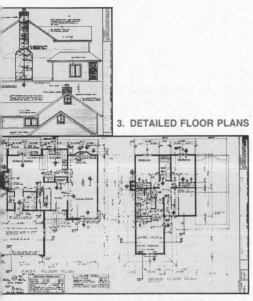

3. DETAILED FLOOR PLANS

5. INTERIOR ELEVATIONS

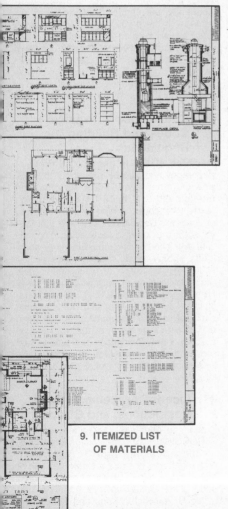

9. ITEMIZED LIST OF MATERIALS

11. HELPFUL "HOW-TO" DIAGRAMS

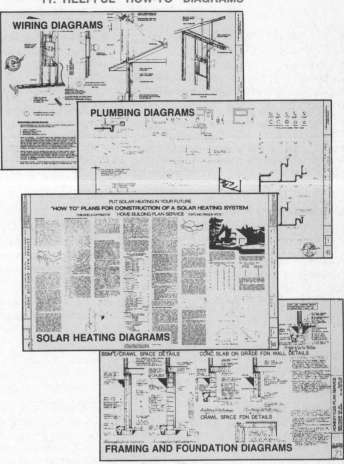

WIRING DIAGRAMS

PLUMBING DIAGRAMS

PUT SOLAR HEATING IN YOUR FUTURE
"HOW TO" PLANS FOR CONSTRUCTION OF A SOLAR HEATING SYSTEM

SOLAR HEATING DIAGRAMS

BSM'T/CRAWL SPACE DETAILS   CONC. SLAB ON GRADE FDN. WALL DETAILS

CRAWL SPACE FDN. DETAILS

FRAMING AND FOUNDATION DIAGRAMS

Important Extras and Helpful Building Aids
(Sold Separately)

Every set of plans that you order will contain all the details that your builder will need. However, "Source 1" provides additional guides and information as follows:

9. **Itemized List of Materials** details the quantity, type, and size of materials needed to build your home. (This list is extremely helpful in acquiring an accurate construction estimate. It is not intended for use to order materials.)

10. **Mirror Reverse Plans** are useful if you want to build your home in the reverse of the plan that is shown. Reverse plans are available for an additional charge. However, since the lettering and dimensions will read backwards, we recommend that you order at least one regular-reading set of blueprints.

11. **Helpful "How-To" Diagrams** — Plumbing, Wiring, Solar Heating, and Framing and Foundation Conversion Diagrams

Each of these diagrams details the basic tools and techniques needed to plumb, wire, and install a solar heating system, convert plans with 2 x 4 exterior walls to 2 x 6 (or vice versa), or adapt a plan for a basement, crawlspace, or slab foundation.

WHAT YOU NEED TO KNOW
BEFORE YOU ORDER

1. HomeStyles "SOURCE 1" Designers' Network

"SOURCE 1" is a consortium of 35 of America's leading residential designers. All the plans presented in this book are designed by licensed architects or members of the A.I.B.D. (American Institute of Building Designers), and each plan is designed to meet the nationally recognized building codes (either the Uniform Building Code, Standard Building Code or Basic Building Code) in effect at the time and place that they are drawn.

2. Blueprint Price Schedule

Our sales volume allows us to offer quality blueprints at a fraction of the cost it takes to develop them. Custom designs cost thousands of dollars, usually 5 to 15 percent of the cost of construction. Design costs for a $100,000 home, for example, can range from $5,000 to $15,000. A HomeStyles "SOURCE 1" plan costs only $165 to $395 depending on the size of the home and the number of sets of blueprints that you order. By ordering a "SOURCE 1" plan, you save enough money to add a deck, swimming pool, beautiful kitchen, luxurious master bedroom, elegant bathroom, or other extras.

The "SOURCE 1" pricing schedule is based on "total finished living space." When we calculate "living space" we do not include garages, porches, decks, unfinished space or unfinished basements. The schedule below outlines the value and savings you get from ordering "SOURCE 1" plans and multiple sets:

NUMBER OF SETS	PRICE CODE GROUP BY SQUARE FEET						
	A Under 1,500	B 1,500-1,999	C 2,000-2,499	D 2,500-2,999	E 3,000-3,499	F 3,500-3,999	G 4,000 & Up
7	$265	$315	$350	$385	$420	$455	$490
4	$235	$275	$305	$340	$375	$410	$445
1	$190	$225	$255	$285	$320	$355	$390

*Prices guaranteed to December 31, 1991.

3. Revisions, Modifications, and Customizing

The tremendous variety of designs available through "SOURCE 1" allows you to choose the home that best suits your lifestyle, budget and building site. Your home can be easily customized through your choice of siding, roof, trim, decorating, color, and other non-structural alterations and materials.

Most "SOURCE 1" plans are easily modified by qualified professionals. Minor changes and material substitutions can be made by any professional builder without the need for expensive blueprint revisions. However, if you are considering making major changes to your design, we strongly recommend that you seek the services of an architect or professional designer to assist you.

Also, every state, county, and municipality has its own codes, zoning requirements, ordinances, and building regulations. Modifications may be necessary to comply with your specific requirements — snow loads, energy codes, seismic zones, etc.

4. Estimating Building Costs

Building costs vary widely depending on style and size, the type of finishing materials you select, and the local rates for labor and building materials. With an average cost per square foot of construction, you can multiply this figure by the total living area of your home and derive a rough estimate. More accurate estimates will require a professional review of the working blueprints and the types of materials you choose. To get a rough estimate, call a local contractor, your state or local Builders Association, the National Association of Home Builders (NAHB), or the AIBD.

5. Foundation Options and Exterior Construction

Depending on your specific geography and climate, your home will be built with either a slab, crawlspace, or basement type foundation and the exterior walls will either be 2 x 4 or 2 x 6. Most professional contractors and builders can easily adapt a home to meet the foundation and exterior wall requirements that you desire. If the specific home that you select does not meet your foundation or exterior wall requirements, "SOURCE 1" has a foundation and framing conversion diagram available.

6. "SOURCE 1" Service Policy and Blueprint Delivery

"SOURCE 1" service representatives are available to answer questions and assist you in placing your blueprint order. All telephone orders are entered directly into our computer. Mail orders are entered upon receipt. We try to process and ship every order within 48 hours. For regular mailing (US First Class Mail or UPS Second Day Air) you should receive your blueprints within 4 to 5 working days. For express mail (UPS Next Day Air or Federal Express) please expect 1 to 2 days for delivery.

7. How Many Blueprints Should I Order?

> **BLUEPRINT CHECKLIST**
> ____ OWNER'S SET(S)
> ____ BUILDER (usually requires at least three sets: one for legal document, one for inspections, and a minimum of one set for subcontractors.)
> ____ BUILDING PERMIT DEPARTMENT (at least one set; check with your local governing body for number of sets required.)
> ____ LENDING INSTITUTION (usually one set for conventional mortgage; three sets for FHA or VA loans.)
> ____ TOTAL NUMBER OF SETS NEEDED

A single set of blueprints is sufficient to study and review a home in greater detail. However, if you are planning to get cost estimates or are planning to build, you will need a minimum of 4 sets and more likely 7 sets — sometimes more. Once you begin the process of building your home, everyone seems to need a set. As the owner, you will want to retain a set (1), your lending institution (2), the local building authorities (3), your builder/contractor (4), and of course, subcontractors — foundation, framing, plumbing, heating, electrical, insulation, etc. (5-10) To help you determine the exact number of sets you will need, please refer to the Blueprint Checklist.

8. Architectural and Engineering Seals

With increased concern over energy costs and safety, many cities and states are now requiring that an architect or engineer review and "seal" a blueprint prior to construction. There may be an additional charge for this service. Please contact your local lumber yard, municipal building department, Builders Association, or local chapters of the AIBD or American Institute of Architecture (AIA). **Note:** (Plans for homes to be built in Nevada may have to be re-drawn and sealed by a Nevada-licensed design professional.)

9. Returns and Exchanges

Each set of "SOURCE 1" blueprints is specially printed and shipped to you in response to your specific order; consequently, we cannot honor requests for refunds. If the prints you order cannot be used, we will be pleased to exchange them. Please return all sets to us within 30 days. For the new set of plans that you select in exchange, there will simply be a flat charge of $50 (plus $5 for each additional set up to the original number of sets ordered).

10. Compliance With Local Codes and Building Regulations

Because of the tremendous variety of geography and climate throughout the U.S. and Canada, every state, county, and municipality will have its own building regulations, codes, zoning requirements and ordinances. Depending on where you live, your plan may need to be modified to comply with your local building requirements — snow loads, energy codes, seismic zones, etc. All of "SOURCE 1" plans are designed to meet the specifications of seismic zones I or II. HomeStyles "SOURCE 1" Designers' Network authorizes the use of our blueprints expressly conditioned upon your obligation and agreement to strictly comply with all local building codes, ordinances, regulations, and requirements — including permits and inspections at the time of and during construction.

11. License Agreement, Copy Restrictions, and Copyright

When you purchase your blueprints from "SOURCE 1," we, as Licensor, grant you, as Licensee, the right to use these documents to construct a single unit. All of the plans in this publication are protected under the Federal Copyright Act, Title XVII of the United States Code and Chapter 37 of the Code of Federal Regulations. Each "Source 1" designer retains title and ownership of the original documents. The blueprints licensed to you cannot be used, resold to any other person, copied or reproduced by any means.

How to Order Your Blueprints

Ordering blueprints is fast and easy. You can order by mail, by fax (use our International Fax number 1-612-338-1626) or call our toll free number **1-800-547-5570.** When ordering by phone, please have your credit card ready. Thank you for your order. Good luck building your dream home.

★ "Source 1" Home Photo Contest — Win $1000 ★

When you build your "Source 1" home, we'd like to give you national recognition. We are always looking for cover photos of finished homes for our home plan magazines. Even if you've made modifications, we would love to see your pictures. Send us snapshots of your finished homes. Photos need not be professionally taken. If we use your home as a cover or inside feature, you will win $250. If we select your home for our Annual cover, you will win $1,000. Please send all photos along with your name, address, phone number and the plan number to the attention of Ms. Pam Tasler, Ass't Editor.

------- BLUEPRINT ORDER FORM -------

Mail to: **For Faster Service**
HomeStyles "Source 1"   **Call Toll-Free**
275 Market St., Suite 521   **1-800-547-5570**
Minneapolis, MN 55405

Please send me the following:

Plan Number _____ Price Code _____

Foundation _____
(Please review your plan carefully for foundation options — basement, crawlspace, or slab. Many plans offer all three options, others offer only one.)

Number of Sets		B	C	D	E	F	G	Amount
☐ 7		$265	$315	$350	$385	$420	$455	$490	$ _____
☐ 4		$235	$275	$305	$340	$375	$410	$445	$ _____
☐ 1		$190	$225	$255	$285	$320	$355	$390	$ _____

*Prices guaranteed to December 31, 1991.

☐ **Additional Sets** of this plan, $25 now; $ _____
$35 later, each. (Number of sets _____)

☐ **Itemized List of Materials,** $30, each $ _____
additional set $10.
Lists are available only for plans with prefix letters AH, AM, B, C, CPS, E, H, I, J, K, N, NW*, P, R, S, SD, U, W)
*Please ask when ordering, not available on all plans

☐ **Description of Materials:** Two sets $25 $ _____
(For use in obtaining FHA or VA financing)
(Only available for Plans with prefix letters C, E, H, J, K, N, P, U)

☐ **Mirror Reverse Surcharge,** $25. $ _____
(Number of sets to be reversed _____.)
*The writing on Mirror Reverse plans will be backwards. Order at least one regular set.

☐ **Typical How-To Diagrams** $ _____
☐ Plumbing ☐ Wiring ☐ Solar Heating
☐ Framing & Foundation Conversion
One set @ $12.50, any two @ $23.00, any three @ $30.00, all four only $35.

☐ **Sales Tax** (MN Residents, please add 6%) $ _____

Please Add Postage Charges (Check One)

☐ First-Class Priority or UPS Blue Label $ _____
(U.S. only), $10.50
Allow 4-5 working days for delivery. *Must have street address for UPS delivery.

☐ First-Class Priority (Canada only) $10.50 $ _____
Allow 2-3 weeks for delivery.

☐ Overnight Express Delivery (U.S. only) $25.00 $ _____
Allow 1-2 working days for delivery. *Must have street address.

☐ Express Delivery (Canada only) $40.00 $ _____
Allow 4-5 working days for delivery. *Must have street address.

☐ Overseas Airmail Delivery $40.00 $ _____
Allow approx. 7 working days.

Payment   TOTAL ORDER $ _____
☐ Check/money order enclosed (in U.S. funds)
☐ VISA ☐ MasterCard ☐ AmEx ☐ Discover   Exp. Date_____

Card Number _____

Signature _____

Name _____

Street _____

City _____ State ___ Zip_____

Daytime Telephone (___) _____

☐ Builder-Contractor ☐ Home Owner ☐ Renter   PG-8

------- BLUEPRINT ORDER FORM -------

Mail to: **For Faster Service**
HomeStyles "Source 1"   **Call Toll-Free**
275 Market St., Suite 521   **1-800-547-5570**
Minneapolis, MN 55405

Please send me the following:

Plan Number _____ Price Code _____

Foundation _____
(Please review your plan carefully for foundation options — basement, crawlspace, or slab. Many plans offer all three options, others offer only one.)

Number of Sets	A	B	C	D	E	F	G	Amount
☐ 7		$265	$315	$350	$385	$420	$455	$490	$ _____
☐ 4		$235	$275	$305	$340	$375	$410	$445	$ _____
☐ 1		$190	$225	$255	$285	$320	$355	$390	$ _____

*Prices guaranteed to December 31, 1991.

☐ **Additional Sets** of this plan, $25 now; $ _____
$35 later, each. (Number of sets _____)

☐ **Itemized List of Materials,** $30, each $ _____
additional set $10.
Lists are available only for plans with prefix letters AH, AM, B, C, CPS, E, H, I, J, K, N, NW*, P, R, S, SD, U, W)
*Please ask when ordering, not available on all plans

☐ **Description of Materials:** Two sets $25 $ _____
(For use in obtaining FHA or VA financing)
(Only available for Plans with prefix letters C, E, H, J, K, N, P, U)

☐ **Mirror Reverse Surcharge,** $25. $ _____
(Number of sets to be reversed _____.)
*The writing on Mirror Reverse plans will be backwards. Order at least one regular set.

☐ **Typical How-To Diagrams** $ _____
☐ Plumbing ☐ Wiring ☐ Solar Heating
☐ Framing & Foundation Conversion
One set @ $12.50, any two @ $23.00, any three @ $30.00, all four only $35.

☐ **Sales Tax** (MN Residents, please add 6%) $ _____

Please Add Postage Charges (Check One)

☐ First-Class Priority or UPS Blue Label $ _____
(U.S. only), $10.50
Allow 4-5 working days for delivery. *Must have street address for UPS delivery.

☐ First-Class Priority (Canada only) $10.50 $ _____
Allow 2-3 weeks for delivery.

☐ Overnight Express Delivery (U.S. only) $25.00 $ _____
Allow 1-2 working days for delivery. *Must have street address.

☐ Express Delivery (Canada only) $40.00 $ _____
Allow 4-5 working days for delivery. *Must have street address.

☐ Overseas Airmail Delivery $40.00 $ _____
Allow approx. 7 working days.

Payment   TOTAL ORDER $ _____
☐ Check/money order enclosed (in U.S. funds)
☐ VISA ☐ MasterCard ☐ AmEx ☐ Discover   Exp. Date_____

Card Number _____

Signature _____

Name _____

Street _____

City _____ State ___ Zip_____

Daytime Telephone (___) _____

☐ Builder-Contractor ☐ Home Owner ☐ Renter   PG-8

Spacious and Stately

- Covered porches front and rear.
- Downstairs master suite with spectacular bath.
- Family/living/dining areas combine for entertaining large groups.
- Classic Creole/plantation exterior.

Plan E-3000

Bedrooms: 4	Baths: 3½

Space:

Upper floor:	1,027 sq. ft.
Main floor:	2,008 sq. ft.
Total living area:	**3,035 sq. ft.**
Porches:	429 sq. ft.
Basement:	2,008 sq. ft.
Garage:	484 sq. ft.
Storage:	96 sq. ft.

Exterior Wall Framing:	2x6

Typical Ceiling Heights:

Upper floor:	8'
Main floor:	9'

Foundation options:
Standard basement.
Crawlspace.
Slab.
(Foundation & framing conversion diagram available — see order form.)

Blueprint Price Code:	E

Plan E-3000

L-Shaped Country-Style Home

PLAN E-1412
WITHOUT BASEMENT

Living	1400 sq. ft.
Utility & Storage	84 sq. ft.
Garage	440 sq. ft.
Porch	80 sq. ft.
Total	2004 sq. ft.

Exterior walls are 2x6 construction.
Specify crawlspace or slab foundation.

Floor plan labels:

GARAGE 22'-0" x 20'-0"

PATIO

DISAPPEARING STAIRS

UTILITY & STORAGE 12'-0" x 7'-0"

DRY.

WASH.

KITCHEN 13'-0" x 12'-0"

RANGE

SINK

DISHWASHER

REFRIGERATOR

BAR

DINING 14'-0" x 12'-0"

BED ROOM 14'-0" x 10'-0"

CLO.

HEAT & A/C

LINEN

BATH

HALL

PANTRY

BROOMS

W.H.

CLO.

CLO.

BATH

FLAT CEILING

BEAM

BEAM

LIVING 18'-0" x 16'-0"

SLOPE CEILING

BOOKS

DESK

CLO.

BED ROOM 12'-0" x 11'-4"

CLO.

MASTER B.R. 15'-0" x 14'-0"

PORCH 20'-0" x 4'-0"

ENTRY

56'-0"

46'-0"

An Energy Efficient Home

Blueprint Price Code A

Plan E-1412

Spacious Country Kitchen

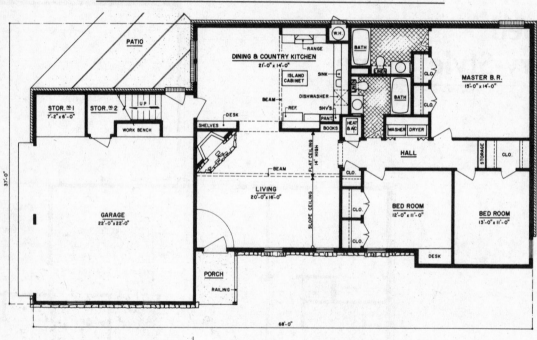

PATIO

STOR. № 1
7'-2" x 6'-0"

STOR. № 2

WORK BENCH

GARAGE
22'-0" x 22'-0"

DINING & COUNTRY KITCHEN
21'-0" x 14'-0"

RANGE
W.H.
BATH

ISLAND CABINET
SINK
KITCH.
MASTER B.R.
15'-0" x 14'-0"
CLO.

BEAM
DISHWASHER
BATH
CLO.

REF.
SHV'S
PANT
BOOKS
WASHER DRYER

DESK
SHELVES
HEAT & A/C

FLAT CEILING 14' HIGH
HALL
STORAGE
CLO.

BEAM
SLOPE CEILING
CLO.

LIVING
20'-0" x 16'-0"
CLO.
BED ROOM
12'-0" x 11'-0"
BED ROOM
13'-0" x 11'-0"

CLO.
DESK

PORCH
RAILING

37'-0"

68'-0"

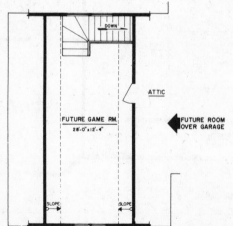

DOWN

ATTIC

FUTURE ROOM
OVER GARAGE

FUTURE GAME RM.
28'-0" x 12'-4"

SLOPE   SLOPE

AREAS

Living	1405 sq. ft.
Garage & Storage	623 sq. ft.
Porch	42 sq. ft.
Total	2070 sq. ft.
Future Game Room	345 sq. ft.

Exterior walls are 2x6 construction.
Specify basement, crawlspace or slab foundation.

An Energy Efficient Home

Blueprint Price Code A

Plan E-1408

**TO ORDER THIS BLUEPRINT,
CALL TOLL-FREE 1-800-547-5570**
(Prices and details on pp. 12-15.)

HomeStyles
SOURCE 1
DESIGNERS NETWORK

The Solid Look of Permanence

- Exterior design lends an air of quality and elegance which is carried on throughout the home.
- Exterior design lends an air of quality and elegance which is carried on throughout the home.
- Large, centered living room decor includes 10' ceilings, detailed fireplace, and ceiling fans.
- Side porch can be entered through living/dining area.
- Minimum halls generate maximum living space.
- Secluded master suite has romantic sitting area and designer bath.

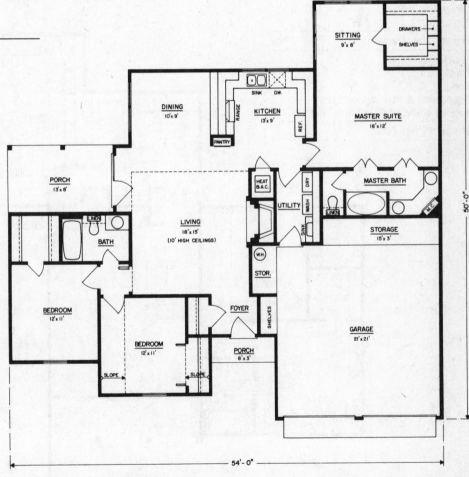

Plan E-1435

Bedrooms: 3	Baths: 2
Space:	
Total living area:	1,442 sq. ft.
Garage and storage:	516 sq. ft.
Porches:	128 sq. ft.
Exterior Wall Framing:	2x4
Foundation options: Crawlspace. Slab. (Foundation & framing conversion diagram available — see order form.)	
Blueprint Price Code:	A

TO ORDER THIS BLUEPRINT, CALL TOLL-FREE 1-800-547-5570 (Prices and details on pp. 12-15.)

Cozy, Compact One-Story Home

- Central living room and attached dining room feature 11' ceilings.
- Cleverly positioned between the main living areas is a unique fireplace, wet bar, and book shelves combination.
- Isolated master suite boasts private bath and large walk-in closet.
- Secondary bedrooms have king-sized closets, and share a full bath.

Plan E-1427

Bedrooms: 3	Baths: 2

Space:

Total living area:	1,444 sq. ft.
Garage and storage:	540 sq. ft.
Porches:	160 sq. ft.

Exterior Wall Framing:	2x6

Foundation options:
Crawlspace.
Slab.
(Foundation & framing conversion diagram available — see order form.)

Blueprint Price Code:	A

MAIN FLOOR

54'-0"

52'-0"

Plan E-1427

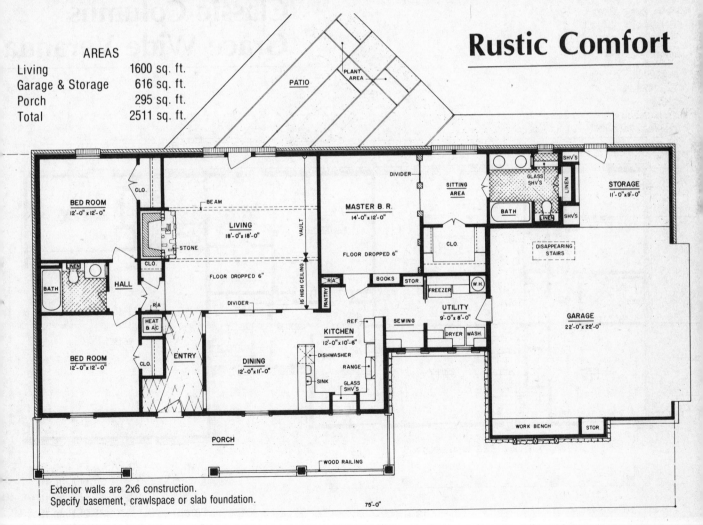

Rustic Comfort

AREAS

Living   1600 sq. ft.
Garage & Storage 616 sq. ft.
Porch   295 sq. ft.
Total   2511 sq. ft.

PATIO

PLANT AREA

BED ROOM
12'-0" x 12'-0"

CLO.

BEAM

LIVING
18'-0" x 18'-0"

STONE

VAULT

FLOOR DROPPED 6"

16' HIGH CEILING

DIVIDER

LINEN

BATH

HALL

R/A

HEAT B A/C

CLO.

ENTRY

BED ROOM
12'-0" x 12'-0"

DINING
12'-0" x 11'-0"

KITCHEN
12'-0" x 10'-6"

DISHWASHER

RANGE

SINK

GLASS SHV'S

REF.

DIVIDER

MASTER B. R.
14'-0" x 12'-0"

FLOOR DROPPED 6"

SITTING AREA

GLASS SHV'S

SHV'S

LINEN

BATH

LINEN

SHV'S

STORAGE
11'-0" x 9'-0"

CLO.

DISAPPEARING STAIRS

PANTRY

R/A

BOOKS

STOR

FREEZER

W.H.

UTILITY
9'-0" x 8'-0"

SEWING

DRYER

WASH.

GARAGE
22'-0" x 22'-0"

PORCH

WOOD RAILING

WORK BENCH

STOR

Exterior walls are 2x6 construction.
Specify basement, crawlspace or slab foundation.

75'-0"

An Energy Efficient Home

Blueprint Price Code B

Plan E-1607

TO ORDER THIS BLUEPRINT,
CALL TOLL-FREE 1-800-547-5570
(Prices and details on pp. 12-15.) 21

Classic Columns
Grace Wide Veranda

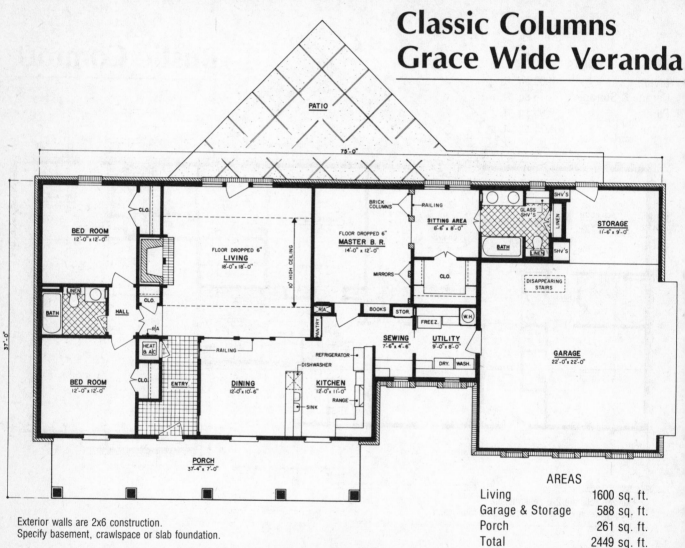

PATIO

75'-0"

37'-0"

BED ROOM
12'-0" x 12'-0"

CLO.

FLOOR DROPPED 6"
LIVING
18'-0" x 18'-0"

10' HIGH CEILING

BRICK
COLUMNS

RAILING

SITTING AREA
8'-6" x 8'-0"

GLASS
SHV'S

SHV'S

FLOOR DROPPED 6"
MASTER B.R.
14'-0" x 12'-0"

BATH

LINEN

SHV'S

STORAGE
11'-6" x 9'-0"

MIRRORS

CLO.

DISAPPEARING
STAIRS

LINEN

BATH

CLO.

R/A

BOOKS

STOR.

PANTRY

FREEZ.

W.H.

GARAGE
22'-0" x 22'-0"

HALL

CLO.

R/A

HEAT
& A/C

SEWING
7'-6" x 4'-6"

UTILITY
9'-0" x 8'-0"

RAILING

REFRIGERATOR

DRY.

WASH.

BED ROOM
12'-0" x 12'-0"

CLO.

ENTRY

DINING
12'-0" x 10'-6"

DISHWASHER

KITCHEN
12'-0" x 11'-0"

SINK

RANGE

PORCH
37'-4" x 7'-0"

AREAS

Living	1600 sq. ft.
Garage & Storage	588 sq. ft.
Porch	261 sq. ft.
Total	2449 sq. ft.

Exterior walls are 2x6 construction.
Specify basement, crawlspace or slab foundation.

An Energy Efficient Home
Blueprint Price Code B

Plan E-1614

HomeStyles
SOURCE 1
DESIGNERS NETWORK

Traditional Design For Narrow Lot

Living:	1,626 sq. ft.
Porch:	216 sq. ft.
Storage:	104 sq. ft.
Carport:	410 sq. ft.
Total:	2,356 sq. ft.

Specify basement, crawlspace or slab foundation.

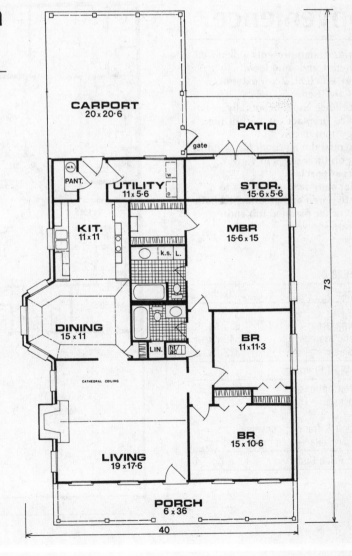

Blueprint Price Code B

Plan J-86161

TO ORDER THIS BLUEPRINT, CALL TOLL-FREE 1-800-547-5570 (Prices and details on pp. 12-15.)

Elegance and Convenience

- Exterior design presents a dignified, distinctive and solid look.
- Energy-efficient, 2 x 6 exterior walls are used.
- 15' ceilings and a beautifully detailed fireplace are part of the living room decor.
- Octagonal dining room has window walls on three sides to view adjacent porches.
- Master suite features access to a private porch and an attached bath with corner marbled tub and separate shower.

Plan E-1628

Bedrooms: 3	Baths: 2

Space:

Total living area:	1,655 sq. ft.
Garage and storage:	549 sq. ft.
Porches:	322 sq. ft.

Exterior Wall Framing:	2x6

Foundation options:
Crawlspace.
Slab.
(Foundation & framing conversion diagram available — see order form.)

Blueprint Price Code:	B

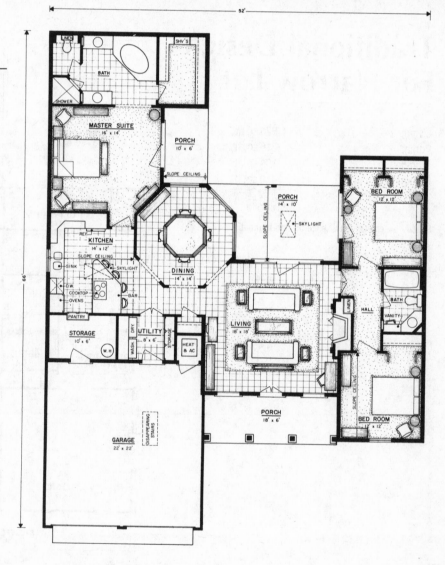

Plan E-1628

HomeStyles
SOURCE
DESIGNERS NETWORK

Deluxe Home with Expansion Potential

AREAS

Living	1681 sq. ft.
Garage, Storage, & Sun Garden	698 sq. ft.
Porches	200 sq. ft.
Total	2579 sq. ft.
Future Room over Garage	381 sq. ft.

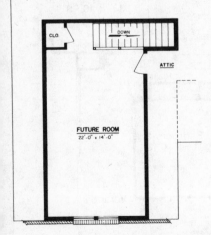

Exterior walls are 2x6 construction.
Specify basement, crawlspace or slab foundation.

An Energy Efficient Home

Blueprint Price Code B

Plan E-1621

TO ORDER THIS BLUEPRINT, CALL TOLL-FREE 1-800-547-5570
(Prices and details on pp. 12-15.)

FRONT VIEW

REAR VIEW

PLAN L-755-VA
WITHOUT BASEMENT
(SLAB-ON-GRADE FOUNDATION)

Graceful One-Story Design

(Plans for a detached two-car garage included with blueprints.)

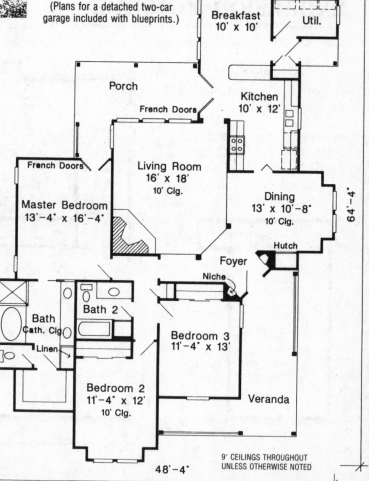

Breakfast
10' x 10'

Util.

Porch

Kitchen
10' x 12'

French Doors

French Doors

Living Room
16' x 18'
10' Clg.

Dining
13' x 10'-8"
10' Clg.

Master Bedroom
13'-4" x 16'-4"

Hutch

Foyer

Niche

Bath
Cath. Clg.

Bath 2

Bedroom 3
11'-4" x 13'

Linen

Bedroom 2
11'-4" x 12'
10' Clg.

Veranda

64'-4"

48'-4"

9' CEILINGS THROUGHOUT
UNLESS OTHERWISE NOTED

Total living area: 1,753 sq. ft.

Blueprint Price Code B
Plan L-755-VA

HomeStyles
SOURCE 1
DESIGNERS' NETWORK

One-Story Victorian

- From the gingerbread shingles above the bay windows to the turnposts on the spacious porches, this country Victorian farm house exudes classic style.
- An unusually large dining room flanks an enormous family room to create a huge space for entertaining.
- The family room features an unusual corner fireplace.
- The elegant kitchen contains a pantry and plenty of counter space.
- The master bedroom boasts a huge bath with two large walk-in closets, and also has direct access to the rear porch.
- Two other bedrooms share a compartmentalized bath with double vanity; the front bedroom is brightened by a large bay window.
- The plan also includes a convenient laundry area.

Plan L-1772

Bedrooms: 3	Baths: 2

Space:

Total living area:	1,772 sq. ft.

Garage: (Plans for a 505 sq. ft. detached two-car garage are included with blueprints.)

Exterior Wall Framing:	2x4

Foundation options:
Slab only.
(Foundation & framing conversion diagram available — see order form.)

Blueprint Price Code:	B

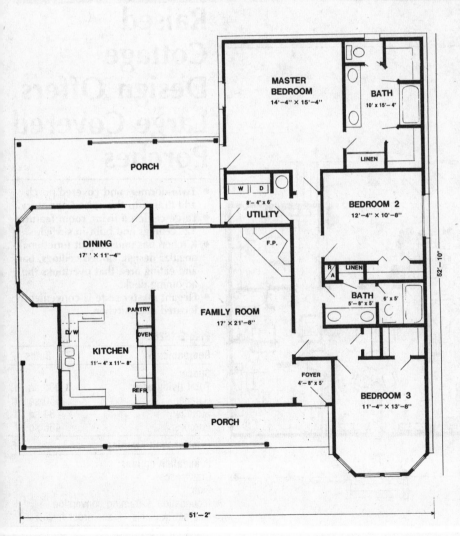

Plan L-1772

TO ORDER THIS BLUEPRINT, CALL TOLL-FREE 1-800-547-5570
(Prices and details on pp. 12-15.) **27**

Raised Cottage Design Offers Large Covered Porches

- Twin dormers and covered porch add drama to this raised one-story.
- Large centered living room features 12′ ceilings and built-in skylights.
- Kitchen has unusual but functional angular design, sloped ceilings, bar, and eating area that overlooks the adjoining deck.
- Elegant master suite is conveniently located near kitchen.

Plan E-1826

Bedrooms: 3	Baths: 2

Space:	
Total living area:	1,800 sq. ft.
Garage:	550 sq. ft.
Storage:	84 sq. ft.
Porches:	466 sq. ft.

Exterior Wall Framing:	2x6

Foundation options:
Crawlspace.
Slab.
(Foundation & framing conversion diagram available — see order form.)

Blueprint Price Code:	B

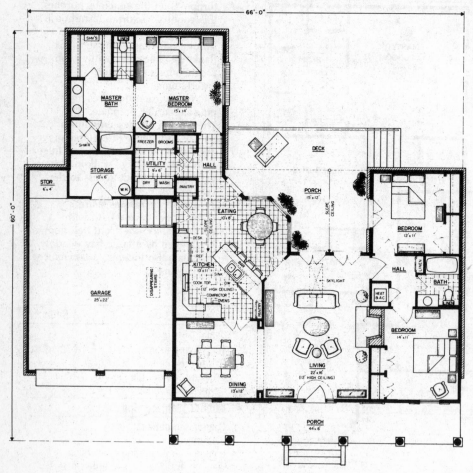

Plan E-1826

Master Bedroom Suite Features "His-and-Hers" Baths

Total living area: 1,860 sq. ft.

Exterior walls are 2x6 construction.
Specify crawlspace or slab foundation.

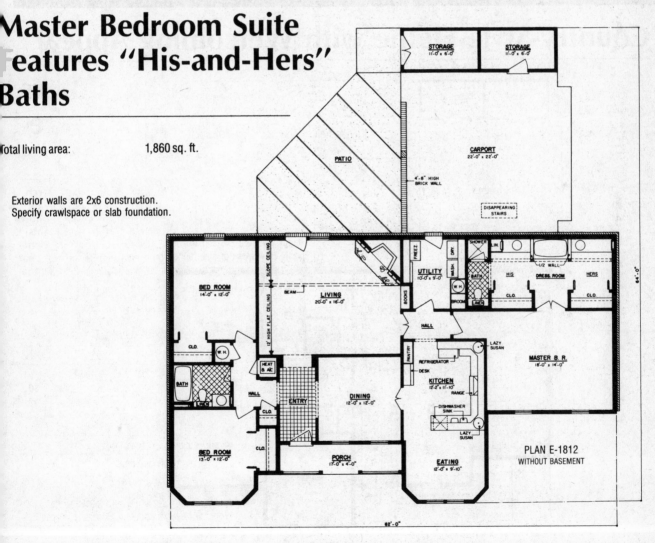

STORAGE
11'-0" x 6'-0"

STORAGE
11'-0" x 6'-0"

PATIO

CARPORT
22'-0" x 22'-0"

4'-8" HIGH
BRICK WALL

DISAPPEARING
STAIRS

BED ROOM
14'-0" x 12'-0"

SLOPE CEILING

12' HIGH FLAT CEILING

BEAM

LIVING
20'-0" x 16'-0"

FREEZ.

UTILITY
10'-0" x 9'-0"

WASH

DRY.

SHOWER

LIN

BATH

HIS

DRESS. ROOM

1/2 WALL

HERS

W.H.

BROOM

LINEN

CLO.

CLO.

BOOKS

CLO.

W.H.

HEAT
& A/C

HALL

BATH

HALL

ENTRY

CLO.

DINING
12'-0" x 12'-0"

PANTRY

DESK

REFRIGERATOR

KITCHEN
12'-2" x 11'-10"

RANGE

DISHWASHER

SINK

LAZY
SUSAN

LAZY
SUSAN

MASTER B. R.
18'-0" x 14'-0"

BED ROOM
13'-0" x 12'-0"

CLO.

PORCH
17'-0" x 4'-0"

EATING
12'-0" x 9'-10"

PLAN E-1812
WITHOUT BASEMENT

62'-0"

64'-0"

An Energy Efficient Home
Blueprint Price Code B
Plan E-1812

TO ORDER THIS BLUEPRINT,
CALL TOLL-FREE 1-800-547-5570
(Prices and details on pp. 12-15.) **29**

HomeStyles
Source1
DESIGNERS NETWORK

Country-Style Home with Welcoming Appeal

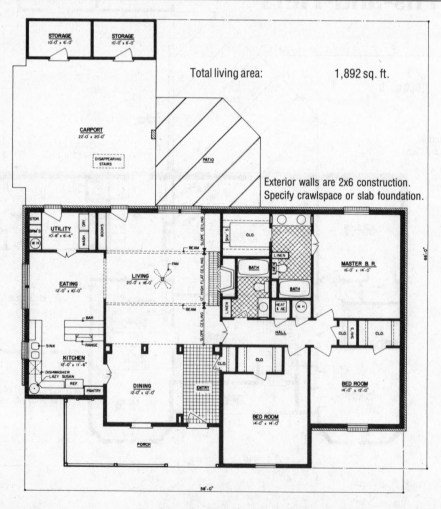

STORAGE
10'-0" x 6'-0"

STORAGE
10'-0" x 6'-0"

Total living area: 1,892 sq. ft.

CARPORT
22'-0" x 20'-0"

DISAPPEARING
STAIRS

PATIO

Exterior walls are 2x6 construction.
Specify crawlspace or slab foundation.

UTILITY
10'-8" x 6'-6"

WASH DRY

BOOKS

CLO.

SKY'S.

BATH

LINEN

MASTER B. R.
16'-0" x 14'-0"

BEAM

FAN

LIVING
20'-0" x 18'-0"

BATH

HEAT
& A.C.

EATING
12'-0" x 10'-0"

BEAM

LINEN

BAR

HALL

CLO.   SKY'S.   CLO.

SINK

KITCHEN
12'-0" x 11'-6"

RANGE

CLO.

CLO.

BED ROOM
14'-0" x 12'-0"

DISHWASHER
LAZY SUSAN

REF

PANTRY

DINING
12'-0" x 12'-0"

ENTRY

BED ROOM
14'-0" x 14'-0"

PORCH

56'-0"

An Energy Efficient Home
Blueprint Price Code B

Plan E-1813

HomeStyles
SOURCE 1
DESIGNERS NETWORK

High Ceilings Add Elegance to a Traditional Design

The raised front porch of this brick home is finely detailed with wood columns, railings, and mouldings. The transom French doors blend well with the subtle stucco finish of the porch.

Living room, dining room and entry have 12-ft. ceilings. Skylights illuminate the living room. The master suite features a raised tray ceiling, and enormous garden bath and large walk-in closet. Typical ceilings are 8-ft. high. The large quarter-circle master bath tub is surrounded with a mirror wall.

Heated area:	1,936 sq. ft.
Unheated area:	791 sq. ft.
Total area: (Not counting garage)	2,727 sq. ft.

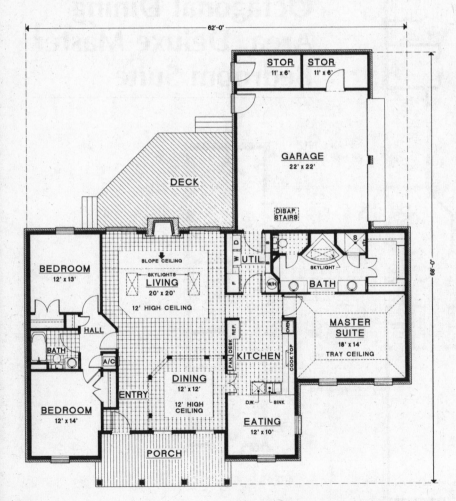

Specify crawlspace or slab foundation.
Exterior walls are 2x6 construction.

Blueprint Price Code B

Plan E-1909

Octagonal Dining Area, Deluxe Master Bedroom Suite

PLAN E-1912
(WITHOUT BASEMENT)

Exterior walls are 2x6 construction.
Specify crawlspace or slab foundation.

AREAS

Living	1946 sq. ft.
Porches	282 sq. ft.
Garage & Storage	562 sq. ft.
Total	2790 sq. ft.

An Energy Efficient Home
Blueprint Price Code B

Plan E-1912

**TO ORDER THIS BLUEPRINT,
CALL TOLL-FREE 1-800-547-5570**

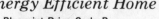

Large Living Room Features Corner Fireplace

- Brick, stucco and wood beams are skillfully combined on this design to create a very interesting and attractive traditional exterior.
- The thoroughly modern interior features a large Great-Room-style living room with a striking corner fireplace, built-in book shelves and beamed ceiling.
- An extremely efficient and functional arrangement of kitchen, dining room and informal eating area is joined by a handy utility area.
- The master suite is especially luxurious for a home of this size, and includes a beautiful private bath, dressing room and two closets.
- The other two bedrooms also feature large closets and abundant window space.
- A covered porch and efficient foyer add a specially inviting touch to the front entry of the home.

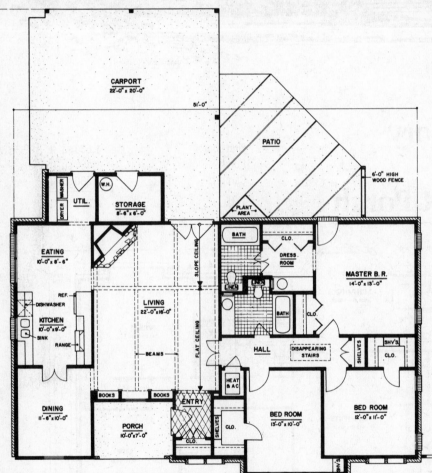

Plan E-1407

Bedrooms: 3	Baths: 2

Space:

Total living area:	1,474 sq. ft.
Porch:	70 sq. ft.
Carport:	482 sq. ft.
Storage:	51 sq. ft.

Exterior Wall Framing: 2x4

Foundation options:
Crawlspace.
Slab.
(Foundation & framing conversion diagram available — see order form.)

Blueprint Price Code: A

HomeStyles
SOURCE
DESIGNERS NETWORK

Plan E-1407

TO ORDER THIS BLUEPRINT, CALL TOLL-FREE 1-800-547-5570 (Prices and details on pp. 12-15.)

Gracious One-Story Traditional with Welcoming Front Porch

First floor:	1,633 sq. ft.
Porch:	195 sq. ft.
Carport:	380 sq. ft.
Total:	2,208 sq. ft.

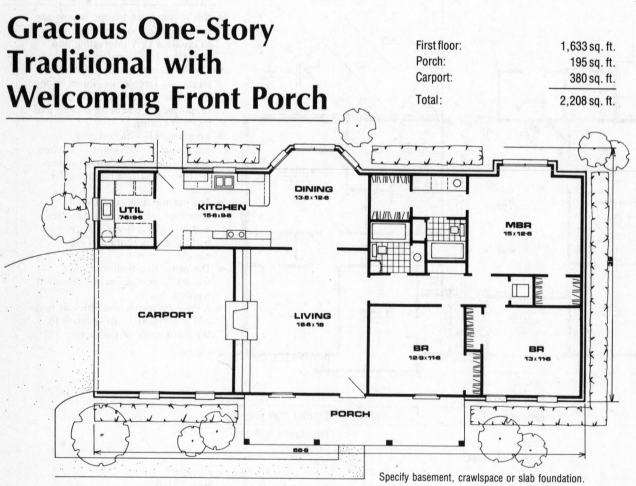

Specify basement, crawlspace or slab foundation.

Blueprint Price Code B
Plan J-8692

HomeStyles
SOURCE 1
DESIGNERS NETWORK

Warm & Friendly Brick Design

The front-facing gables of this stylish residence quickly create a feeling of friendliness and warmth. Light from the front door transom and sidelights add cheer to the foyer. The transoms are repeated over the French doors in the Great Room that open to the long back porch.

The Great Room features arches that frame the bookshelves and cased openings on each side of the fireplace. Just across the hall is a generous dining room, which has a separate entrance to the kitchen. The spacious kitchen leads to a laundry room with access to the covered back porch.

The master bedroom also has a door opening to the porch, and the private bath includes a spa tub. The two smaller bedrooms share a compartmentalized bath.

PLAN V-1403
WITHOUT BASEMENT
(CRAWLSPACE FOUNDATION)

Total living area: 1,403 sq. ft.

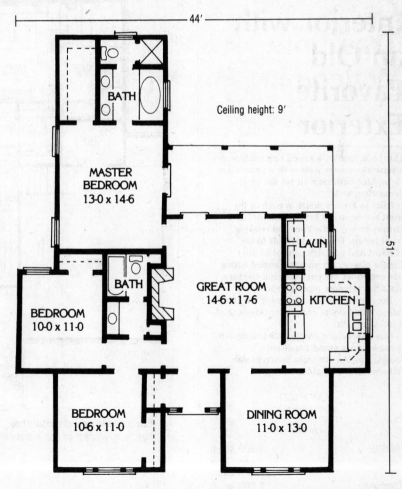

Ceiling height: 9'

44'

51'

BATH

MASTER
BEDROOM
13-0 x 14-6

BEDROOM
10-0 x 11-0

BATH

LAUN

GREAT ROOM
14-6 x 17-6

KITCHEN

BEDROOM
10-6 x 11-0

DINING ROOM
11-0 x 13-0

HomeStyles
SOURCE 1
DESIGNERS NETWORK

Blueprint Price Code A
Plan V-1403

TO ORDER THIS BLUEPRINT,
CALL TOLL-FREE 1-800-547-5570
(Prices and details on pp. 12-15.)   **35**

Fresh New Interior with an Old Favorite Exterior

This Louisiana-style raised cottage features a separate master suite with a connecting showplace bathroom fit for the most demanding taste.

Pairs of French doors in each of the front rooms invite family members and visitors to enjoy the cool and relaxing front porch. The tin roof adds to the comfort and nostalgic appeal of this Creole classic. An unusual, angled eating bar overlooks the cozy covered terrance via a bay window morning room.

The secondary bedroom wing has two full-size bedrooms, maximum closets, and a full-size bath.

This full-feature energy-efficient design is drawn on a raised crawlspace foundation. An alternate concrete slab foundation is available.

PLAN E-1823
WITHOUT BASEMENT

Areas:

Heated:	1,800 sq. ft.
Unheated:	1,100 sq. ft.
Total area:	2,900 sq. ft.

Exterior walls are 2x6 construction.
Specify crawlspace or slab foundation.

An Energy Efficient Home

Blueprint Price Code B

Plan E-1823

Classic, Cozy, Charming

Plan L-848-FA

Bedrooms: 3	**Baths:** 2

Total living area: 1,846 sq. ft.

Features:
Exterior features solidity and warmth of traditional brick.
Spacious living room features 10′ ceiling.
Kitchen opens to sunny breakfast nook.
Foyer flows into dining or living rooms.

Exterior Wall Framing: 2x4

Foundation options:
Slab only.
(Foundation & framing conversion diagram available — see order form.)

Blueprint Price Code: B

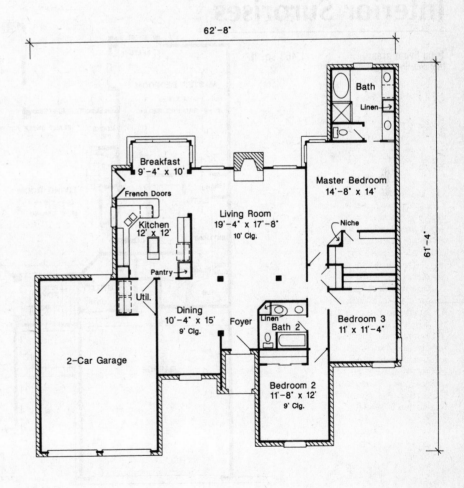

62′-8″

61′-4″

Bath
Linen

Breakfast
9′-4″ x 10′

French Doors

Kitchen
12′ x 12′

Master Bedroom
14′-8″ x 14′

Living Room
19′-4″ x 17′-8″
10′ Clg.

Niche

Pantry

Util.

Dining
10′-4″ x 15′
9′ Clg.

Foyer

Linen
Bath 2

Bedroom 3
11′ x 11′-4″

2-Car Garage

Bedroom 2
11′-8″ x 12′
9′ Clg.

Plan L-848-FA

TO ORDER THIS BLUEPRINT,
CALL TOLL-FREE 1-800-547-5570
(Prices and details on pp. 12-15.)

Secluded Entry, Interior Surprises

Total living area: 1,468 sq. ft.
(Not counting garage)

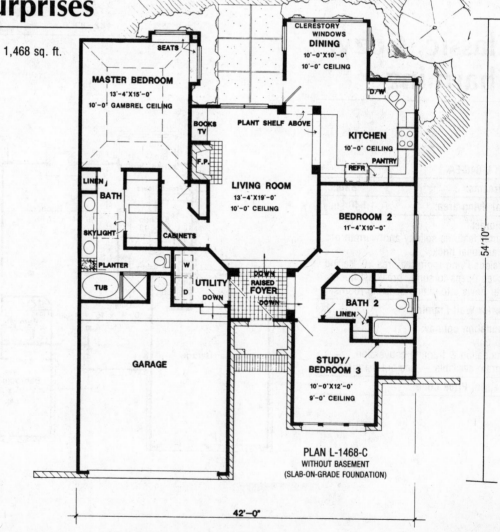

MASTER BEDROOM
13'-4"X15'-0"
10'-0" GAMBREL CEILING

SEATS

CLERESTORY WINDOWS
DINING
10'-0"X10'-0"
10'-0" CEILING

BOOKS
TV

PLANT SHELF ABOVE

D/W

KITCHEN
10'-0" CEILING

PANTRY

REFR

F.P.

LIVING ROOM
13'-4"X19'-0"
10'-0" CEILING

LINEN
BATH

SKYLIGHT

CABINETS

BEDROOM 2
11'-4"X10'-0"

PLANTER

TUB

W
D

UTILITY

DOWN

DOWN
RAISED
FOYER
DOWN

BATH 2

LINEN

GARAGE

STUDY/
BEDROOM 3
10'-0"X12'-0"
9'-0" CEILING

54'10"

42'-0"

PLAN L-1468-C
WITHOUT BASEMENT
(SLAB-ON-GRADE FOUNDATION)

TO ORDER THIS BLUEPRINT,
CALL TOLL-FREE 1-800-547-5570
(Prices and details on pp. 12-15.)

Blueprint Price Code A
Plan L-1468-C

Secluded Entryway

AREAS

Living	1678 sq. ft.
Garage & Storage	528 sq. ft.
Porches	139 sq. ft.
Total	2345 sq. ft.

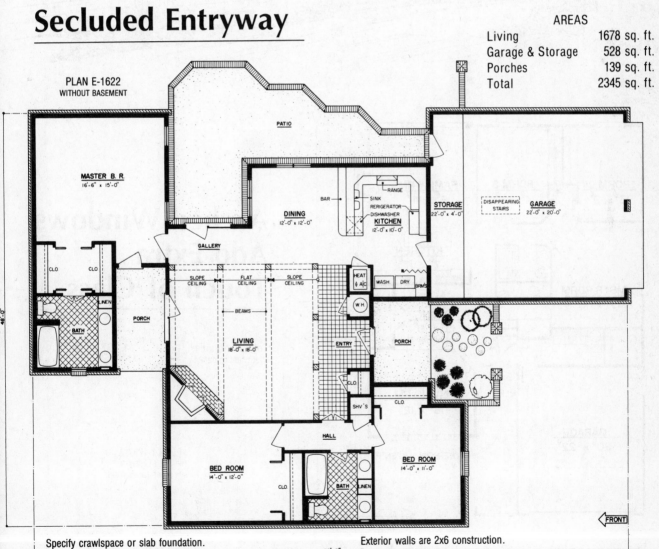

PLAN E-1622
WITHOUT BASEMENT

MASTER B. R.
16'-6" x 15'-0"

CLO   CLO

LINEN

BATH

PORCH

PATIO

DINING
12'-0" x 12'-0"

GALLERY

SLOPE CEILING   FLAT CEILING   SLOPE CEILING

BEAMS

LIVING
18'-0" x 18'-0"

BAR

SINK
RERIGERATOR
DISHWASHER
KITCHEN
12'-0" x 10'-0"

RANGE

STORAGE
22'-0" x 4'-0"

DISAPPEARING STAIRS

GARAGE
22'-0" x 20'-0"

HEAT & A/C   WASH   DRY   BRMS

W. H.

ENTRY

PORCH

CLO

SHV'S

CLO

BED ROOM
14'-0" x 12'-0"

CLO

HALL

BATH   LINEN

BED ROOM
14'-0" x 11'-0"

48'-0"

72'-0"

FRONT

Specify crawlspace or slab foundation.

Exterior walls are 2x6 construction.

An Energy Efficient Home

Blueprint Price Code B

**TO ORDER THIS BLUEPRINT,
CALL TOLL-FREE 1-800-547-5570**
(Prices and details on pp. 12-15.)

Plan E-1622

HomeStyles
SOURCE 1
DESIGNERS NETWORK

Arched Windows
Add Extra
Touch of Class

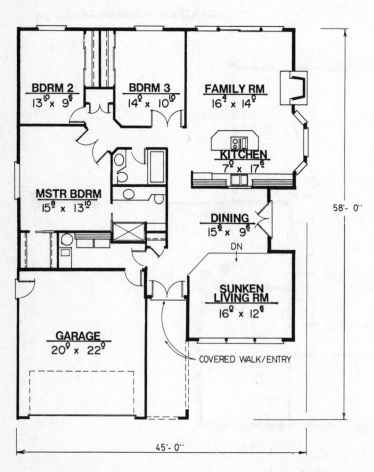

58'- 0"

45'- 0"

BDRM 2
13¹⁰ x 9⁶

BDRM 3
14⁰ x 10¹⁰

FAMILY RM
16⁴ x 14⁰

KITCHEN
7⁰ x 17⁶

MSTR BDRM
15⁸ x 13¹⁰

DINING
15⁸ x 9⁶

DN

SUNKEN
LIVING RM
16⁰ x 12⁶

GARAGE
20⁰ x 22⁰

COVERED WALK/ENTRY

Total living area: 1,737 sq. ft.
(Not counting garage)

PLAN I-1737-A
WITHOUT BASEMENT
(CRAWLSPACE FOUNDATION)

Blueprint Price Code B
Plan I-1737-A

Spacious Living/Dining Area Features High Ceilings

Total living area: 1,529 sq. ft.
(Not counting garage)

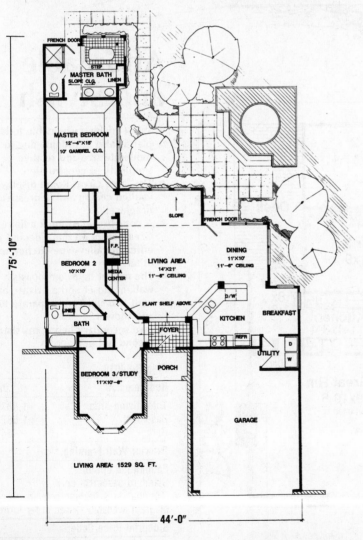

PLAN L-509-A
WITHOUT BASEMENT
(SLAB-ON-GRADE FOUNDATION)

FRENCH DOOR

STEP

MASTER BATH
SLOPE CLG.   LINEN

MASTER BEDROOM
12'-4"×15'
10' GAMBREL CLG.

SLOPE

FRENCH DOOR

F.P.

BEDROOM 2
10'×10'

MEDIA
CENTER

LIVING AREA
14'×21'
11'-6" CEILING

DINING
11'×10'
11'-6" CEILING

PLANT SHELF ABOVE

D/W

LINEN

BATH

FOYER

KITCHEN

BREAKFAST

REFR

BEDROOM 3/STUDY
11'×10'-6"

PORCH

UTILITY

D W

GARAGE

LIVING AREA: 1529 SQ. FT.

75'-10"

44'-0"

HomeStyles
SOURCE 1
DESIGNERS NETWORK

Affordable and Stylish

- While highly fashionable today, this plan is also affordable due to its moderate size and relative simplicity of construction.
- The large Great Room displays a vaulted ceiling and impressive fireplace.
- A cozy breakfast nook adjoins the Great Room on one side and the efficient galley-type kitchen on the other.
- The master bedroom boasts a huge walk-in closet and a private bath with two sinks and separate tub and shower.
- Two secondary bedrooms share a second full bath.

Plan B-89018

Bedrooms: 3	Baths: 2
Total living area:	1,587 sq. ft.
Basement:	1,587 sq. ft.
Garage:	484 sq. ft.

Exterior Wall Framing:	2x4

Foundation options:
Standard basement only.
(Foundation & framing conversion diagram available — see order form.)

Blueprint Price Code: B

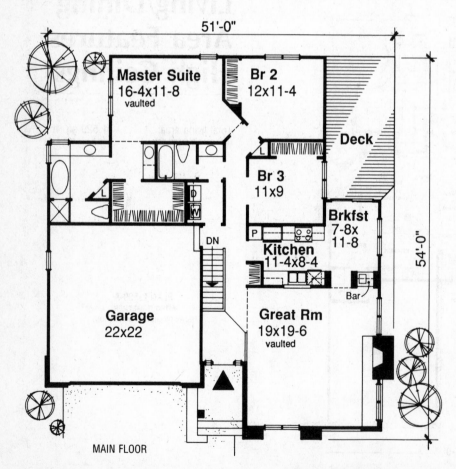

51'-0"

Master Suite
16-4x11-8
vaulted

Br 2
12x11-4

Deck

Br 3
11x9

Brkfst
7-8x 11-8

Kitchen
11-4x8-4

Bar

DN

Garage
22x22

Great Rm
19x19-6
vaulted

54'-0"

MAIN FLOOR

Plan B-89018

HomeStyles **SOURCE 1** DESIGNERS NETWORK

A Garden Home With A View

This clever design proves that privacy doesn't have to be compromised even in high-density urban neighborhoods. From within, all views are oriented to the sideyard and to a lush entry courtyard. From the outside, the home is sheltered yet maintains a warm, welcoming look.

The centrally located kitchen is designed to direct traffic flow away from the working area while still serving all of the major living areas. The adjacent morning room, with its interesting angled walls, offers a commanding view of the courtyard. A railing separates the hall and kitchen from the sunken family room, which features vaulted ceilings and a fireplace flanked by built-in cabinets. The formal dining room overlooks the living room, and both rooms view to a sideyard porch.

The master suite is only a few steps away from the kitchen. It features an elegant bath complete with whirlpool tub. Packed with extras, the master bath includes built-in shelves and a dual-sink vanity. The front room can be used as a third bedroom or as a formal living room.

This energy-efficient home is designed with 9' high ceilings. The front porch and the family room have raised ceilings.

Heated area:	1,891 sq. ft.
Unheated area:	720 sq. ft.
Total area:	2,611 sq. ft.

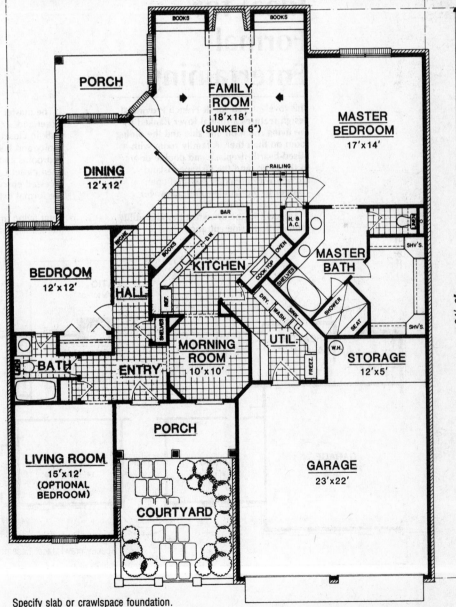

Specify slab or crawlspace foundation.

HomeStyles Source 1 Designers Network

Blueprint Price Code B

Plan E-1824

TO ORDER THIS BLUEPRINT,
CALL TOLL-FREE 1-800-547-5570
(Prices and details on pp. 12-15.)

43

Ideal for Formal Entertaining

This lovely 1,940 sq. ft. French Provincial design features a formal foyer flanked by the living room on one side and the dining room on the other. A family room with a raised-hearth fireplace and double doors to the patio, and the L-shaped island kitchen with breakfast bay and open counter to the family room, allow for more casual living.

Adjacent to the breakfast bay is a utility room with outside entrance.

The master suite includes one double closet and a compartmentalized bath with walk-in closet, step-up garden tub, double vanity and linen closet. Two front bedrooms and a second full bath with linen closet complete the design. A recessed entry and circular porch add to the formal exterior.

Total living area: 1,940 sq. ft.
(Not counting basement or garage)

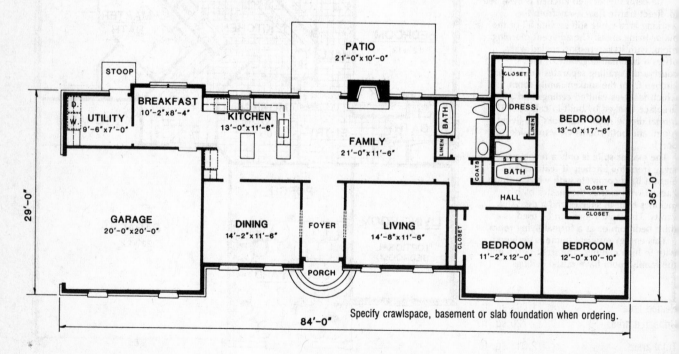

Specify crawlspace, basement or slab foundation when ordering.

TO ORDER THIS BLUEPRINT, CALL TOLL-FREE 1-800-547-5570
(Prices and details on pp. 12-15.)

Blueprint Price Code B
Plan C-8103

Classic and Charming

Total living area: 1,822 sq. ft.
(Not counting garage)

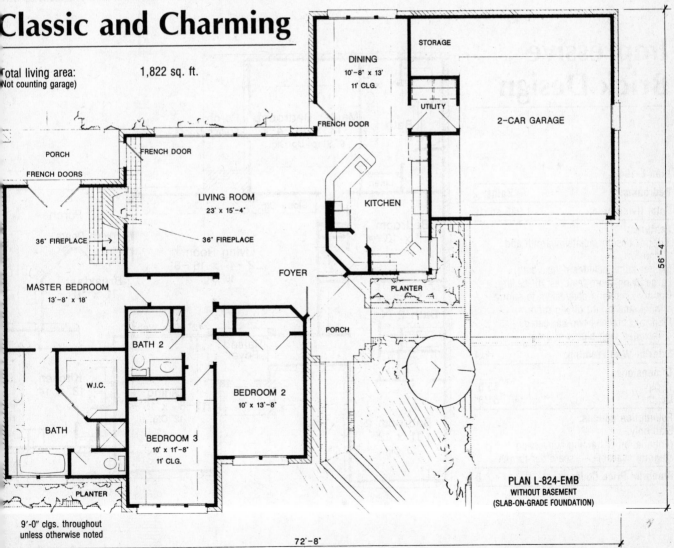

STORAGE

DINING
10'-8" x 13'
11' CLG.

2-CAR GARAGE

FRENCH DOOR

UTILITY

PORCH

FRENCH DOOR

FRENCH DOORS

LIVING ROOM
23' x 15'-4"

KITCHEN

36" FIREPLACE

36" FIREPLACE

FOYER

PLANTER

MASTER BEDROOM
13'-8" x 18'

PORCH

BATH 2

W.I.C.

BEDROOM 2
10' x 13'-8"

BATH

BEDROOM 3
10' x 11'-8"
11' CLG.

PLANTER

56'-4"

PLAN L-824-EMB
WITHOUT BASEMENT
(SLAB-ON-GRADE FOUNDATION)

9'-0" clgs. throughout
unless otherwise noted

72'-8"

HomeStyles
Source 1
DESIGNERS NETWORK

Blueprint Price Code B

Plan L-824-EMB

45

Impressive Brick Design

Plan L-1943

Bedrooms: 3	Baths: 2
Total living area:	1,943 sq. ft.

Features:
Exterior design radiates warmth and
comfort.
Master suite includes deluxe bath.
Large living room features 10' ceiling.
Roomy kitchen is convenient to sunny
nook and bright dining room.
Plan for detached two-car garage
included with blueprint order.

Exterior Wall Framing:	2x4

Dimensions:
Width: 55'0"
Depth: 51'8"

Foundation options:
Slab only.
(Foundation & framing conversion
diagram available — see order form.)

Blueprint Price Code: B

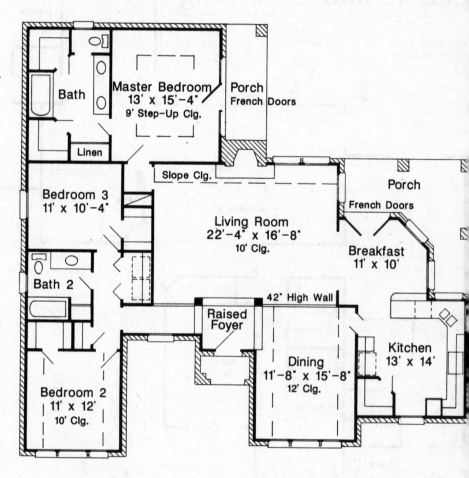

Plan L-1943

A Cozy, Permanent Look

Total living area:	1,996 sq. ft.
Porches:	278 sq. ft.
Garage:	449 sq. ft.
Total slab:	2,723 sq. ft.

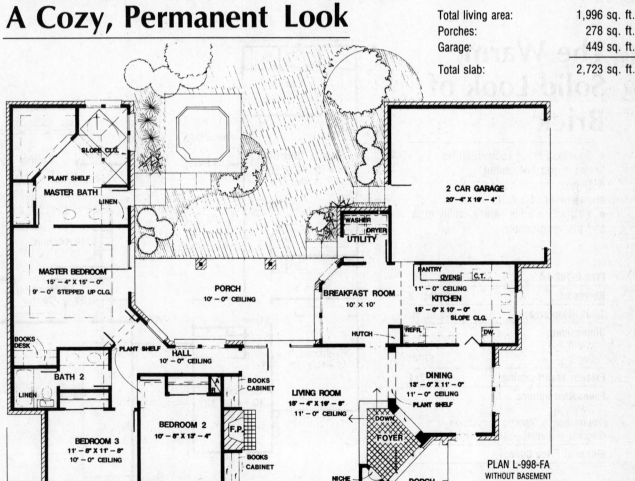

MASTER BATH

PLANT SHELF

SLOPE CLG.

LINEN

MASTER BEDROOM
15'—4" X 15'—0"
9'—0" STEPPED UP CLG.

BOOKS
DESK

PLANT SHELF

BATH 2

LINEN

HALL
10'—0" CEILING

BOOKS
CABINET

BEDROOM 3
11'—8" X 11'—8"
10'—0" CEILING

BEDROOM 2
10'—8" X 13'—4"

F.P.

BOOKS
CABINET

NICHE

PORCH
10'—0" CEILING

LIVING ROOM
15'—4" X 19'—8"
11'—0" CEILING

DOWN

FOYER

PORCH

2 CAR GARAGE
20'—4" X 19'—4"

WASHER   DRYER

UTILITY

BREAKFAST ROOM
10' X 10'

HUTCH

PANTRY
OVENS   C.T.

KITCHEN
15'—0" X 10'—0"
SLOPE CLG.

11'—0" CEILING

REFR.   DW.

DINING
13'—0" X 11'—0"
11'—0" CEILING
PLANT SHELF

PLAN L-998-FA
WITHOUT BASEMENT
(SLAB-ON-GRADE FOUNDATION)

71'—4"

Blueprint Price Code B

Plan L-998-FA

TO ORDER THIS BLUEPRINT,
CALL TOLL-FREE 1-800-547-5570
(Prices and details on pp. 12-15.)   **47**

The Warm, Solid Look of Brick

- Spacious living room features fireplace and 10′ ceiling.
- Deluxe master suite has 9′ ceiling and large private bath.
- Kitchen includes pantry, utility area and planning center.

Plan L-782-FA

Bedrooms: 3	**Baths: 2**
Total living area:	1,780 sq. ft.

Dimensions:
Width	50′8″
Depth	58′4″

Exterior Wall Framing: 2x4

Foundation options:
Slab only.
(Foundation & framing conversion diagram available — see order form.)

Blueprint Price Code: B

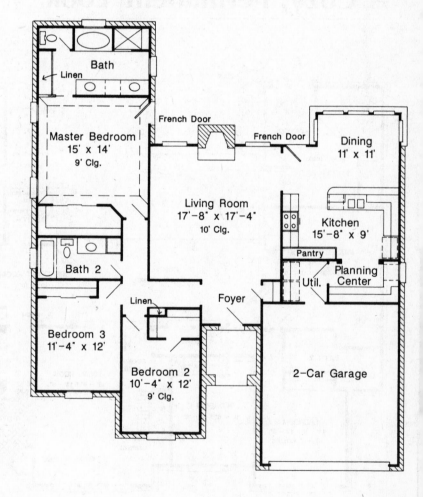

Plan L-782-FA

Great Room Featured

this rustic design, the centrally located reat Room features a cathedral ceiling ith exposed wood beams. Living and ning areas are separated by a massive replace.

The isolated master suite features a alk-in closet and compartmentalized bath. The gallery type kitchen is between the eakfast room and formal dining area. A rge utility room and storage room omplete the garage area.

On the opposite side of the Great Room are two additional bedrooms and a second full bath. All of this is included in only 1,670 square feet of heated living area.

Total living area: 1,670 sq. ft.
(Not counting basement or garage)
(Specify crawlspace, basement or slab foundation when ordering.)

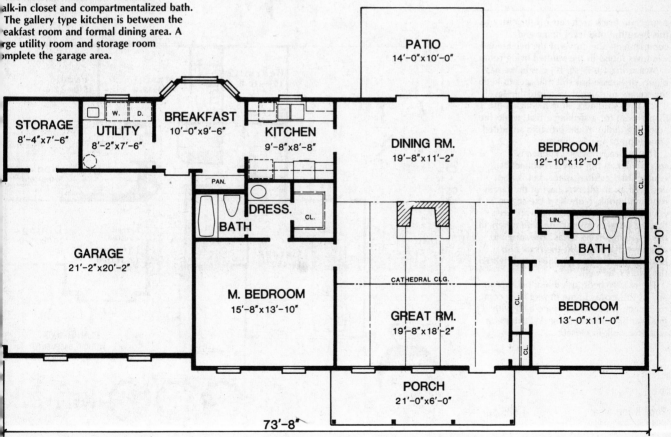

Grace and Finesse

A graceful brick arch sets off the entry to this beautiful one level home and complements the curve of the heightened windows found in the vaulted living room.

Measuring 1,685 sq. ft., this home has plenty of finesse but still manages to keep the square footage at an affordable level.

A barrel vaulted ceiling highlights the living room for a striking effect, while the adjoining dining room provides an added dimension of spaciousness.

The centrally located kitchen is spectacular. It not only has abundant counter and cabinet space, but is also designed as an integral part of the family room and nook. Note how the angled counter provides the cook a work area that encourages interaction with others in the adjoining living areas. The solarium windows that highlight the nook also provide plenty of natural light to brighten the kitchen as well.

The master bedroom doesn't skimp on any of the extras home buyers have come to expect. It boasts a private bath with dual vanities, illuminating skylight and a fantastic walk-in closet.

Total living area: 1,685 sq. ft.
(Not counting garage)

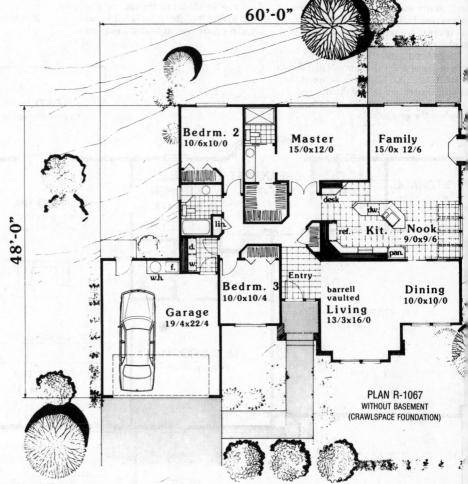

PLAN R-1067
WITHOUT BASEMENT
(CRAWLSPACE FOUNDATION)

TO ORDER THIS BLUEPRINT,
CALL TOLL-FREE 1-800-547-5570
50 (Prices and details on pp. 12-15.)

Blueprint Price Code B
Plan R-1067

Rustic Home With Porches Means Relaxation

A spacious screened porch serves as a great place to eat out during warm summer days and nights, while the front porch is ideal for relaxed rocking or a swing. The Great Room to the left of the entry has a fireplace and connects to the dining area and country kitchen. The large master bedroom features a private bath and ample closets.

For entertaining large groups, the combined dining area, living room and screened porch provide lots of space. Also note the large kitchen/utility and pantry area.

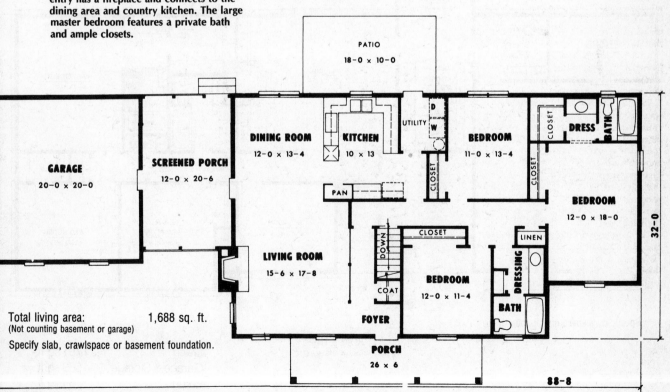

PATIO
18-0 x 10-0

DINING ROOM
12-0 x 13-4

KITCHEN
10 x 13

UTILITY

D
W

BEDROOM
11-0 x 13-4

CLOSET

CLOSET

DRESS

BATH

CLOSET

BEDROOM
12-0 x 18-0

GARAGE
20-0 x 20-0

SCREENED PORCH
12-0 x 20-6

PAN

LIVING ROOM
15-6 x 17-8

DOWN

CLOSET

LINEN

DRESSING

COAT

BEDROOM
12-0 x 11-4

BATH

FOYER

PORCH
26 x 6

32-0

88-8

Total living area: 1,688 sq. ft.
(Not counting basement or garage)

Specify slab, crawlspace or basement foundation.

Efficient Dining-Kitchen-Nook Combination

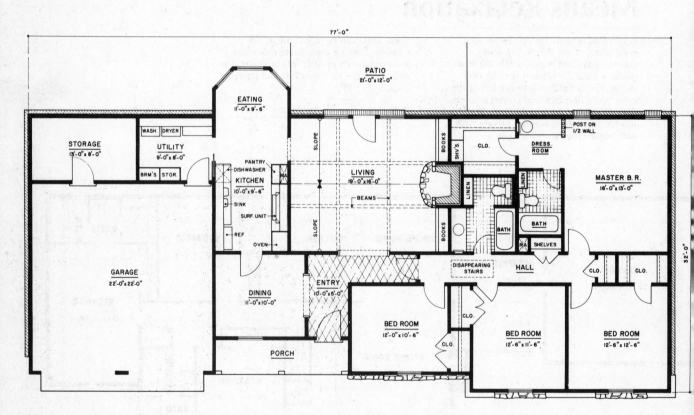

77'-0"

PATIO
21'-0"x12'-0"

EATING
11'-0"x 9'-6"

WASH. DRYER

STORAGE
13'-0"x 8'-0"

UTILITY
9'-0"x 8'-0"

BRM'S. STOR.

PANTRY
DISHWASHER

KITCHEN
10'-0"x 9'-6"

SINK

SURF. UNIT

REF

OVEN

SLOPE

SLOPE

LIVING
19'-0"x16'-0"

BEAMS

BOOKS

BOOKS

SHV'S.

CLO.

LINEN

LINEN

BATH

BATH

SHELVES

POST ON 1/2 WALL

DRESS. ROOM

MASTER B.R.
16'-0"x 13'-0"

32'-0"

GARAGE
22'-0"x 22'-0"

DINING
11'-0"x10'-0"

ENTRY
10'-0"x 5'-0"

DISAPPEARING STAIRS

HALL

CLO.

CLO.

BED ROOM
12'-0"x10'-6"

CLO.

CLO.

BED ROOM
12'-6"x11'-6"

BED ROOM
12'-6"x12'-6"

PORCH

Specify crawlspace or slab foundation.

PLAN E-1702
WITHOUT BASEMENT

AREAS

Living	1751 sq. ft.
Garage & Storage	589 sq. ft.
Porch	64 sq. ft.
Total	2404 sq. ft.

Blueprint Price Code B
Plan E-1702

HomeStyles
SOURCE 1
DESIGNERS NETWORK

Rustic Home
for Relaxed Living

A screened-in breezeway provides a cool place to dine out on warm summer days and nights, and the rustic front porch is ideal for relaxed rocking or a swing. A Great Room to the left of the entry has a fireplace and connects the dining area to the country kitchen.

The large master suite contains separate shower, garden tub, vanities and walk-in closets.

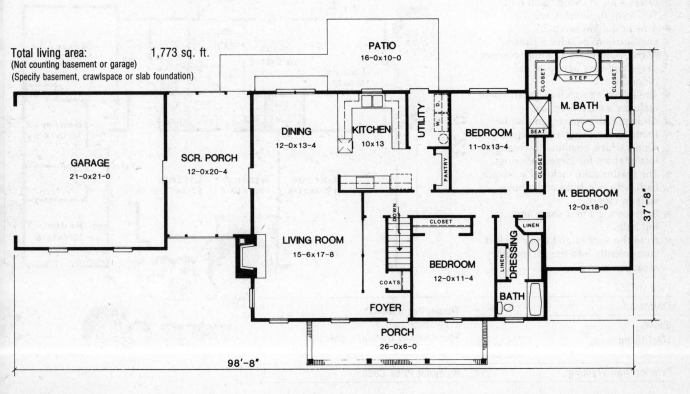

Total living area: 1,773 sq. ft.
(Not counting basement or garage)
(Specify basement, crawlspace or slab foundation)

PATIO
16-0x10-0

GARAGE
21-0x21-0

SCR. PORCH
12-0x20-4

DINING
12-0x13-4

KITCHEN
10x13

UTILITY

W. D.

PANTRY

BEDROOM
11-0x13-4

CLOSET

M. BATH

SEAT

CLOSET

M. BEDROOM
12-0x18-0

LIVING ROOM
15-6x17-8

DOWN

CLOSET

BEDROOM
12-0x11-4

LINEN

DRESSING

LINEN

COATS

BATH

FOYER

PORCH
26-0x6-0

37'-8"

98'-8"

Blueprint Price Code B
Plan C-8650

TO ORDER THIS BLUEPRINT,
CALL TOLL-FREE 1-800-547-5570
(Prices and details on pp. 12-15.) **53**

Deluxe Kitchen

- This attractive and functional home offers a lot of living room on a 1,774 sq. ft. foundation.
- A beautiful kitchen/nook combination includes a pantry, island, built-in desk, ample counter space and easy access to the outdoors.
- The adjoining spacious family room includes a cozy fireplace.
- An impressive space can also be found in the living and dining rooms which combine to create lots of room for large gatherings.
- The master suite includes a private bath with two sinks and a huge walk-in closet.
- Bedrooms 2 and 3 share another full bath.
- Note the washer and dryer tucked conveniently into the garage entry area.

Plan R-1062

Bedrooms: 3	Baths: 2

Space:

Total living area:	1,774 sq. ft.
Garage:	408 sq. ft.

Exterior Wall Framing:	2x4

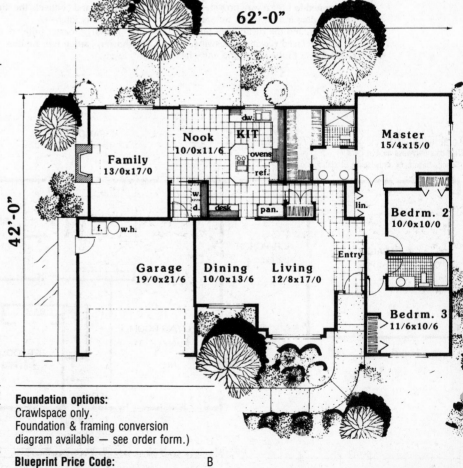

Foundation options:
Crawlspace only.
Foundation & framing conversion diagram available — see order form.)

Blueprint Price Code: B

Plan R-1062

Classic Country Style

AREAS

Living	1800 sq. ft.
Equipment Rm	22 sq. ft.
Garage & Storage	605 sq. ft.
Porches	354 sq. ft.
Total	2781 sq. ft.

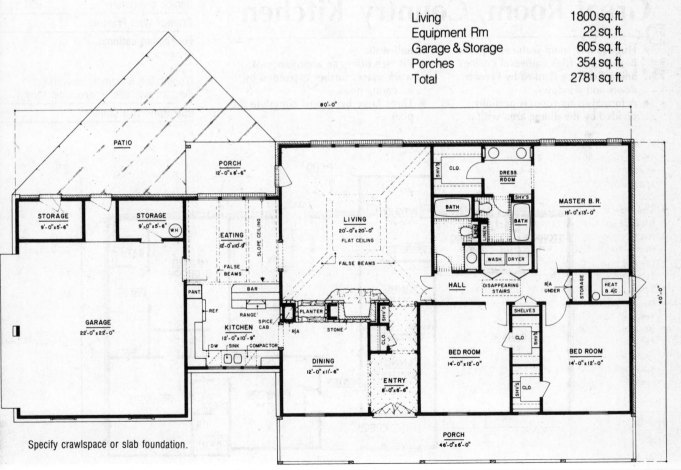

Specify crawlspace or slab foundation.

PATIO

PORCH
12'-0" x 6'-6"

STORAGE
9'-0" x 5'-6"

STORAGE
9'-0" x 5'-6"

WH

EATING
12'-0" x 10'-9"

FALSE BEAMS

SLOPE CEILING

LIVING
20'-0" x 20'-0"
FLAT CEILING

FALSE BEAMS

CLO.

DRESS ROOM

BATH

SHV'S

BATH

MASTER B.R.
16'-0" x 13'-0"

LINEN

WASH   DRYER

HALL

DISAPPEARING STAIRS

R/A UNDER

STORAGE

HEAT & A/C

GARAGE
22'-0" x 22'-0"

PANT

REF

BAR

RANGE

SPICE CAB

PLANTER

STONE

R/A

SHV'S

CLO.

SHELVES

CLO.

BED ROOM
14'-0" x 12'-0"

CLO.

BED ROOM
14'-0" x 12'-0"

DW

SINK

COMPACTOR

KITCHEN
12'-0" x 10'-9"

DINING
12'-0" x 11'-6"

ENTRY
8'-0" x 6'-6"

SHV'S

CLO.

PORCH
46'-0" x 6'-0"

80'-0"

40'-0"

Blueprint Price Code B
Plan E-1808

**TO ORDER THIS BLUEPRINT,
CALL TOLL-FREE 1-800-547-5570**
(Prices and details on pp. 12-15.)

Charming Traditional With Great Room, Country Kitchen

- Huge family room features exposed beams in its high cathedral ceilings and a fireplace flanked by French doors and windows.
- A formal living room is partially divided by the dining area with a half-wall.
- Kitchen offers an abundance of work space, further expanded by an eating nook.
- Three large bedrooms complete the plan.

Plan E-1815

Bedrooms: 3	Baths:
Space:	
Total living area:	1,898 sq. ft
Garage and porch:	608 sq. ft
Exterior Wall Framing:	2x
Foundation options: Crawlspace. Slab. (Foundation & framing conversion diagram available — see order form.)	
Blueprint Price Code:	

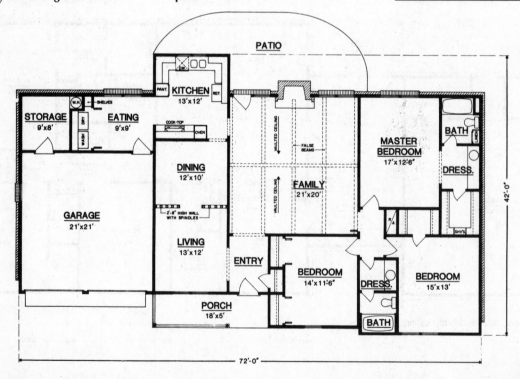

Plan E-1815

Cozy L-Shaped Bungalow

This pleasing L-shaped design packs a smooth-flowing floor plan into 1,950 sq. ft. The master suite includes garden tub, shower, his and her vanities and separate walk-in closets. Two other bedrooms and a full bath complete the sleeping wing.

A large family room, foyer and separate living-dining room combine to form the center section. U-shaped kitchen, breakfast nook with bay window and separate utility complete the plan.

Total living area: 1,950 sq. ft.
(Not counting basement or garage)

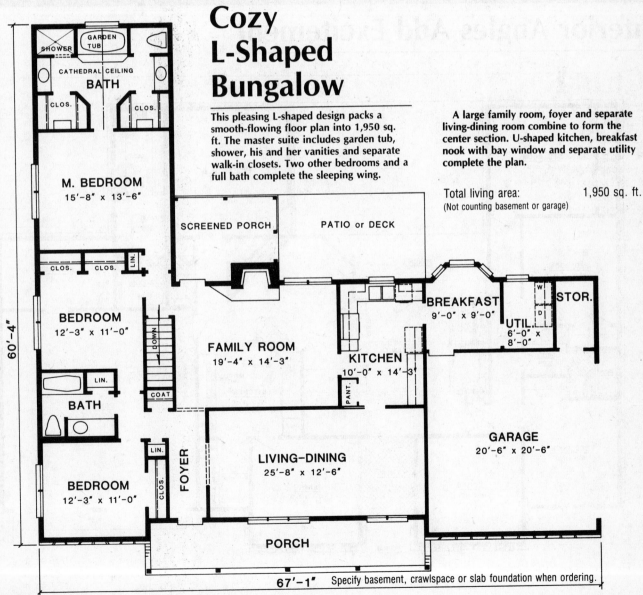

BATH
CATHEDRAL CEILING
SHOWER
GARDEN TUB
CLOS.
CLOS.

M. BEDROOM
15'-8" x 13'-6"

CLOS. CLOS. LIN.

BEDROOM
12'-3" x 11'-0"

DOWN

COAT

BATH
LIN.

BEDROOM
12'-3" x 11'-0"

LIN.
CLOS.

FOYER

60'-4"

SCREENED PORCH

PATIO or DECK

FAMILY ROOM
19'-4" x 14'-3"

KITCHEN
10'-0" x 14'-3"
PANT.

LIVING-DINING
25'-8" x 12'-6"

BREAKFAST
9'-0" x 9'-0"

UTIL.
6'-0" x 8'-0"

STOR.
W D

GARAGE
20'-6" x 20'-6"

PORCH

67'-1" Specify basement, crawlspace or slab foundation when ordering.

HomeStyles
Source 1
DESIGNERS NETWORK

Blueprint Price Code B
Plan C-8620

Interior Angles Add Excitement

70'-0"

48'-0"

BED ROOM 12'-6" x 12'-0"

PATIO

MASTER B. R. 14'-0" x 14'-0"

CLO.

CLO.

SHV'S

CLO.

DRESS. ROOM

BED ROOM 12'-0" x 11'-0"

PORCH

EATING 11'-0" x 10'-0"

CHINA

CLO.

STORAGE 13'-0" x 8'-0"

BATH

BATH

W.H.

CLO.

HALL

SHV'S

SHELVES

DRESS. ROOM

BATH

LINEN

CLO.

FAMILY 18'-6" x 15'-0"

SINK

SLOPE CEILING

DISHWASHER

SURFACE UNIT

KITCHEN 14'-0" x 12'-0"

REFRIGERATOR

PANT.

DISAPPEARING STAIRS

GARAGE 22'-0" x 22'-0"

SHV'S

BEAMS

SLOPE CEILING

OVEN

BRM'S

BED ROOM 12'-0" x 11'-0"

LIVING 12'-6" x 12'-0"

ENTRY

DINING 12'-6" x 12'-0"

UTILITY 8'-0" x 6'-0"

DRYER

WASHER

PORCH

Specify crawlspace or slab foundation.

AREAS

Living	1997 sq. ft.
Garage & Storage	588 sq. ft.
Porches	157 sq. ft.
Total	2742 sq. ft.

TO ORDER THIS BLUEPRINT, CALL TOLL-FREE 1-800-547-5570 (Prices and details on pp. 12-15.)

Blueprint Price Code B

Plan E-1904

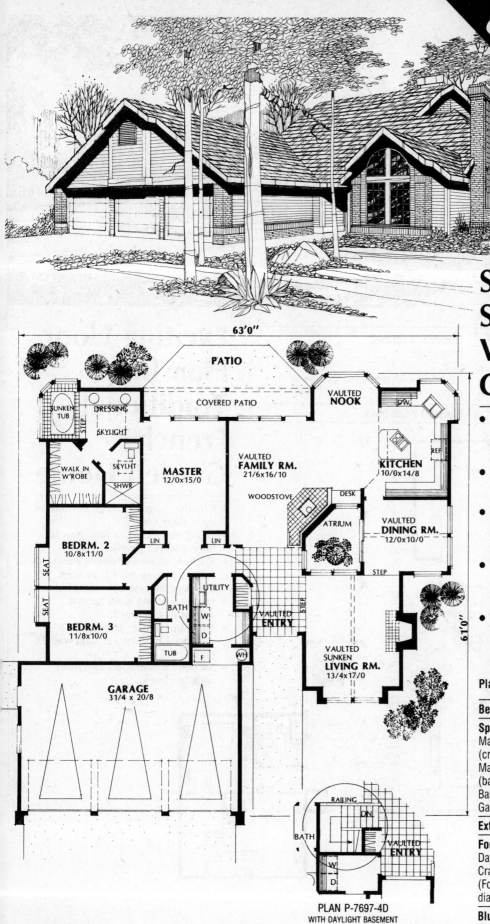

Soaring Spaces under Vaulted Ceilings

- A dignified exterior and a gracious, spacious interior combine to make this an outstanding plan for today's families.
- The living, dining, family rooms and breakfast nook all feature soaring vaulted ceilings.
- An interior atrium provides an extra touch of elegance, with its sunny space for growing plants and sunbathing.
- The master suite is first class all the way, with a spacious sleeping area, opulent bath, large skylight and enormous walk-in closet.
- A gorgeous kitchen includes a large work/cooktop island, corner sink with large corner windows and plenty of counter space.

Plans P-7697-4A & -4D

Bedrooms: 3	Baths: 2

Space:

Main floor (crawlspace version):	2,003 sq. ft.
Main floor (basement version):	2,030 sq. ft.
Basement:	2,015 sq. ft.
Garage:	647 sq. ft.

Exterior Wall Framing:	2x4

Foundation options:
Daylight basement (Plan P-7697-4D).
Crawlspace (Plan P-7697-4A).
(Foundation & framing conversion diagram available — see order form.)

Blueprint Price Code:	C

PATIO

COVERED PATIO

VAULTED NOOK

SUNKEN TUB   DRESSING   SKYLIGHT

WALK IN W'ROBE   SKYLHT   SHWR

MASTER 12/0x15/0

VAULTED FAMILY RM. 21/6x16/10

KITCHEN 10/0x14/8   REF   DW

WOODSTOVE   DESK

ATRIUM

VAULTED DINING RM. 12/0x10/0

BEDRM. 2 10/8x11/0

LIN   LIN

UTILITY

BATH   W   D

VAULTED ENTRY

STEP

BEDRM. 3 11/8x10/0

SEAT   SEAT

TUB   F   WH

VAULTED SUNKEN LIVING RM. 13/4x17/0

GARAGE 31/4 x 20/8

63'0"

61'0"

RAILING
DN
BATH
VAULTED ENTRY
W
D

PLAN P-7697-4D
WITH DAYLIGHT BASEMENT

Plans P-7697-4A & -4D

Plan E-2004

Bedrooms: 3	**Baths:** 2

Space:

Total living area:	2,023 sq. ft.
Garage:	484 sq. ft.
Storage & Porches:	423 sq. ft.

Exterior Wall Framing: 2x6

Foundation options:
Crawlspace.
Slab.
(Foundation & framing conversion diagram available — see order form.)

Blueprint Price Code: C

Exciting Floor Plan In Traditional French Garden Home

- Creative, angular design permits an open floor plan.
- Living and dining rooms open to a huge covered porch.
- Kitchen, living and dining rooms feature impressive 12' ceilings accented by extensive use of glass.
- Informal eating nook faces a delightful courtyard.
- Luxurious master bath offers a whirlpool tub, shower, and walk-in closet.
- Secondary bedrooms also offer walk-in closets.

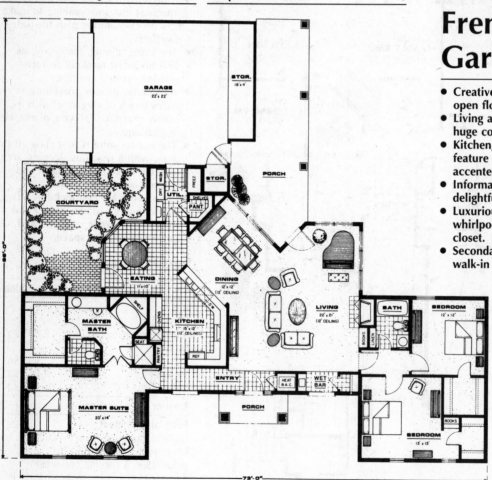

TO ORDER THIS BLUEPRINT,
CALL TOLL-FREE 1-800-547-5570
60 (Prices and details on pp. 12-15.)

Plan E-2004

Charming Exterior, Exciting Interior

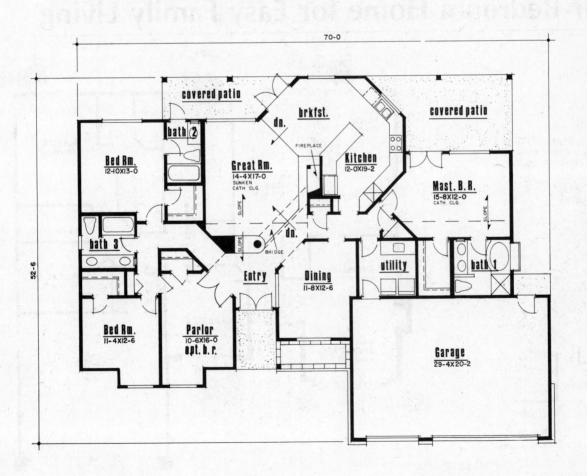

70-0

52-6

covered patio

bath 2

Bed Rm.
12-10X13-0

brkfst.

dn.

fireplace

covered patio

Great Rm.
14-4X17-0
SUNKEN
CATH. CLG.

Kitchen
12-0X19-2

Mast. B. R.
15-8X12-0
CATH. CLG.

SLOPE

SLOPE

SLOPE

bath 3

dn.

BRIDGE

Entry

Dining
11-8X12-6

utility

bath 1

Bed Rm.
11-4X12-6

Parlor
10-6X16-0
opt. b. r.

Garage
29-4X20-2

Total living area: 2,033 sq. ft.
(Not counting garage)

Plan Q-2033-1A
WITHOUT BASEMENT
(SLAB-ON-GRADE FOUNDATION)

HomeStyles
SOURCE 1
DESIGNERS NETWORK

Blueprint Price Code C
Plan Q-2033-1A

TO ORDER THIS BLUEPRINT,
CALL TOLL-FREE 1-800-547-5570
(Prices and details on pp. 12-15.)

61

Four-Bedroom Home for Easy Family Living

PLAN P-7696-4A
WITHOUT BASEMENT
(CRAWLSPACE FOUNDATION)

Total living area: 2,047 sq. ft.
(Not counting garage)

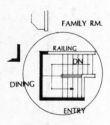

PLAN P-7696-4D
WITH DAYLIGHT BASEMENT

Main floor: 2,047 sq. ft.
(Not counting garage)

Basement level: 2,047 sq. ft.

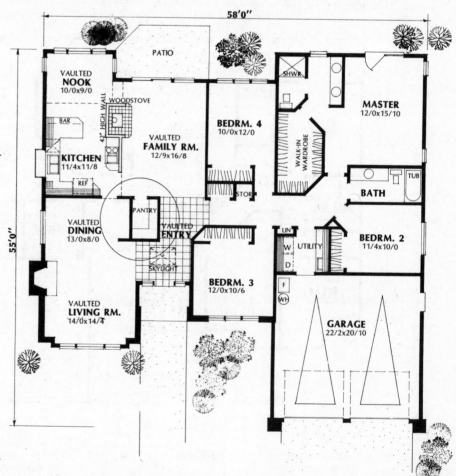

58'0"

55'0"

PATIO

VAULTED
NOOK
10/0x9/0

WOODSTOVE

42" HIGH WALL

BAR

KITCHEN
11/4x11/8

REF

VAULTED
FAMILY RM.
12/9x16/8

BEDRM. 4
10/0x12/0

SHWR

MASTER
12/0x15/10

WALK-IN
WARDROBE

STOR

BATH

TUB

PANTRY

VAULTED
DINING
13/0x8/0

VAULTED
ENTRY

LIN

W D
UTILITY

BEDRM. 2
11/4x10/0

SKYLIGHT

BEDRM. 3
12/0x10/6

F
WH

VAULTED
LIVING RM.
14/0x14/4

GARAGE
22/2x20/10

Blueprint Price Code C

Plans P-7696-4A & P-7696-4D

HomeStyles
SOURCE 1
DESIGNERS NETWORK

One Level, Three Bedrooms

WINDOW SEATS

FAMILY ROOM
14'-4" x 15'
10'-0" CEILING

MASTER BATH
SLOPE CLG.

FRENCH DOORS

BREAKFAST AREA

LINEN

PLANT SHELF

PORCH
FRENCH DOORS

42" HIGH COUNTER

4" WHEELSTOP

2 CAR GARAGE

SLOPE CLG.

MASTER BEDROOM
14'-10" X 14'-0"

DINING
11'-4" X 14'-0"
10'-0" CEILING

DW.

KITCHEN

PANTRY

SLOPE CLG.

REFR.

10'-0" CEILING

PANTRY

OVENS

HALL

DRYER

UTILITY

WASHER

FOYER

LIVING ROOM
13'-4" X 21'-0"
10'-0" CEILING

PLAN L-062-FAB
WITHOUT BASEMENT
(SLAB-ON-GRADE FOUNDATION)

BATH 2

BEDROOM 2
10'-4" X 11'-4"
10' VAULTED CEILING

SLOPE CLG.

BEDROOM 3
12'-0" X 10'-0"
10' CEILING

PORCH

61'-8"

64'-0"

Total living area: **2,060 sq. ft.**
(Not counting garage)

Blueprint Price Code C

Plan L-062-FAB

TO ORDER THIS BLUEPRINT,
CALL TOLL-FREE 1-800-547-5570
(Prices and details on pp. 12-15.)

Deluxe, Isolated Master Suite

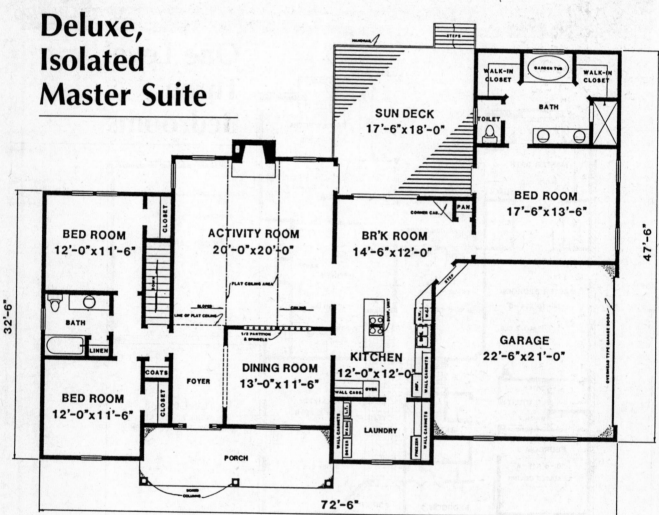

SUN DECK 17'-6"x18'-0"

WALK-IN CLOSET **GARDEN TUB** **WALK-IN CLOSET**

TOILET **BATH**

BED ROOM 17'-6"x13'-6"

BED ROOM 12'-0"x11'-6"

CLOSET

ACTIVITY ROOM 20'-0"x20'-0"

BR'K ROOM 14'-6"x12'-0"

CORNER CAB. PAN.

FLAT CEILING AREA

SLOPED CEILING
LINE OF FLAT CEILING

1/2 PARTITION & SPINDLES

BATH

LINEN

KITCHEN 12'-0"x12'-0"

GARAGE 22'-6"x21'-0"

OVERHEAD TYPE GARAGE DOOR

BED ROOM 12'-0"x11'-6"

COATS

CLOSET

FOYER

DINING ROOM 13'-0"x11'-6"

WALL CASS. OVEN
WALL CABINETS

LAUNDRY

WALL CABINETS FREEZER WALL CABINETS

PORCH

32'-6"

47'-6"

72'-6"

House:	2,130 sq. ft.
Garage:	491 sq. ft.
Porch:	168 sq. ft.
Sun Deck:	313 sq. ft.
Basement:	1,208 sq. ft.

PLAN W-2167
WITH BASEMENT

Blueprint Price Code C
Plan W-2167

HomeStyles
Source 1
DESIGNERS NETWORK

LEFT SIDE

Mediterranean Splendor

Sunny living spaces are found inside and out in this delightful design. The handsome stucco exterior enfolds a beautiful courtyard and spa tucked to one side of the home. The sun-drenched arbor is topped with a trellis roof, while a covered porch, or loggia, provides a sheltered outdoor living area.

The front of the home is just as inviting, with its arched transoms above the French windows and double-door entry. Both the front door and the service door in the garage open to the loggia. From here, French doors with an arched transom beckon guests into the foyer. The tiled foyer is lined with windows overlooking the courtyard area. Another pair of French doors opens to the arbor.

The formal living and dining rooms are designed to view toward the courtyard. Stately columns with overhead plant shelves outline the dining room. The living room features a built-in media center and a fireplace. The generous window allotment continues with the bay window in the kitchen/breakfast area. A wet bar serves both the indoor and outdoor entertainment areas.

The Ultimate Bathroom off the master bedroom is a special highlight of this home plan. The huge tiled bathing area includes a shower, a raised spa tub and two-way fireplace. A TV/VCR cabinet rotates to provide viewing from the sleeping area or the bath. The window facing the courtyard is placed high for privacy. Topping off the master bath area are a huge his-and-hers walk-in closet and a private commode.

A second bedroom features a delightful window seat, a walk-in closet and a private bath. The third bedroom also has a walk-in closet. Note the laundry closet, which is convenient to all three bedrooms.

Living area: 2,176 sq. ft.
(Not counting garage)

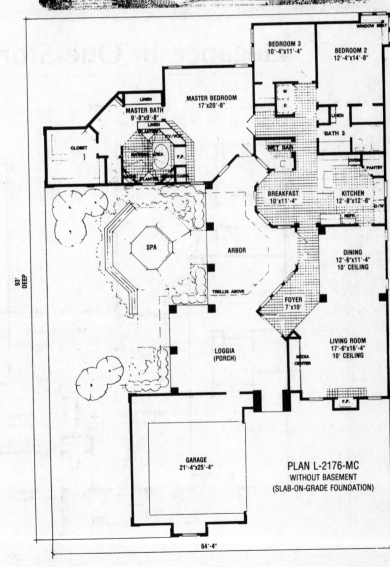

PLAN L-2176-MC
WITHOUT BASEMENT
(SLAB-ON-GRADE FOUNDATION)

Blueprint Price Code C
Plan L-2176-MC

TO ORDER THIS BLUEPRINT,
CALL TOLL-FREE 1-800-547-5570
(Prices and details on pp. 12-15.)

Elegance In One-Story Design

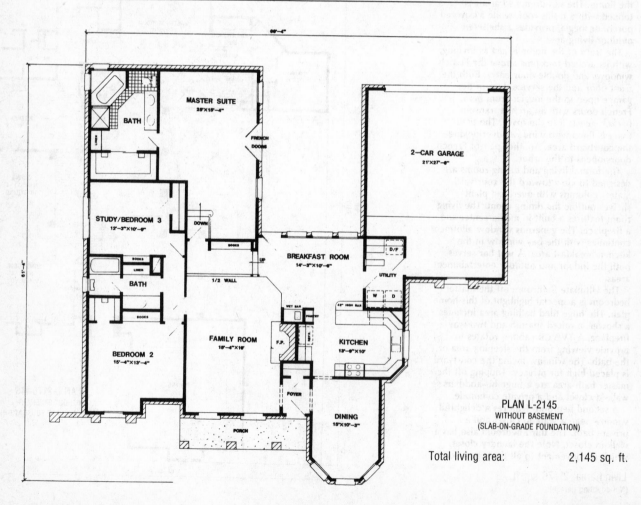

MASTER SUITE
25'X15'-4"

BATH

LINEN

FRENCH DOORS

2-CAR GARAGE
21'X27'-6"

STUDY/BEDROOM 3
12'-3"X10'-9"

DOWN

BOOKS

UP

BREAKFAST ROOM
14'-3"X10'-6"

D/F

BOOKS

LINEN

BATH

UTILITY

1/2 WALL

BOOKS

WET BAR

PANTRY

42" HIGH BAR

W   D

BEDROOM 2
15'-4"X13'-4"

FAMILY ROOM
19'-4"X16'

F.P.

MICRO

KITCHEN
13'-9"X10'

FOYER

DINING
15'X10'-3"

PORCH

PLAN L-2145
WITHOUT BASEMENT
(SLAB-ON-GRADE FOUNDATION)

Total living area: 2,145 sq. ft.

TO ORDER THIS BLUEPRINT,
CALL TOLL-FREE 1-800-547-5570
66 (Prices and details on pp. 12-15.)

Blueprint Price Code C
Plan L-2145

HomeStyles
Source
DESIGNERS NETWORK

Southern Country

- This home is distinctly Southern Country in style, from its wide front porch to its multi-paned and shuttered windows.
- The living room boasts a 12' cathedral ceiling, a fireplace and French doors to the rear patio.
- The dining room is open, but defined by three massive columns with overhead beams.
- The delightful kitchen/nook area is spacious and well-planned for both efficiency and pleasant kitchen working conditions.
- A handy utility room and half-bath are on either side of a short hallway leading to the carport.
- The master suite offers his and hers walk-in closets and an incredible bath which incorporates a plant shelf above the garden tub.

Plan J-86140	
Bedrooms: 3	Baths: 2½
Total living area:	2,177 sq. ft.
Basement:	2,177 sq. ft.
Carport:	440 sq. ft.
Storage:	120 sq. ft.
Porch:	233 sq. ft.
Exterior Wall Framing:	2x4
Ceiling Heights:	9'

Foundation options:
Standard basement.
Crawlspace.
Slab.
(Foundation & framing conversion diagram available — see order form.)

Blueprint Price Code: C

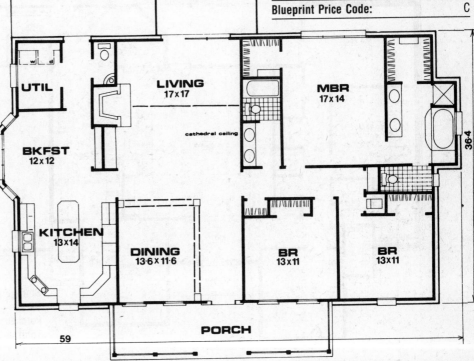

Isolated Master Bedroom Suite

Exterior walls are 2x6 construction.
Specify basement, crawlspace or slab foundation.

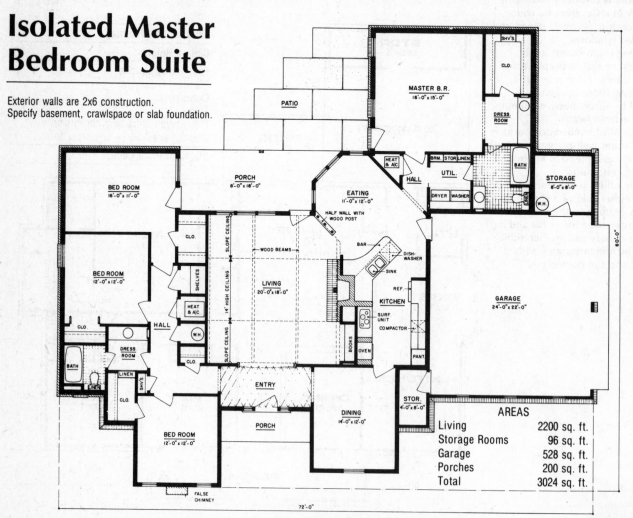

AREAS	
Living	2200 sq. ft.
Storage Rooms	96 sq. ft.
Garage	528 sq. ft.
Porches	200 sq. ft.
Total	3024 sq. ft.

An Energy Efficient Home

Blueprint Price Code C

Plan E-2206

Classy Rambler
Features Practical Floor Plan

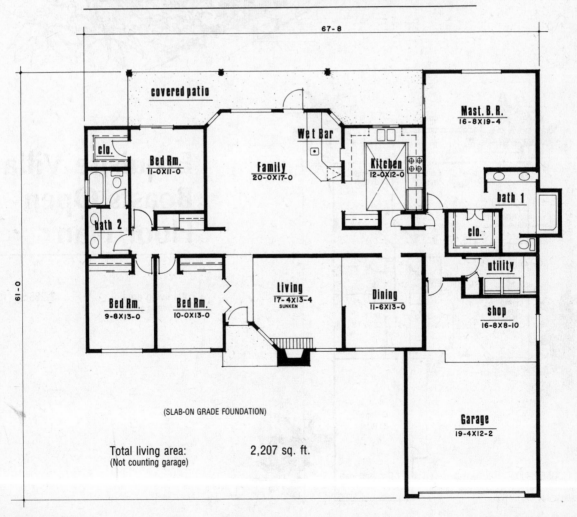

67-8

61-0

covered patio

clo.

Bed Rm.
11-0X11-0

Family
20-0X17-0

Wet Bar

Kitchen
12-0X12-0

Mast. B. R.
16-8X19-4

bath 1

clo.

bath 2

utility

Bed Rm.
9-8X13-0

Bed Rm.
10-0X13-0

Living
17-4X13-4
SUNKEN

Dining
11-6X13-0

shop
16-8X8-10

(SLAB-ON GRADE FOUNDATION)

Garage
19-4X12-2

Total living area:
(Not counting garage)

2,207 sq. ft.

Blueprint Price Code C
Plan Q-2207-1A

TO ORDER THIS BLUEPRINT,
CALL TOLL-FREE 1-800-547-5570
(Prices and details on pp. 12-15.)

Exquisite Villa Boasts Open Floor Plan

Total living area:
(Not counting garage)

2,235 sq. ft.

Floor Plan Labels:

- Pool
- Breakfast 9x10
- Family 18x17-2
- Master Suite 14-6x15-6
- Kitchen 16x11-4
- Bar
- Dining 14x11
- Garden
- Living 12-8x16
- Den/Br 3 10-8x13
- Mech
- Br 2 12-9x13
- Garage 23-6x24
- 1 Car (optional) 20x10
- 50'-0"
- 83'-0"

PLAN B-89003
WITHOUT BASEMENT
(SLAB-ON-GRADE FOUNDATION)

**TO ORDER THIS BLUEPRINT,
CALL TOLL-FREE 1-800-547-5570**
(Prices and details on pp. 12-15.)

Blueprint Price Code C
Plan B-89003

An Exciting Place to Live

- Long, graceful lines and multiple gables on a full-hip roof are highlights of this attractive design.
- Brick quoins at the corners add further accents to the facade.
- A recessed front entry leads into an exciting and spacious floor plan.
- The foyer divides the home into the sleeping area at the left, formal entertaining in the middle and family living on the right.
- The formal area includes the sunken living room, dining room and library.
- In the casual family living area, you'll find a large family room, sunny breakfast nook and open, island-type kitchen.
- The master suite sports a luxurious bath with spa tub and separate shower, plus a large walk-in closet and a private deck.

Plan I-2242-A

Bedrooms: 3	Baths: 2
Total living area:	2,242 sq. ft.
Garage:	744 sq. ft.
Exterior Wall Framing:	2x4

Foundation options:
Crawlspace.
Slab.
(Foundation & framing conversion diagram available — see order form.)

Blueprint Price Code: C

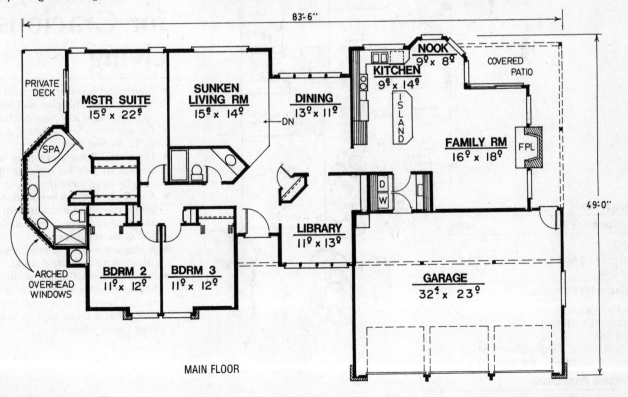

MAIN FLOOR

Plan I-2242-A

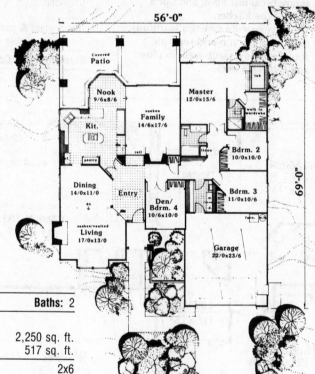

56'-0"

Covered Patio

Nook
9/6x8/6

Master
12/0x15/6

tub

walk in wardrobe

Kit.

sunken Family
14/6x17/6

linen

Bdrm. 2
10/0x10/0

pantry

rail

69'-0"

Dining
14/0x11/0

Entry

Den/ Bdrm. 4
10/6x10/0

Bdrm. 3
11/0x10/6

furn.

dn

sunken/vaulted Living
17/0x13/0

Garage
22/0x23/6

Plan R-1054

Bedrooms: 3-4	**Baths:** 2

Space:

Total living area:	2,250 sq. ft.
Garage:	517 sq. ft.

Exterior Wall Framing: 2x6

Ceiling Heights:
Foundation options:
Slab only.
(Foundation & framing conversion diagram available — see order form.)

Blueprint Price Code: C

Spanish-Style for Gracious Living

- A beautiful Spanish style with modern lines, this plan will be appreciated in any neighborhood.
- The interior offers a roomy 2,250 sq. ft. on one floor.
- The formal living and dining rooms are side by side for easy use of both by large gatherings.
- A well-planned kitchen/nook and family room combination provide adequate space for family dining and other activities.
- A pleasant master suite offers a private bath and large closet.
- A den provides the option of having a fourth bedroom or guest room if needed, or a great home office that is more appropriate for your family situation.

Plan R-1054

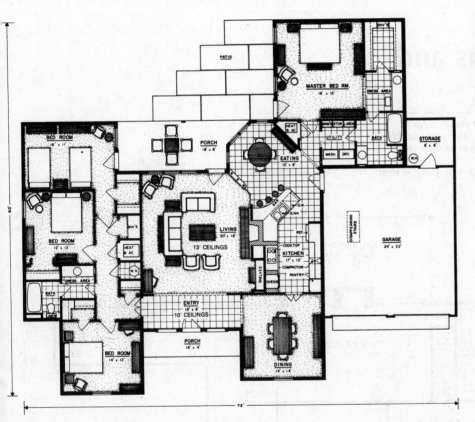

Luxury Living on One Level

- **Exterior presents a classic air of quality and distinction in design.**
- **Spacious one-story interior provides space for family life and entertaining.**
- **The large central living room boasts a 13' ceiling and large hearth.**
- **A roomy formal dining room adjoins the foyer.**
- **The gorgeous kitchen/nook combination provides a sunny eating area along with an efficient and attractive kitchen with eating bar and abundant counter space.**
- **The master suite is isolated from the other bedrooms for more privacy, and includes a luxurious bath and dressing area.**
- **Three additional bedrooms make up the left side of the plan, and share a second bath.**
- **The garage is off the kitchen for maximum convenience in carrying in groceries; also note the storage space off the garage.**

Plan E-2208

Bedrooms: 4	Baths: 2
Total living area:	2,252 sq. ft.
Garage:	528 sq. ft.
Storage:	64 sq. ft.
Exterior Wall Framing:	2x6

Typical Ceiling Heights:
8' unless otherwise noted.

Foundation options:
Standard basement.
Crawlspace.
Slab.
(Foundation & framing conversion diagram available — see order form.)

Blueprint Price Code: C

Plan E-2208

Spacious and Inviting

The four-column front porch, picture window, siding, brick, stone and cupola combine for a pleasing exterior for this three-bedroom home.

Extra features include a fireplace, screen porch, deluxe master bath and a large separate breakfast room.

Total living area: 2,306 sq. ft.
(Not counting basement or garage)

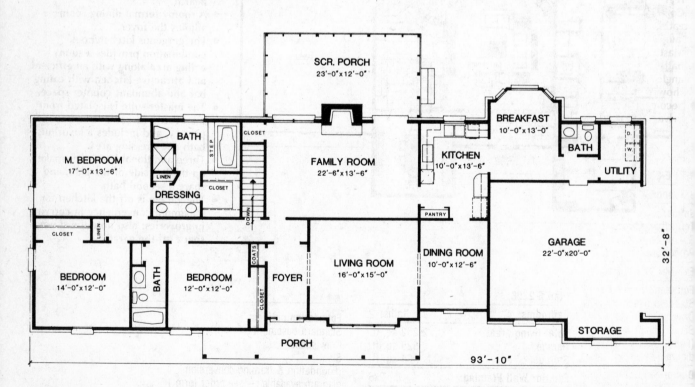

SCR. PORCH
23'-0" x 12'-0"

BATH

CLOSET

STEP

LINEN

M. BEDROOM
17'-0" x 13'-6"

FAMILY ROOM
22'-6" x 13'-6"

BREAKFAST
10'-0" x 13'-0"

KITCHEN
10'-0" x 13'-6"

BATH

D.
W.

DRESSING

CLOSET

DOWN

UTILITY

CLOSET

LINEN

BEDROOM
14'-0" x 12'-0"

BATH

BEDROOM
12'-0" x 12'-0"

COATS

FOYER

PANTRY

LIVING ROOM
16'-0" x 15'-0"

DINING ROOM
10'-0" x 12'-6"

GARAGE
22'-0" x 20'-0"

32'-8"

CLOSET

PORCH

STORAGE

93'-10"

Specify basement, crawlspace or slab foundation.

Blueprint Price Code C
Plan C-8625

High Luxury in One-Story Plan

- 12' ceilings are featured in the entryway and living room.
- 400 sq. ft. living room boasts a massive fireplace and access to the rear porch.
- Corridor-style kitchen has angled eating bar and convenient nearby laundry facilities.
- Master suite incorporates unusual bath arrangement consisting of an angled whirlpool tub and separate shower.
- Secondary bedrooms are zoned for privacy and climate control.

Plan E-2302

Bedrooms: 4	Baths: 2

Space:

Total living area:	2,396 sq. ft.
Garage and storage:	590 sq. ft.
Porches:	216 sq. ft.
Exterior Wall Framing:	2x6

Foundation options:
Standard basement.
Crawlspace.
Slab.
(Foundation & framing conversion diagram available — see order form.)

Blueprint Price Code:	C

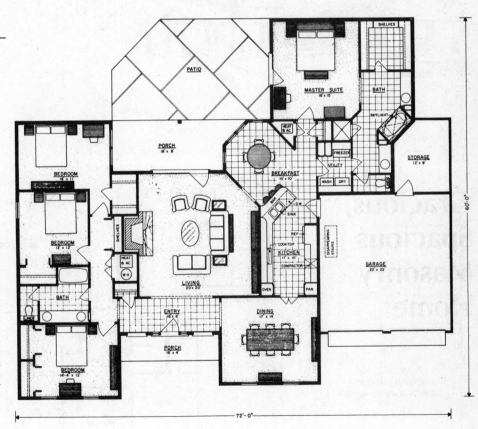

Plan E-2302

REAR VIEW

Gracious, Spacious Masonry Home

PLAN L-483-HB
WITHOUT BASEMENT
(SLAB-ON-GRADE FOUNDATION)

Total living area: 2,481 sq. ft.

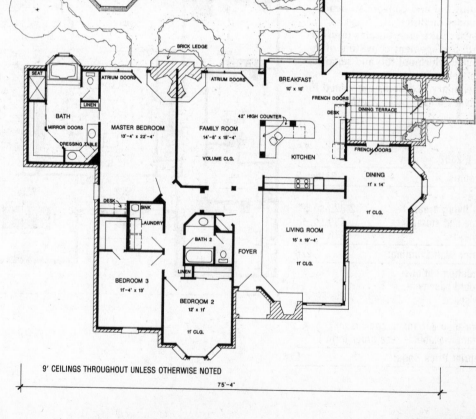

3-CAR GARAGE

BREAKFAST
10' x 10'

FRENCH DOORS

DESK

DINING TERRACE

BRICK LEDGE

ATRIUM DOORS   ATRIUM DOORS

42" HIGH COUNTER

SEAT

LINEN

BATH
MIRROR DOORS
DRESSING TABLE

MASTER BEDROOM
13'-4" x 22'-4"

FAMILY ROOM
14'-6" x 19'-4"

VOLUME CLG.

KITCHEN

FRENCH DOORS

DINING
11' x 14'

11' CLG.

DESK
SINK
LAUNDRY

BATH 2
LINEN

FOYER

LIVING ROOM
15' x 19'-4"

11' CLG.

BEDROOM 3
11'-4" x 13'

BEDROOM 2
12' x 11'

11' CLG.

9' CEILINGS THROUGHOUT UNLESS OTHERWISE NOTED

75'-4"

80'-8"

Blueprint Price Code C
Plan L-483-HB

HomeStyles
SOURCE 1
DESIGNERS NETWORK

"Down-Home" Country Flavor

AREAS	
Living	2522 sq. ft.
Garage	484 sq. ft.
Porches	444 sq. ft.
Storage Rooms	90 sq. ft.
Total	3540 sq. ft.

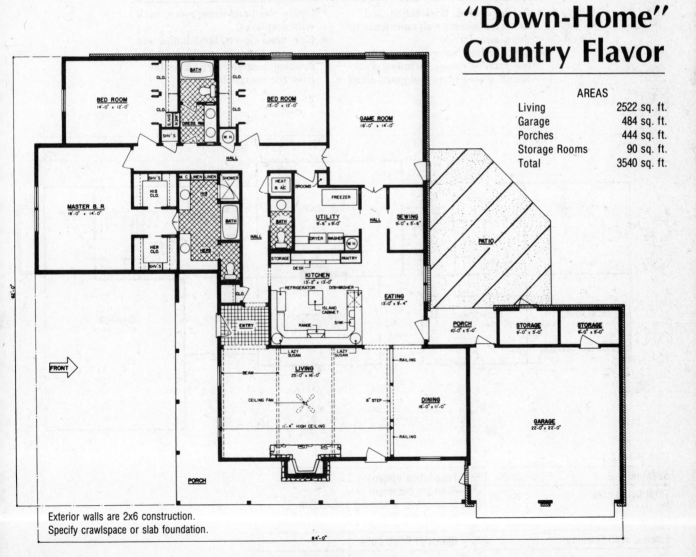

Exterior walls are 2x6 construction.
Specify crawlspace or slab foundation.

An Energy Efficient Home

Blueprint Price Code C

Plan E-2502

Southern Colonial with Authentic Style

- Porch columns, brick siding, and shuttered windows all contribute to this classic facade.
- This spacious home features large but detailed rooms, including a formal dining room and grand-sized

family room and living room, each with fireplaces.
- King-sized closets, large baths, and generous bedrooms make up the sleeping quarters, well separated from the main living areas.

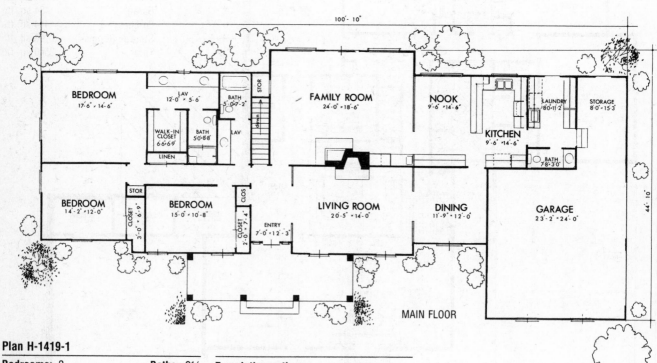

MAIN FLOOR

Plan H-1419-1

Bedrooms: 3	Baths: 2½
Total living area:	2,558 sq. ft.
Basement:	approx. 2,558 sq. ft.
Garage:	556 sq. ft.
Exterior Wall Framing:	2x6

Foundation options:
Standard basement only.
(Foundation & framing conversion diagram available — see order form.)

Blueprint Price Code: C

Plan H-1419-1

HomeStyles SOURCE 1 DESIGNERS' NETWORK

FRONT VIEW

REAR VIEW

Spacious Western Ranch

- A three-bedroom sleeping wing is separated from the balance of the home, with the master suite featuring a raised tub below skylights and a walk-in dressing room.
- Sunken living room is enhanced by a vaulted ceiling and fireplace with raised hearth.
- Family room is entered from the central hall through double doors; a wet bar and a second fireplace grace this gathering spot.
- Kitchen has functional L-shaped arrangement, attached nook, and pantry.

Plan H-3701-1A	
Bedrooms: 4	**Baths:** 3½
Total living area: Garage:	3,735 sq. ft. 830 sq. ft.
Exterior Wall Framing:	2x4

Foundation options:
Crawlspace only.
(Foundation & framing conversion
diagram available — see order form.)

Blueprint Price Code: F

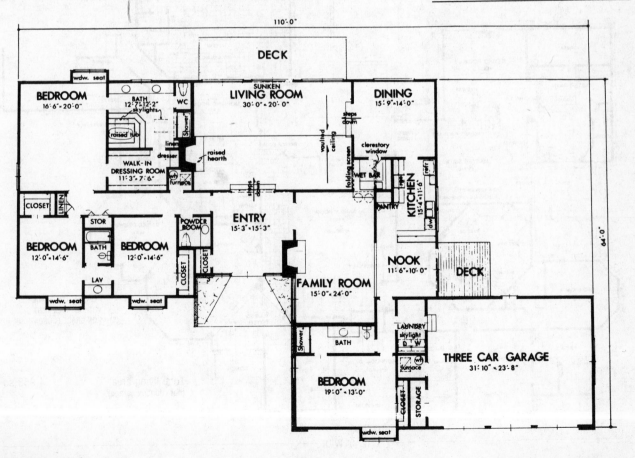

Plan H-3701-1A

In A Class by Itself

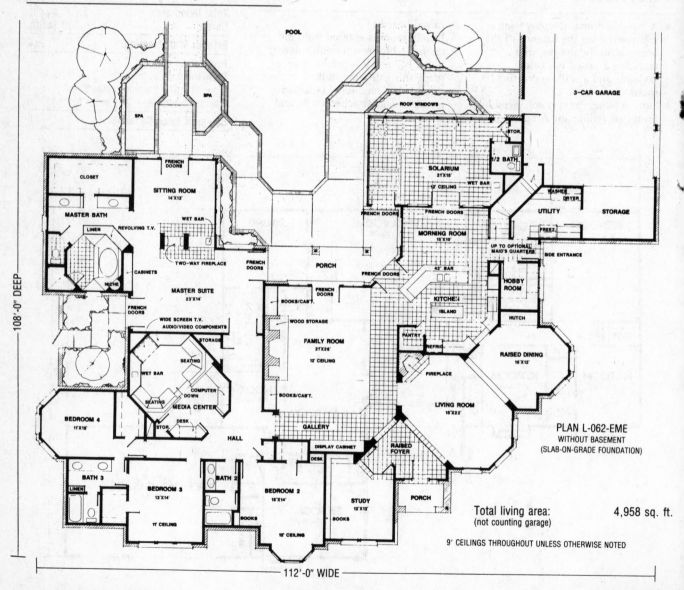

POOL

3-CAR GARAGE

SPA

SPA

CLOSET

FRENCH DOORS

SITTING ROOM
14'X13'

MASTER BATH

ROOF WINDOWS

STOR.

1/2 BATH

SOLARIUM
21'X15'

LINEN

REVOLVING T.V.

WET BAR

12' CEILING

WET BAR

WASHER DRYER

CABINETS

TWO-WAY FIREPLACE

FRENCH DOORS

FRENCH DOORS

MORNING ROOM
15'X10'

UTILITY

STORAGE

NICHE

FREEZ.

UP TO OPTIONAL MAID'S QUARTERS

SIDE ENTRANCE

FRENCH DOORS

MASTER SUITE
23'X14'

42" BAR

HOBBY ROOM

WIDE SCREEN T.V.
AUDIO/VIDEO COMPONENTS

FRENCH DOORS

BOOKS/CAB'T.

PORCH

FRENCH DOORS

KITCHEN

ISLAND

HUTCH

STORAGE

WOOD STORAGE

FAMILY ROOM
21'X26'

PANTRY

REFRIG.

WET BAR

SEATING

12' CEILING

RAISED DINING
16'X12'

COMPUTER DOWN

FIREPLACE

SEATING

BOOKS/CAB'T.

MEDIA CENTER

BEDROOM 4
11'X15'

DESK

STOR.

LIVING ROOM
15'X22'

HALL

GALLERY

PLAN L-062-EME
WITHOUT BASEMENT
(SLAB-ON-GRADE FOUNDATION)

DISPLAY CABINET

RAISED FOYER

DESK

BATH 3

LINEN

BEDROOM 3
13'X14'

BATH 2

BEDROOM 2
18'X14'

STUDY
12'X13'

PORCH

11' CEILING

BOOKS

12' CEILING

BOOKS

Total living area: **4,958 sq. ft.**
(not counting garage)

9' CEILINGS THROUGHOUT UNLESS OTHERWISE NOTED

108'-0" DEEP

112'-0" WIDE

Blueprint Price Code G

Plan L-062-EME

HomeStyles
SOURCE
DESIGNERS' NETWORK

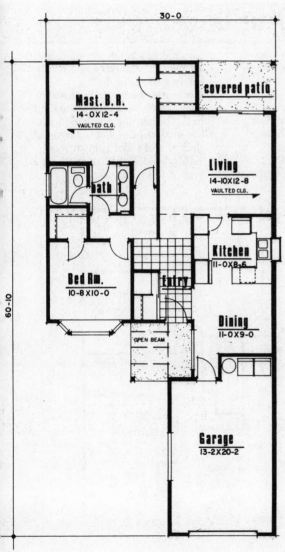

Tight-Lot Excitement on A Tight Budget

- This plan packs plenty of exciting living spaces into 989 square feet and just 30 feet of width.
- The entry features an arbor for drama and opens into the foyer with a spacious closet and a view into the vaulted living room.
- The galley kitchen serves a sunny dining area which opens up to the front yard.
- The master bedroom features a vaulted ceiling, walk-in closet, and private access to the bath.
- The second bedroom has a bay window seat and a full walk-in closet.

Plan Q-989-1A

Bedrooms: 2	**Baths:** 1

Space:	
Total living area:	989 sq. ft.
Garage:	266 sq. ft.

Exterior Wall Framing:	2x4

Foundation options:
Slab.
(Foundation & framing conversion diagram available — see order form.)

Blueprint Price Code:	A

Plan L-186-CSA

Bedrooms: 3	**Baths:** 2

Space:

Total living area:	1,186 sq. ft.
Garage and storage:	503 sq. ft.

Exterior Wall Framing:	2x4
Ceiling Heights:	9'

Foundation options:
Slab.
(Foundation & framing conversion
diagram available — see order form.)

Blueprint Price Code:	A

Luxury on One Level

- An exciting living room greets your first glance at the pleasantries that appear throughout this lovely Victorian home; a 42"-high wall reveals a fireplace, built-in media center and front-facing bay window.
- French doors in the attached dining room open onto a rear covered porch.
- A pass-thru and eating bar separate the dining area from the kitchen,

which offers ample counter space, a view to the porch and a handy utility room close by.
- The master bedroom features its own French doors for private entry to the porch; the adjoining bath has dual vanities and separate tub, shower and toilet compartment.
- Two secondary bedrooms share a second full bath.

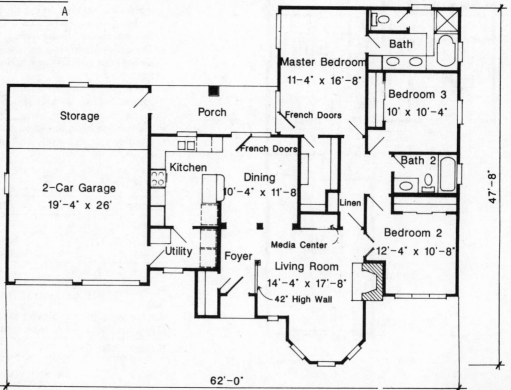

Plan L-186-CSA

Maximum Value and Excitement

- This well-planned 1,231 sq. ft. ranch design gives the first-time home buyer the most value and excitement for the dollar.
- The front porch, stone chimney, divided windows, and gable louvre all highlight a nostalgic charm.
- The interior spaces feature vaulted ceilings for an airy feel.
- The den could serve several functions, including guest quarters or a formal dining room.
- The master bedroom has a full-wall closet and a divided bath with private toilet.

Plan B-88021

Bedrooms: 2-3	Baths: 2
Space:	
Total living area:	1,231 sq. ft.
Basement:	1,231 sq. ft.
Garage:	400 sq. ft.
Exterior Wall Framing:	2x4
Foundation options:	

Standard basement.
(Foundation & framing conversion diagram available — see order form.)

Blueprint Price Code:	A

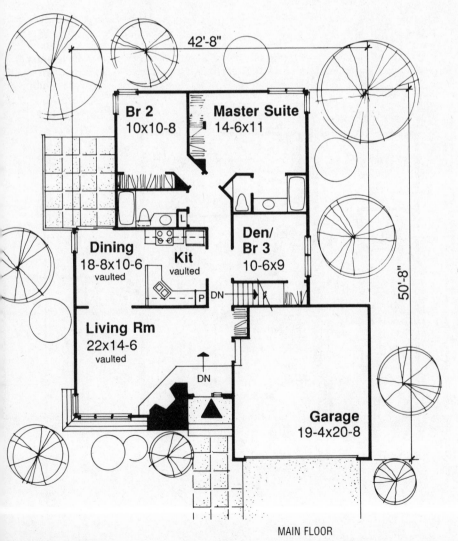

42'-8"

50'-8"

Br 2
10x10-8

Master Suite
14-6x11

Dining
18-8x10-6
vaulted

Kit
vaulted

Den/ Br 3
10-6x9

Living Rm
22x14-6
vaulted

P

DN

DN

Garage
19-4x20-8

MAIN FLOOR

Plan B-88021

TO ORDER THIS BLUEPRINT, CALL TOLL-FREE 1-800-547-5570
(Prices and details on order form.)

C-3

Cottage in the Country

- A nostalgic cottage exterior look would be appealing whether built in the country or the suburbs.
- The interior offers excitement and efficiency in its 1,497 sq. ft.
- A formal living room and interesting octagonal dining room greet guests from the entry.
- The kitchen overlooks the family room with cathedral ceiling, fireplace, and sliders to a covered patio.
- The master suite includes a vaulted ceiling, walk-in closet and private bath.

Plan Q-1497-1A

Bedrooms: 3	Baths: 2

Space:

Total living area:	1,497 sq. ft.
Garage:	383 sq. ft.

Exterior Wall Framing:	2x4

Foundation options:
Slab.
(Foundation & framing conversion diagram available — see order form.)

Blueprint Price Code:	A

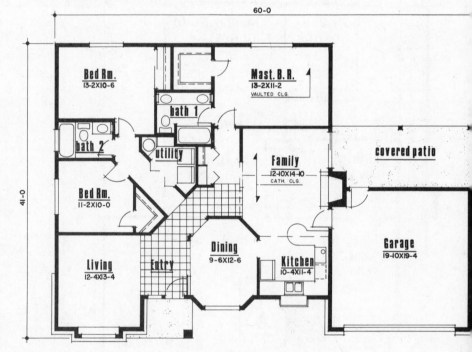

TO ORDER THIS BLUEPRINT, CALL TOLL-FREE 1-800-547-5570
(Prices and details on order form.)

Plan Q-1497-1A

Rustic Ranch Look

- A rustic exterior look combines with an open, flowing interior to offer buyers an exciting, livable package.
- The entry opens up to dramatic views into the formal living/dining rooms with fireplace to the left, and straightahead into the informal family room.
- The U-shaped kitchen overlooks the informal family living area.
- The master bedroom includes a dressing area and a private bath.
- The third bedroom can serve as a study with double doors opening to the entry.

Plan Q-1554-1A

Bedrooms: 2-3	Baths: 2
Space:	
Total living area:	1,554 sq. ft.
Garage:	469 sq. ft.
Exterior Wall Framing:	2x4

Foundation options:
Slab.
(Foundation & framing conversion diagram available — see order form.)

Blueprint Price Code: B

Plan Q-1554-1A

Room To Grow

- Though modest in square footage, this ranch design offers the growing family four bedrooms and plenty of living space.
- The plan includes a large, front-facing formal living room and an open kitchen/dining/family room combination informal living area to the rear.
- The family room is lowered a step for drama, and offers a craft room with bi-fold doors to tuck away masterpieces-in-progress.
- The spacious master suite includes a large dressing area and a private bath.

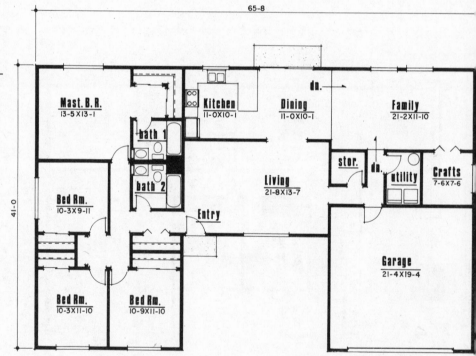

Plan Q-1891-1A

Bedrooms: 4	Baths: 2
Space:	
Total living area:	1,891 sq. ft.
Garage:	412 sq. ft.
Exterior Wall Framing:	2x4

Foundation options:
Slab.
(Foundation & framing conversion diagram available — see order form.)

Blueprint Price Code: B

TO ORDER THIS BLUEPRINT,
CALL TOLL-FREE 1-800-547-5570
(Prices and details on order form.)

Plan Q-1891-1A

Country Charm Revisited

- A covered front porch, dormers, multi-paned windows and two projected windows at the dining room and study offer a welcoming front exterior with country charm revisited.
- The Great Room is the heart of this plan, featuring a cathedral ceiling, fireplace with flanking bookshelves and direct access to the rear sun room through dual sliders.
- The kitchen with cooking island serves both the formal dining room and the breakfast eating area.
- The master suite opens onto the rear deck via sliders.
- The master bath has double vanities and separate shower and tub under corner windows.
- Two other bedrooms are located at the other end of the house for privacy, with the front bedroom doubling as a study.

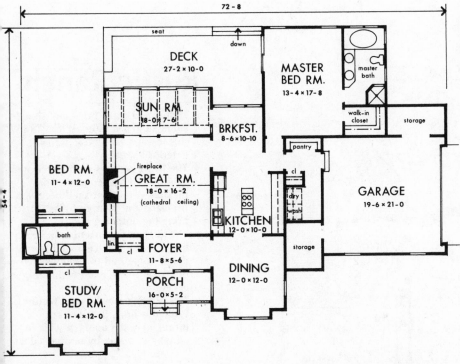

Plan DG-161

Bedrooms: 2-3	Baths: 2

Space:

Total living area:	1,899 sq. ft.
Garage:	410 sq. ft.
Storage area:	approx. 125 sq. ft.

Exterior Wall Framing:	2x4

Foundation options:
Crawlspace.
(Foundation & framing conversion diagram available — see order form.)

Blueprint Price Code:	B

REAR VIEW

Plan DG-161

Rustic Ranch

- Half-round glass, brick and shingle siding, and a full-round louver give this ranch a rustic traditional exterior appeal.
- The living room is dramatized with vaulted ceilings, column room dividers with plant shelf details, a fireplace and plenty of glass to bring the outdoors in.
- The kitchen is conveniently situated between the tray-ceilinged formal dining room and the sunny breakfast room, each with deck access.
- The exciting master suite features a vaulted ceiling, private deck through French doors, a walk-in closet and a splashy master bath.

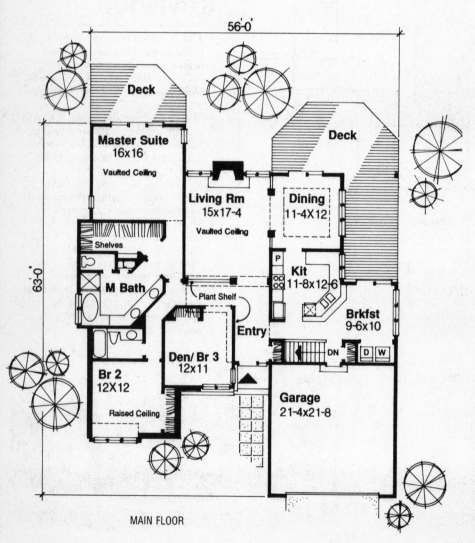

MAIN FLOOR

Plan UDG-90001

Plan UDG-90001	
Bedrooms: 3	**Baths:** 2

Total living area:	1,958 sq. ft.
Basement:	1,958 sq. ft.
Garage:	462 sq. ft.

Exterior Wall Framing:	2x4

Foundation options:
Standard basement.
(Foundation & framing conversion diagram available — see order form.)

Blueprint Price Code:	B

TO ORDER THIS BLUEPRINT,
CALL TOLL-FREE 1-800-547-5570
(Prices and details on order form.)

Plan UDG-90001

Look No Further

- If you are looking for a move-up ranch with plenty of move-up features look no further.
- The excitement begins with the covered porch entry which opens up to a dramatic view of the vaulted living room with fireplace and French door to the deck and greenspaces beyond.
- The formal dining room keeps the excitement rising, with a generous wall overlooking the deck.
- The kitchen opens up to a large vaulted space which includes a family room, breakfast area, desk and a second fireplace.
- The three bedrooms are all on one side of the house, which the parents of small children will especially appreciate. The vaulted master bedroom has plenty of privacy, however, and its features include French doors to the deck, a large walk-in closet, an exciting master bath with separate tub and shower, compartmented toilet, and double vanity.

Plan B-118-86

Bedrooms: 3	Baths: 2½

Space:

Total living area:	2,004 sq. ft.
Basement:	2,004 sq. ft.
Garage:	609 sq. ft.

Exterior Wall Framing:	2x4

Foundation options:
Standard basement.
(Foundation & framing conversion
diagram available — see order form.)

Blueprint Price Code:	C

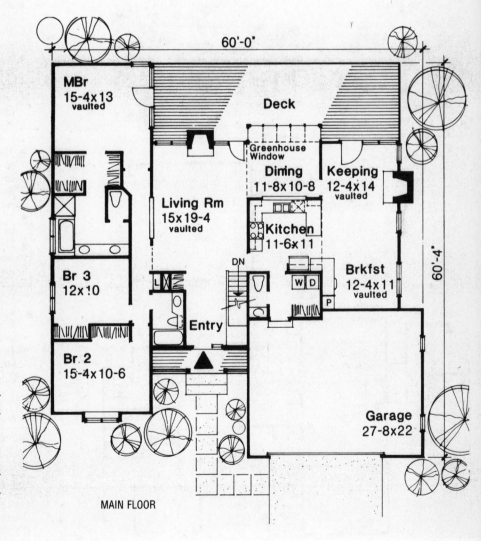

MAIN FLOOR

60'-0"

60'-4"

MBr
15-4x13
vaulted

Deck

Greenhouse
Window

Dining
11-8x10-8

Keeping
12-4x14
vaulted

Living Rm
15x19-4
vaulted

Kitchen
11-6x11

Br 3
12x10

DN

Brkfst
12-4x11
vaulted

W D

P

Br 2
15-4x10-6

Entry

Garage
27-8x22

Plan B-118-86

C-9

REAR VIEW

Sunny Delight

- This three-bedroom country cottage home with a sunroom at the front takes advantage of south-facing lots.
- A generous entrance foyer allows direct access to Great Room, dining room, and sun room.
- A country kitchen with breakfast bar and cooking island provides an abundance of cabinet space and views into the Great Room.
- The Great Room, with direct access to deck and sun room, is oversized to offer a sense of spaciousness. Both the Great Room and the sun room have cathedral ceilings.
- The sun room also has four skylights to allow penetration of the sunlight.
- The master bedroom is on opposite side of house from other bedrooms for privacy. Note the double door entrance from the Great Room. Walk-in closets and a master bath with whirlpool tub, shower and double bowl vanity provide the latest in desired amenities.
- The garage is connected to the house by a covered breezeway.

Plan DG-179

Bedrooms: 3	Baths: 2

Space:	
Total living area:	2,053 sq. ft.
Garage:	447 sq. ft.

Exterior Wall Framing:	2x4

Foundation options:
Crawlspace.
(Foundation & framing conversion diagram available — see order form.)

Blueprint Price Code:	C

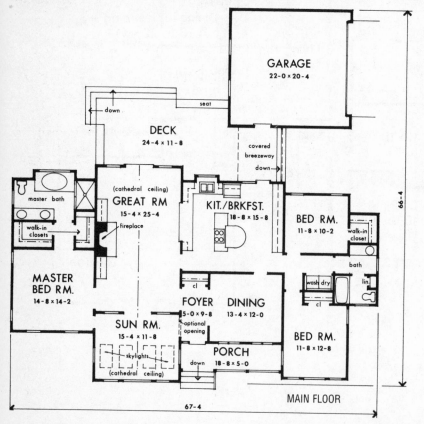

GARAGE
22-0 x 20-4

DECK
24-4 x 11-8

seat

covered
breezeway

down

down

(cathedral ceiling)
GREAT RM
15-4 x 25-4

fireplace

KIT./BRKFST.
18-8 x 15-8

BED RM.
11-8 x 10-2

walk-in
closet

master bath

walk-in
closets

bath

66-4

MASTER
BED RM.
14-8 x 14-2

cl

FOYER
5-0 x 9-8

DINING
13-4 x 12-0

wash dry

lin.

cl

SUN RM.
15-4 x 11-8

optional
opening

skylights

(cathedral ceiling)

PORCH
18-8 x 5-0

down

BED RM.
11-8 x 12-8

67-4

MAIN FLOOR

Plan DG-179

Sprawling Excitement

- This sprawling ranch design offers plenty of room to roam for the growing family.
- The formal parlor and dining room are the central area of the home, and offer a dramatic entry appeal for guests.
- The kitchen and family room make up the informal family living area. A sewing room and half bath add to the informal function.
- The sleeping wing of the plan includes three bedrooms and two full baths.
- The master suite offers the excitement of double-doors, a fireplace, access to a rear covered patio, a walk-in closet and a private bath.

Plan Q-2067-1A

Bedrooms: 3	Baths: 2½
Space:	
Total living area:	2,067 sq. ft.
Garage:	390 sq. ft.
Exterior Wall Framing:	2x4

Foundation options:
Slab.
(Foundation & framing conversion diagram available — see order form.)

Blueprint Price Code:	C

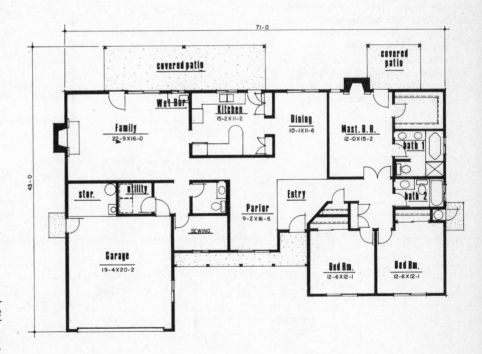

Plan Q-2067-1A

Cozy, Economical

- This economical two-story is available with an optional arbor.
- The country kitchen facing the backyard features a unique built-in breakfast booth wrapped with windows. A corner pantry and pass-thru/eating counter separate the kitchen from the adjoining living room.
- The central living room accommodates a fireplace and a book library.
- The spacious master suite is located on the first floor for privacy; included is a generous walk-in closet and personal bath.
- Another bath and two secondary bedrooms, one with sloped ceilings, are located upstairs, along with a balcony stoop to view the living room below.

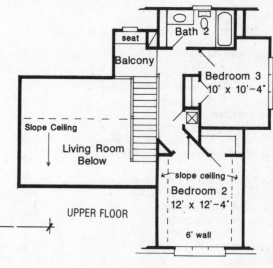

UPPER FLOOR

MAIN FLOOR

Plan L-372-CSA

Bedrooms: 3	Baths: 2½
Space:	
Upper floor:	509 sq. ft.
Main floor:	861 sq. ft.
Total living area:	1,370 sq. ft.
Garage:	406 sq. ft.
Exterior Wall Framing:	2x4
Ceiling Heights:	
Upper floor:	8'
Main floor:	9'

Foundation options:
Slab.
(Foundation & framing conversion diagram available — see order form.)

Blueprint Price Code: A

Plan L-372-CSA

HomeStyles SOURCE 1 DESIGNERS NETWORK

Plan UDG-90004

Bedrooms: 3	**Baths:** 1½

Space:

Upper floor:	709 sq. ft.
Main floor:	672 sq. ft.
Total living area:	1,381 sq. ft.
Basement	672 sq. ft.
Garage:	528 sq. ft.
Exterior Wall Framing:	2x4

Foundation options:
Standard basement.
(Foundation & framing conversion
diagram available — see order form.)

Blueprint Price Code: A

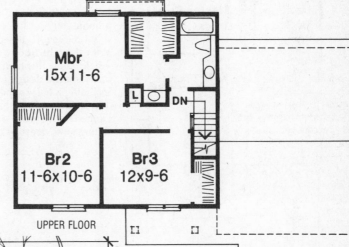

Mbr
15x11-6

Br2
11-6x10-6

Br3
12x9-6

DN

L

UPPER FLOOR

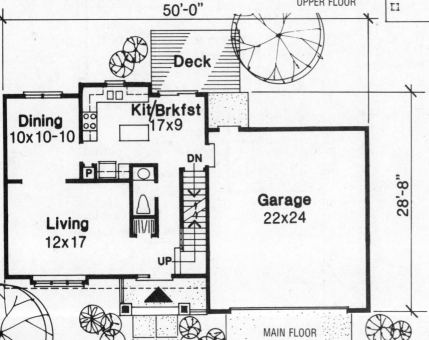

50'-0"

Deck

Dining
10x10-10

Kit/Brkfst
17x9

P

DN

Living
12x17

UP

Garage
22x24

28'-8"

MAIN FLOOR

The Two-Story within Reach

- For the young family on-the-grow who wants a traditional two-story home but finds most out of reach, here is the house you have been looking for.
- The exciting main floor includes a formal living room, formal dining room and island kitchen with informal breakfast eating area.
- The upper floor includes three bedrooms and a private access to the bath from the master bedroom.
- In a few years when funds allow, a family room can be easily added on behind the garage, completing a dream two-story plan.

HomeStyles
SOURCE 1
DESIGNERS' NETWORK

Plan UDG-90004

Den/Br 3
10x12

Master Suite
14-4x12
vaulted

DN

Br 2
13x11

UPPER FLOOR

Narrow Width, Wide Appeal

- Restricted lot conditions may require cutting down the width of a home, but not the excitement in this 1,525 sq. ft. design.
- With three bedrooms and two-and-a-half baths, this home contains many special design features, including a half-round gable detail, a breakfast eating area in the kitchen with corner windows, sliding glass doors to the rear deck and yard and a fireplace with a corner window in the living room.
- The second floor has a master bedroom with a vaulted ceiling and private bath.
- The second bedroom has a window seat, and the foyer could be closed off to serve as a third bedroom or left open as a den, reading area, playroom or TV watching area.

Plan B-88048

Bedrooms: 3	Baths: 2½
Space:	
Upper floor:	760 sq. ft.
Main floor:	765 sq. ft.
Total living area:	1,525 sq. ft.
Basement:	765 sq. ft.
Garage:	430 sq. ft.
Exterior Wall Framing:	2x4

Foundation options:
Standard basement.
(Foundation & framing conversion diagram available — see order form.)

Blueprint Price Code:	B

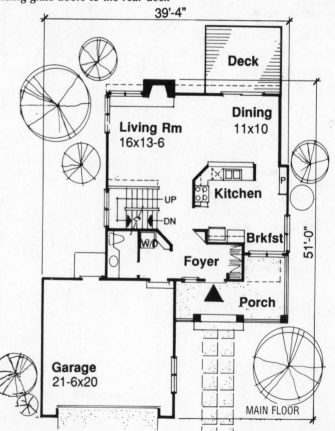

39'-4"

Deck

Living Rm
16x13-6

Dining
11x10

Kitchen

UP
DN

Brkfst

W/D

Foyer

51'-0"

Porch

Garage
21-6x20

MAIN FLOOR

C-14

Plan B-88048

Country Comfort

- Today's strong re-emphasis on country design is reflected in this comfortable two-story home with divided sash transom glass, louvered front porch with glass door and sidelight, tiered planters and stone kneewall.
- From the entry, guests are met with a dramatic view of the living room with vaulted ceiling and loft option above, corner transom windows, and a dining room with sliders to the rear deck beyond the shared see-through fireplace.
- The country kitchen layout allows the family to share precious time together in the breakfast/informal living area, which also has rear deck access.
- There are three bedrooms upstairs, including a master suite with private bath complete with shower and walk-in closet.

Plan B-88004

Bedrooms: 3	Baths: 2½
Space:	
Upper floor:	777 sq. ft.
Main floor:	888 sq. ft.
Total living area:	1,665 sq. ft.
Basement:	888 sq. ft.
Garage:	407 sq. ft.
Exterior Wall Framing:	2x4

Foundation options:
Standard basement.
(Foundation & framing conversion diagram available — see order form.)

Blueprint Price Code:	B

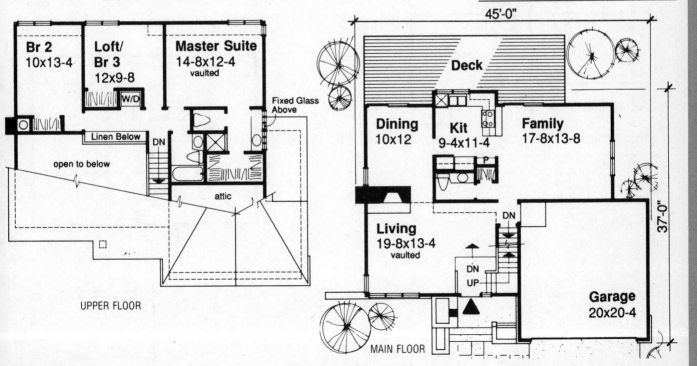

Br 2 10x13-4

Loft/ Br 3 12x9-8

Master Suite 14-8x12-4 vaulted

W/D

Fixed Glass Above

Linen Below

DN

open to below

attic

UPPER FLOOR

45'-0"

Deck

Dining 10x12

Kit 9-4x11-4

Family 17-8x13-8

P

Living 19-8x13-4 vaulted

DN

DN UP

Garage 20x20-4

37'-0"

MAIN FLOOR

Plan B-88004

C-15

Casual Living

- This enjoyable two-story features a unique, relaxing family room on the second level, bordered on one side by an open railing providing a view to the Great Room below.
- The open first floor features an extended living/dining area with fireplace and porch access.
- The attached kitchen houses a handy pantry and an eating bar.
- Located on the main level, the master bedroom features a functional dressing area and its own private entrance to the main bath.
- A second bedroom on this level and a third upstairs complete the living areas.

Plan CPS-1043-D

Bedrooms: 3	Baths: 2
Space:	
Upper floor:	582 sq. ft.
Main floor:	1,085 sq. ft.
Total living area:	1,667 sq. ft.
Basement:	1,085 sq. ft.
Garage:	506 sq. ft.
Exterior Wall Framing:	2x6

Foundation options:
Standard basement.
(Foundation & framing conversion diagram available — see order form.)

Blueprint Price Code: B

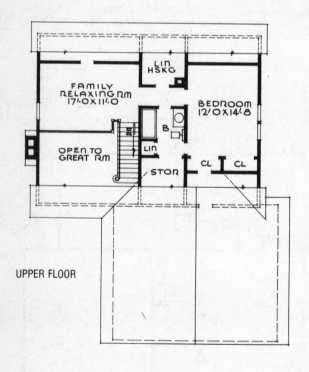

UPPER FLOOR

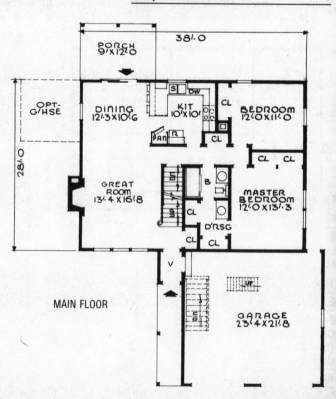

MAIN FLOOR

TO ORDER THIS BLUEPRINT, CALL TOLL-FREE 1-800-547-5570
(Prices and details on order form.)

Plan CPS-1043-D

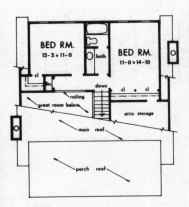

UPPER FLOOR

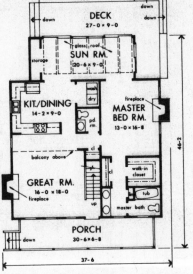

MAIN FLOOR

Plan DG-165

Bedrooms: 3　　　　　**Baths: 2½**

Space:

Upper floor:	492 sq. ft.
Main floor:	1,228 sq. ft.
Total living area:	**1,720 sq. ft.**

Exterior Wall Framing:　　　2x4

Foundation options:
Crawlspace.
(Foundation & framing conversion
diagram available — see order form.)

Blueprint Price Code:　　　　B

Compact Country Style

- An open and spacious interior with an up-to-date floor plan offers a new excitement to this delightful compact country-style home.
- The oversized Great Room with a fireplace has a sloping ceiling up to the second floor, allowing a balcony above.
- The country kitchen offers a dining area within that space, plus direct access to the sun room for an alternate dining and entertainment area.
- The generous master bedroom with its own fireplace also has direct access to the sun room. The master suite has a private master bath containing a double bowl vanity and garden tub. There is plenty of closet space with the walk-in closet.
- The second floor has two large bedrooms sharing a full bath with a separate vanity area for privacy.
- Exterior covered front porch and rear deck provide plenty of outdoor living area.

Plan DG-165

Front Porch Pleaser

- A covered front porch with Victorian trim, triple dormers, and a bay window combine for a pleasing, charming exterior look.
- The front half of the plan incorporates the formal living and dining rooms for entertaining guests.
- The informal family living area faces the rear patio and includes a spacious kitchen with pantry, a built-in snack bar and a large family room.
- The main-floor master suite includes a dressing area next to the walk-in closet and a compartmented bath and toilet.
- There are two additional bedrooms with a full bath upstairs.
- The optional garage features a loft/bonus room overhead.

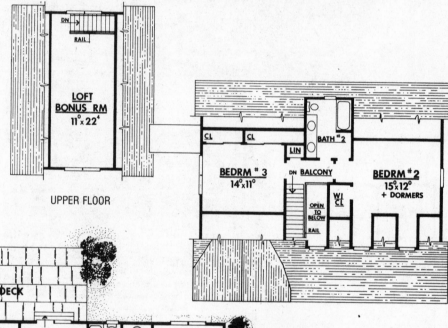

LOFT BONUS RM
11⁰x22⁴

UPPER FLOOR

CL   CL   BATH #2   LIN

BEDRM #3
14⁰x11⁰

DN BALCONY

OPEN TO BELOW
RAIL

WI CL

BEDRM #2
15⁰x12⁰
+ DORMERS

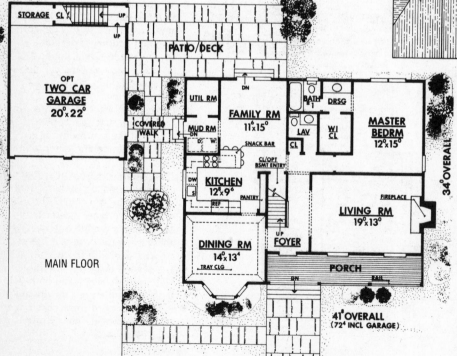

STORAGE CL   UP
UP

OPT
TWO CAR GARAGE
20⁰x22⁰

COVERED WALK

PATIO/DECK

UTIL RM

MUD RM
DN

FAMILY RM
11⁶x15⁰

SNACK BAR

KITCHEN
12⁵x9⁶

PANTRY
REF
DW

DINING RM
14⁰x13⁴
TRAY CLG

DN

BATH #1

LAV

CL

DRSG

WI CL

CL/OPT BSMT ENTRY

UP FOYER

MASTER BEDRM
12⁰x15⁰

LIVING RM
19⁰x13⁰

FIREPLACE

PORCH
RAIL

DN

34⁰ OVERALL

41⁰ OVERALL
(72⁴ INCL GARAGE)

MAIN FLOOR

Plan AX-8272-A

Bedrooms: 3	Baths: 2½

Space:

Upper floor:	616 sq. ft.
Main floor:	1,295 sq. ft.

Total living area:	**1,911 sq. ft.**
Basement:	1,283 sq. ft.
Optional garage:	537 sq. ft.
Optional bonus room/loft area:	303 sq. ft.

Exterior Wall Framing:	2x4

Foundation options:
Standard basement.
Crawlspace.
Slab.
(Foundation & framing conversion diagram available — see order form.)

Blueprint Price Code:	B

Plan AX-8272-A

HomeStyles
SOURCE 1
DESIGNERS NETWORK

Flexible Floor Plan Functions

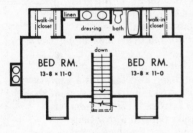

UPPER FLOOR

- In this flexible plan, the Great Room/dining room can be used as one large Great Room with the dining room relocated to the family room.
- A rear-facing sunroom with space for a hot tub is a focal point of the plan.
- The kitchen has combination cooking island and breakfast bar.

- The master bedroom has fireplace, walk-in closet, double bowl vanity with separate bath area, and private access to the sun room.
- Two second-level bedrooms are equal in size and share a full bath with double bowl vanity and linen in separate room. Both bedrooms have a dormer window and a walk-in closet.
- A screened porch with view of front and rear, sheltered front porch and open rear deck offer maximum flexibility for outside living. Skylights provide natural light to the screened porch.

Plan DG-152

Bedrooms: 3	**Baths:** 2½

Space:

Upper floor:	536 sq. ft.
Main floor:	1,377 sq. ft.
Total living area:	**1,913 sq. ft.**
Basement:	1,177 sq. ft.
Garage:	484 sq. ft.
Storage area:	approx. 85 sq. ft.

Exterior Wall Framing: 2x4

Foundation options:
Standard basement.
Crawlspace.
(Foundation & framing conversion diagram available — see order form.)

Blueprint Price Code: D

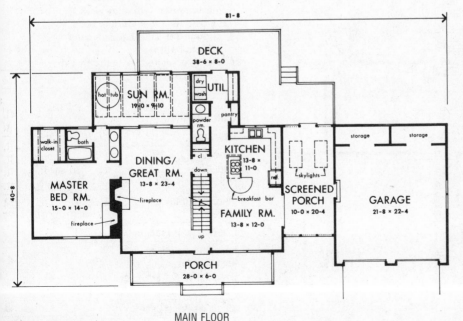

MAIN FLOOR

Plan DG-152

TO ORDER THIS BLUEPRINT,
CALL TOLL-FREE 1-800-547-5570
(Prices and details on order form.) C-19

UPPER FLOOR

Br 2
10-6x14

Br 3
12x10-6

Master Suite
14x14
vaulted

D
W

DN

open to below

Plant Shelf

Raised
Ceiling

Room to Roam

- For the family on the grow, this 2,141 sq. ft. home allows plenty of room to roam.
- The formal living and dining areas are easily accessible from the kitchen.
- The living area features a vaulted ceiling with balcony and plant shelf.
- The kitchen/breakfast area has a sliding door to a rear deck.
- A two-way fireplace is enjoyed by both the breakfast area and the family room.
- The second floor contains the master suite, two additional bedrooms and a laundry area.
- The master suite has a dynamic private bath.
- The two secondary bedrooms share a hall bath.

MAIN FLOOR

53'-0"

39'-0"

Deck

Dining
10x12-4

Kit/Brkfst

Family Rm
17-6x14

P

DN

Living Rm
18x16-4
vaulted

Plant Shelf

UP

Garage
21-4x21-6

Plan B-88069

Bedrooms: 3	Baths: 2½
Space:	
Upper floor:	936 sq. ft.
Main floor:	1,205 sq. ft.
Total living area:	2,141 sq. ft.
Garage:	459 sq. ft.
Exterior Wall Framing:	2x4

Foundation options:
Standard basement.
(Foundation & framing conversion
diagram available — see order form.)

Blueprint Price Code:	C

C-20

Plan B-88069

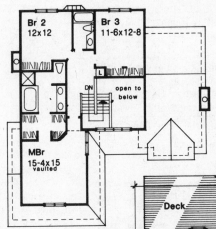

UPPER FLOOR

lan B-106-86

edrooms: 3	Baths: 2½

pace:

pper floor:	1,001 sq. ft.
ain floor:	1,169 sq. ft.
otal living area:	**2,170 sq. ft.**
asement:	1,169 sq. ft.
arage:	390 sq. ft.

xterior Wall Framing: 2x4

oundation options:
tandard basement.
Foundation & framing conversion
iagram available — see order form.)

Blueprint Price Code: C

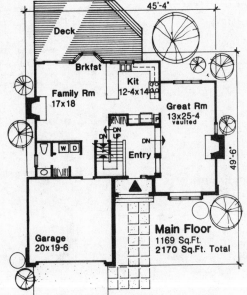

MAIN FLOOR

Creative Country Appeal

- This traditional two-story has the look and the livability just right for a move-up family on the grow.
- The brick, narrow lap siding, and repeated half-circle windows with divided panes give a look of importance and traditional character.
- Moving inside, we enter the large, vaulted entry with open stairs and balcony overlook, as well as a dramatic two-step-down view into the vaulted formal Great Room, with handsome fireplace and pop-out front window with high transom glass.
- The main floor also includes the informal living areas of the kitchen, breakfast, and family room with its own cozy fireplace and outdoor living area access.
- On the upper floor, there are two large bedrooms plus the vaulted master suite, with high transom glass, a plant shelf, double walk-in closets and a lavish master bath.

Plan B-106-86

Inspiring Traditional

- A covered front porch, bay windows, Victorian trim, and a grand spire give this traditional home class and charm.
- A spacious entry greets guests and leads into the Great Room with fireplace or formal dining room with bay windows.
- The island kitchen serves the sunny, octagonal breakfast room.
- Upstairs, the master bathroom is situated in the octagonal spire, with a dramatic platform tub under the glass.
- The master bedroom also features a walk-in closet and a private balcony.

Plan V-2243-F

Bedrooms: 3	**Baths:** 2½

Space:
Upper floor: 1,095 sq. ft.
Main floor: 1,148 sq. ft.
Total living area: 2,243 sq. ft.

Exterior Wall Framing: 2x6

Ceiling Heights:
Upper floor: 9'
Main floor: 10'

Foundation options:
Crawlspace.
(Foundation & framing conversion diagram available — see order form.)

Blueprint Price Code: C

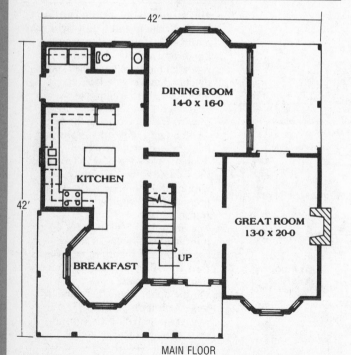

MAIN FLOOR

- DINING ROOM 14-0 x 16-0
- KITCHEN
- GREAT ROOM 13-0 x 20-0
- BREAKFAST
- UP
- 42'
- 42'

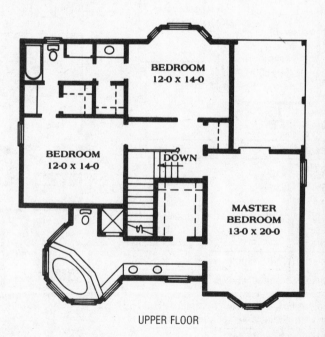

UPPER FLOOR

- BEDROOM 12-0 x 14-0
- BEDROOM 12-0 x 14-0
- DOWN
- MASTER BEDROOM 13-0 x 20-0

Plan V-2243-F

Expandable Plan for the Growing Family

For the growing family who wants to anticipate their changing lifestyle needs and build affordably now, this expandable design is the ticket. Note how the plan can start as an economical yet stylish two-bedroom two-story.

- As funds allow, a lavish main floor master suite can be added. A two-car garage with optional bonus room above can be built attached to the kitchen/utility room or to the optional family room with cathedral ceiling and second fireplace. All options are included in the blueprints. Floor plan shown for Alternate B.

Alternate A

Alternate C

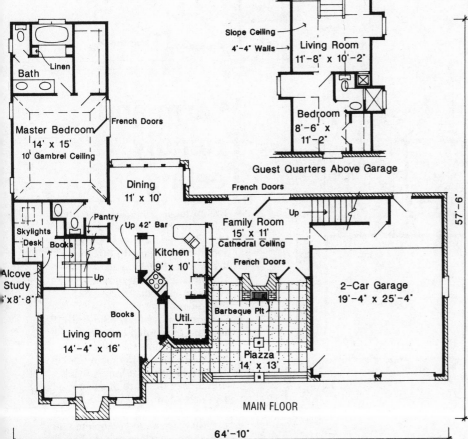

Alternate B

Slope Ceiling
4'-4" Walls

Living Room
11'-8" x 10'-2"

Bedroom
8'-6" x 11'-2"

Guest Quarters Above Garage

French Doors

Bath

Linen

Master Bedroom
14' x 15'
10' Gambrel Ceiling

French Doors

Dining
11' x 10'

Pantry

Up 42" Bar

Skylights

Desk

Books

Alcove
Study
'x8'-8"

Up

Kitchen
9' x 10'

Books

Util.

Living Room
14'-4" x 16'

Family Room
15' x 11'
Cathedral Ceiling

French Doors

Up

2-Car Garage
19'-4" x 25'-4"

Barbeque Pit

Piazza
14' x 13'

MAIN FLOOR

64'-10"

57'-6"

Plan L-711-CSD	
Bedrooms: 2-3	**Baths:** 1½-2½

Space:

Alternate A:

Upper floor:	520 sq. ft.
Main floor:	814 sq. ft.
Total living area:	**1,334 sq. ft.**
Optional Master Suite:	372 sq. ft.
Garage:	495 sq. ft.

Alternate B
(With master suite, family room and attached garage)

Main floor:	1,186 sq. ft.
Family room:	211 sq. ft.
Upper floor:	520 sq. ft.
Guest quarters:	345 sq. ft.
Total living area:	**2,262 sq. ft.**

Alternate C
(With master suite and garage; without family room)

Main floor:	1,186 sq. ft.
Upper floor:	520 sq. ft.
Total living area:	**1,706 sq. ft.**
Exterior Wall Framing:	2x4

Foundation options:
Slab.
(Foundation & framing conversion diagram available — see order form.)

Blueprint Price Code:	C

Plan L-711-CSD

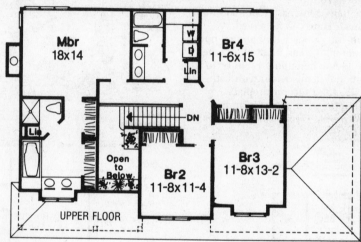

UPPER FLOOR

Plan UDG-90013

Bedrooms: 4	Baths: 2½

Space:

Upper floor:	1,248 sq. ft.
Main floor:	1,059 sq. ft.
Total living area:	**2,307 sq. ft.**
Basement:	1,059 sq. ft.
Garage:	460 sq. ft.

Exterior Wall Framing:	2x4

Foundation options:
Standard basement.
(Foundation & framing conversion
diagram available — see order form.)

Blueprint Price Code:	C

MAIN FLOOR

Upper floor rooms:
- Mbr 18x14
- Br4 11-6x15
- Br2 11-8x11-4
- Br3 11-8x13-2
- Open to Below

Main floor rooms:
- 55'-4"
- Deck
- Family 20x13-6
- Kit / Brkfst 21x12
- 35'-8"
- Living 12-8x13-8
- Dining 13-8x11
- Garage 23x20

Warm and Friendly Feeling

- The nostalgic front porch, multiple gables, divided light windows and lap siding lend a warm, friendly and inviting feeling to this four-bedroom two-story plan.
- The volumetric entry foyer gives guests an immediate sense of spaciousness.
- Columns, rather than solid walls, separate the formal living room and dining rooms from the entry.
- The entire rear of the main floor is devoted to informal family living with a cozy fireplace and sunny breakfast room with deck access.
- The four upstairs bedrooms include a lavish master suite complete with a stunning, spacious private bath.

TO ORDER THIS BLUEPRINT,
CALL TOLL-FREE 1-800-547-5570
(Prices and details on order form.)

REAR VIEW

MASTER BED RM.
15-0 × 12-0

whirlpool

master bath

walk-in closet

fireplace

bath

cl

BED RM.
12-0 × 10-0

lin.

down

cl

cl

cl

BED RM.
13-0 × 10-4

cl

BED RM.
12-0 × 12-0

UPPER FLOOR

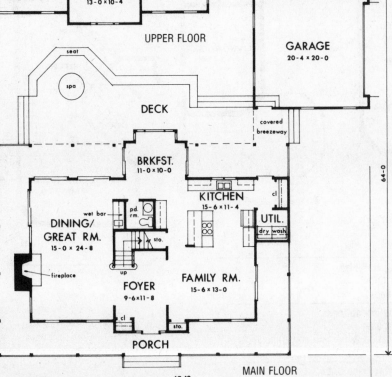

seat

spa

DECK

GARAGE
20-4 × 20-0

covered breezeway

BRKFST.
11-0 × 10-0

KITCHEN
15-6 × 11-4

UTIL.

dry wash

cl

wet bar

pd. rm.

sto.

DINING/ GREAT RM.
15-0 × 24-8

fireplace

up

FOYER
9-6 × 11-8

FAMILY RM.
15-6 × 13-0

cl

sto.

PORCH

67-10

64-0

MAIN FLOOR

Style and Charm on all Four Sides

- This stylish country farm house displays its exterior beauty both front and rear.
- A wrap-around porch allows sheltered access to all first-level areas along with a covered breezeway to the garage.
- The first level boasts a spacious open plan layout with all the latest features.
- The Great Room has a fireplace and plenty of glass.
- The kitchen overlooks the family room and rear yard.
- The Master bedroom on second level has fireplace, large walk-in closet, and master bath with shower, whirlpool tub and double bowl vanity. The other three bedrooms share a full bath with double bowl vanity.
- An expansive deck allows space for a spa tub.

Plan DG-199

Bedrooms: 4	Baths: 2½

Space:

Upper floor:	1,060 sq. ft.
Main floor:	1,254 sq. ft.

Total living area:	2,314 sq. ft.
Garage:	407 sq. ft.

Exterior Wall Framing:	2x4

Foundation options:
Crawlspace.
(Foundation & framing conversion diagram available — see order form.)

Blueprint Price Code:	C

Plan DG-199

Sunny, Spacious Interior

- This breathtaking Victorian begins with a dramatic foyer open all the way up to the tower ceiling.
- The multitude of windows floods the entire house with light; sunny days can also be enjoyed outside on the multi-angled porch or built-in gazebo.
- The spectacular interior includes a huge central Great Room with fireplace, a spacious kitchen with breakfast area and a snack bar, and formal dining and living rooms.
- Upstairs you'll find a master suite with private sitting area or exercise room and an added dressing room.

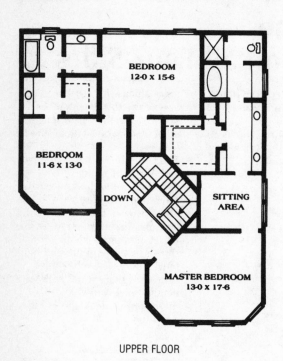

UPPER FLOOR

BEDROOM
12-0 x 15-6

BEDROOM
11-6 x 13-0

DOWN

SITTING AREA

MASTER BEDROOM
13-0 x 17-6

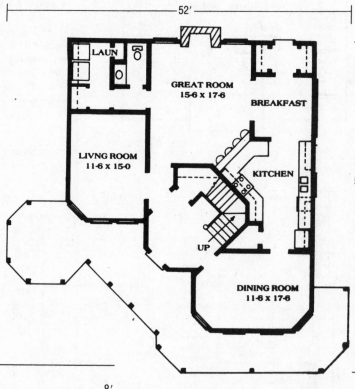

52'

51'

LAUN

GREAT ROOM
15-6 x 17-6

BREAKFAST

LIVNG ROOM
11-6 x 15-0

KITCHEN

UP

DINING ROOM
11-6 x 17-6

MAIN FLOOR

Plan V-2647-F

Bedrooms: 3	Baths: 2½

Space:	
Upper floor:	1,283 sq. ft.
Main floor:	1,364 sq. ft.
Total living area:	**2,647 sq. ft.**

Exterior Wall Framing:	2x6

Ceiling Heights:

Upper floor:	8'
Main floor:	10'

Foundation options:
Crawlspace.
(Foundation & framing conversion diagram available — see order form.)

Blueprint Price Code:	D

TO ORDER THIS BLUEPRINT,
CALL TOLL-FREE 1-800-547-5570
(Prices and details on order form.)

Plan V-2647-F

A Grand Entrance

- Though colonial in style and traditional in form, this dramatic two-story has many contemporary qualities.

- The spacious living and dining room combination is perfect for entertaining large or small groups.
- Recessed two steps below the loggia lies a large family room with a fireplace and sliding glass doors opening to the adjoining covered terrace.
- The roomy kitchen is nestled between a convenient utility room and a breakfast area with its own terrace access.
- A study merges with the large master suite, which offers two walk-in closets, a dressing area and a bath with large corner tub.
- The upper floor has three additional bedrooms, each with abundant storage.

Plan DD-2806-A

Bedrooms: 4	Baths: 2½
Space:	
Upper floor:	803 sq. ft.
Main floor:	2,003 sq. ft.
Total living area:	2,806 sq. ft.
Garage:	431 sq. ft.
Exterior Wall Framing:	2x4

Foundation options:
Slab.
(Foundation & framing conversion diagram available — see order form.)

Blueprint Price Code:	D

UPPER FLOOR

Floor plan labels:
BEDROOM 4 11⁰x13⁰, BATH 2, BEDROOM 3 13⁰x15⁰, UPPER FOYER, BEDROOM 2 12⁰x19⁰

MAIN FLOOR

Floor plan labels:
STORAGE, UTILITY, COVERED TERRACE, BREAKFAST, FAMILY 17⁹x20⁰, BATH 1, DRESSING, POWDER, KITCHEN 11⁶x13⁰ 10⁰x10⁰, DOUBLE GARAGE 20⁶x21⁰, DINING, LOGGIA, LIVING 11⁰x13⁰, FOYER, MASTER BEDROOM 13⁰x17⁶, STUDY 10⁰x11⁰, PORCH, 79⁰, 39⁰

Plan DD-2806-A

UPPER FLOOR

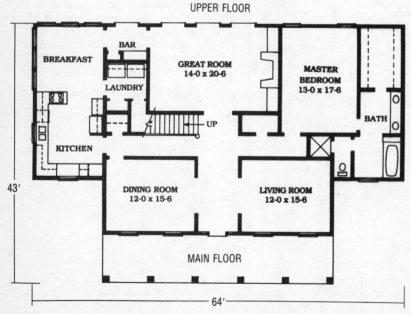

MAIN FLOOR

43'

64'

Colonial Classic

- Classic colonial proportions, details, and trim recall the best of "Deep South" architecture.
- A full-width front porch conjures up images of long summer evenings shared with family and friends.
- The symmetrical main floor plan includes a dramatic entrance hall with views into the living, dining and Great rooms.
- The kitchen overlooks a sunny breakfast room with corner window-walls.
- The main-floor master bedroom suite features a spacious dressing area, walk-in closet and private bath.
- There are three bedrooms and two bathrooms upstairs.

Plan V-2848-LC

Bedrooms: 4	Baths: 3
Space:	
Upper floor:	824 sq. ft.
Main floor:	2,024 sq. ft.
Total living area:	**2,848 sq. ft.**
Exterior Wall Framing:	2x6
Ceiling Heights:	
Upper floor:	8'
Main floor:	10'

Foundation options:
Crawlspace.
(Foundation & framing conversion diagram available — see order form.)

Blueprint Price Code: D

TO ORDER THIS BLUEPRINT, CALL TOLL-FREE 1-800-547-5570
(Prices and details on order form.)

Plan V-2848-LC

HomeStyles
Source 1
DESIGNERS' NETWORK

Plan DD-3172-A

Bedrooms: 4	Baths: 3

Space:

Upper floor:	1,051 sq. ft.
Main floor:	2,134 sq. ft.
Total living area:	3,185 sq. ft.
Garage:	393 sq. ft.

Exterior Wall Framing:	2x4

Ceiling Heights:

Upper floor:	8'
Main floor:	9'

Foundation options:
Slab.
(Foundation & framing conversion diagram available — see order form.)

Blueprint Price Code:	E

UPPER FLOOR

Open, Family Living

- This country-style rambler offers traditional features, such as a front, covered porch and dormer windows.
- Large living areas border the tiled kitchen, morning room, bath and utility areas, the dining/living rooms to the left and the family room to the right.
- Each of the living areas offers access to the rear deck.
- Privacy is achieved by placing the master suite on the main level with its own access to the deck and a bath with a garden tub and separate shower and commode.
- Three additional bathrooms and a playnook with dormers and vaulted ceilings are located on the upper level.

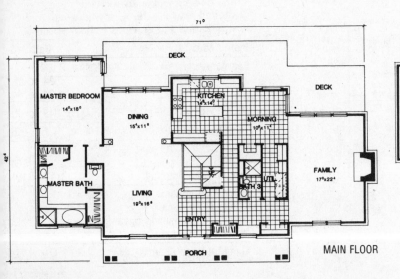

MAIN FLOOR

HomeStyles Source 1 Designers Network

Plan DD-3172-A

TO ORDER THIS BLUEPRINT,
CALL TOLL-FREE 1-800-547-5570
(Prices and details on order form.) **C-29**

Air of Substance

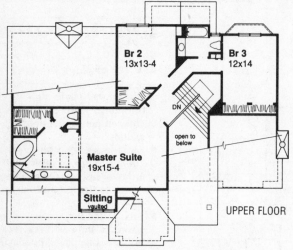

Br 2
13x13-4

Br 3
12x14

DN

open to below

Master Suite
19x15-4

Sitting
vaulted

UPPER FLOOR

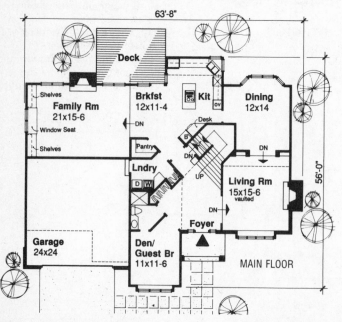

63'-8"

Deck

Shelves

Family Rm
21x15-6

Window Seat

Shelves

Brkfst
12x11-4

Kit

ov

Dining
12x14

Desk

B

DN

Pantry

Lndry

D   W

UP

Living Rm
15x15-6
vaulted

DN

Garage
24x24

Den/
Guest Br
11x11-6

Foyer

56'-0"

MAIN FLOOR

- Exterior detailing includes massive stone masonry walls, roof planes and trim timbers, exuding a rich air of substance.
- Entry excitement is enhanced by an elegant staircase. Views are available through the home from one space into another or beyond through windows, wall cutouts, and glass doors.
- The upper landing offers views of the sunken, vaulted living room as well as the foyer below.
- Many rooms enjoy a visual access to the outside, merging indoor and outdoor living.
- The informal zone of this home includes the kitchen, breakfast and family rooms.
- The owners will enjoy a lavish vaulted master suite with windowed sitting area and gracious walk-in wardrobe.

Plan B-89052-L

Bedrooms: 4	**Baths:** 2½

Space:

Upper floor:	1,347 sq. ft.
Main floor:	1,839 sq. ft.
Total living area:	**3,186 sq. ft.**
Basement:	1,839 sq. ft.
Garage:	576 sq. ft.

Exterior Wall Framing:	2x4

Foundation options:
Standard basement.
(Foundation & framing conversion diagram available — see order form.)

Blueprint Price Code:	E

**TO ORDER THIS BLUEPRINT,
CALL TOLL-FREE 1-800-547-5570**
(Prices and details on order form.)

Plan B-89052-L

Fascinating Views

- An old-fashioned covered porch welcomes visitors to this beautiful four-bedroom home.
- Inside, the vaulted entry and formal dining room are overlooked by an open staircase and balcony; the open railing at the end of the upstairs hall also allows a view of the vaulted family room.
- Pillars separate the family room from the nook and kitchen area without restricting the flow of space or vision.
- Double doors open into the spacious master bedroom with an arched opening to the attached private bath; a relaxing spa tub, dual vanities and a walk-in closet are featured.
- A guest room or extra bedroom has private access to the main bath and is entered through beautiful double doors.
- The upstairs offers accommodations for two bedrooms, a bath, lots of storage space and an added bonus area.

Plan CDG-2011

Bedrooms: 4-5	Baths: 3½

Space:	
Upper floor:	719 sq. ft.
Main floor:	2,164 sq. ft.
Bonus room:	344 sq. ft.

Total living area:	**3,227 sq. ft.**
Garage:	564 sq. ft.

Exterior Wall Framing:	2x4

Foundation options:
Crawlspace.
(Foundation & framing conversion diagram available — see order form.)

Blueprint Price Code:	E

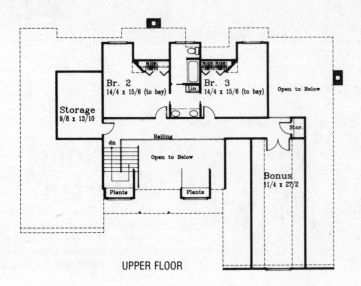

UPPER FLOOR

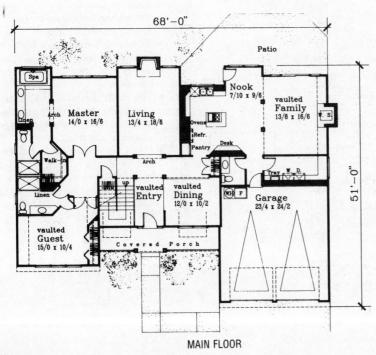

MAIN FLOOR

Plan CDG-2011

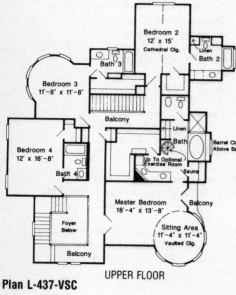

UPPER FLOOR

Plan L-437-VSC

Bedrooms: 4	Baths: 4½

Space:

Upper floor:	1,818 sq. ft.
Main floor:	1,617 sq. ft.
Total living area:	**3,435 sq. ft.**
Garage and storage:	638 sq. ft.

Exterior Wall Framing:	2x4
Ceiling Heights:	9'

Foundation options:
Slab.
(Foundation & framing conversion diagram available — see order form.)

Blueprint Price Code:	E

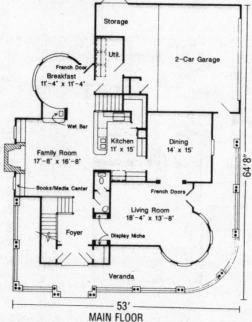

53'
MAIN FLOOR

Vivacious Victorian

- **Distinctive characteristics reminiscent of the Queen Anne era** include a rounded tower, curved veranda and steeply intersecting pitched roofs.
- **Leaded glass front doors open to a grand foyer** with an elegant staircase and overlooking balcony.
- **The large living room features a rounded sitting area and French doors** that open to the lovely side veranda.
- **The centrally located kitchen overlooks the family room,** which boasts a built-in media center and relaxing wet bar.
- **From the second-floor balcony, double doors lead to the private master bedroom,** featuring a vaulted sitting room and attached bath with room for a sauna and optional exercise room.

Optional Loft
12' x 11'-4"
136 Sq. Ft.

Plan L-437-VSC

Cottage Design Offers Comfort and Style

- Upper balcony bedroom overlooks living room below.
- Combined living/dining area makes great space for entertaining.
- Unique kitchen arrangement includes laundry area.
- Master suite features bay window sitting area.

Plan E-1002

Bedrooms: 1-2	Baths: 2

Space:	
Upper floor:	267 sq. ft.
Main floor:	814 sq. ft.
Total living area:	**1,081 sq. ft.**
Unheated area:	59 sq. ft.
Exterior Wall Framing:	**2x4**

Foundation options:
Crawlspace.
Slab.
(Foundation & framing conversion diagram available — see order form.)

Blueprint Price Code:	A

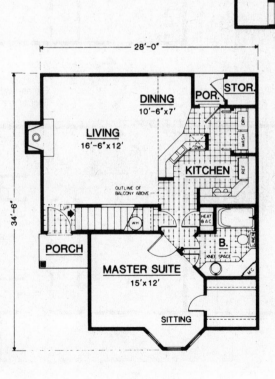

SLOPED CEILING · FLAT CEILING · SLOPED CEILING

OPEN TO LIVING BELOW

HALF WALL

BALCONY/ BEDROOM
13'x10'

OUTLINE OF DORMER

HALF WALL

DN

B.

DESK · SHWR · LINEN

ATTIC

UPPER FLOOR

28'-0"

34'-6"

DINING
10'-6"x7'

POR. | STOR.

DRY | WASH

LIVING
16'-6"x12'

KITCHEN

REF

OUTLINE OF BALCONY ABOVE

UP

WH

HEAT & AC

B.

KNEE SPACE

PORCH

MASTER SUITE
15'x12'

SITTING

MAIN FLOOR

Plan E-1002

Compact Traditional Classic

AREAS

Living-Lower	767 sq. ft.
Living-Upper	720 sq. ft.
Total Living	1487 sq. ft.
Garage & Storage	565 sq. ft.
Atrium	72 sq. ft.
Porch	180 sq. ft.
Total	2304 sq. ft.

▲ UPPER LEVEL

Exterior walls are 2x6 construction.
Specify crawlspace or slab foundation.

▲ LOWER LEVEL

An Energy Efficient Home
Blueprint Price Code A

Plan E-1409

HomeStyles
SOURCE 1
DESIGNERS NETWORK

Expandable Traditional

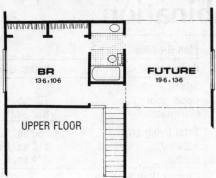

UPPER FLOOR

- BR 13·6 x 10·6
- FUTURE 19·6 x 13·6

- This homey traditional will be at home in any neighborhood, rural or urban.
- A gracious porch leads into the large living room which features a cozy fireplace.
- A sunny breakfast nook provides space for family and guest dining.

- The galley type kitchen opens onto a back porch.
- The master suite is generously sized and exhibits a raised ceiling; a private bath and large closet are also part of the master suite.
- A second bedroom, another bath and convenient utility areas complete the first floor.
- Upstairs, you'll find a third bath and third bedroom, plus a large space which could be finished in the future for any number of purposes.

MAIN FLOOR

- PORCH
- KIT 10 x 8
- BKFST 13 x 11
- BR 11·6 x 10·3
- MBR 16·6 x 13 — RAISED CEILING
- UTIL
- LIVING 15·6 x 15
- GARAGE 19·3 x 19·3
- PORCH 20 x 6

50·4

40

Plan J-8636

Bedrooms: 3	**Baths:** 3

Space:

Upper floor:	270 sq. ft.
Main floor:	1,253 sq. ft.

Total living area:	1,523 sq. ft.
Bonus area:	263 sq. ft.
Basement:	1,253 sq. ft.
Garage:	370 sq. ft.
Storage/utility:	34 sq. ft.
Porch:	155 sq. ft.

Exterior Wall Framing:	2x4

Foundation options:
Standard basement.
Crawlspace.
Slab.
(Foundation & framing conversion diagram available — see order form.)

Blueprint Price Code:	B

HomeStyles SOURCE 1 DESIGNERS NETWORK

Plan J-8636

TO ORDER THIS BLUEPRINT, CALL TOLL-FREE 1-800-547-5570
(Prices and details on pp. 12-15.) **115**

Open Kitchen/Family Room Combination

- This compact plan is designed to provide maximum casual living space for a small but busy family.
- A large family room/kitchen combination opens onto a large deck.
- The great room features an impressive corner fireplace and a vaulted ceiling and adjoins the

dining room to create a liberal space for entertaining.
- Upstairs, the master suite includes a private bath and large closet.
- Bedroom 2 boasts a large gable window, two closets and easy access to a second upstairs bath.
- The loft area is available for study, play, an exercise area or third bedroom.

Plan B-88006

Bedrooms: 2-3	Baths: 2½

Space:

Upper floor:	732 sq. ft.
Main floor:	818 sq. ft.

Total living area:	**1,550 sq. ft.**
Basement:	818 sq. ft.
Garage:	374 sq. ft.

Exterior Wall Framing:	2x4

Foundation options:
Standard basement only.
(Foundation & framing conversion diagram available — see order form.)

Blueprint Price Code:	B

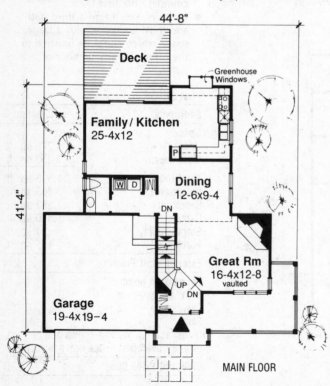

MAIN FLOOR

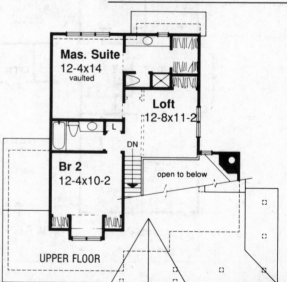

UPPER FLOOR

TO ORDER THIS BLUEPRINT,
CALL TOLL-FREE 1-800-547-5570

116 (Prices and details on pp. 12-15.)

Plan B-88006

Deluxe Downstairs Master Bedroom Suite

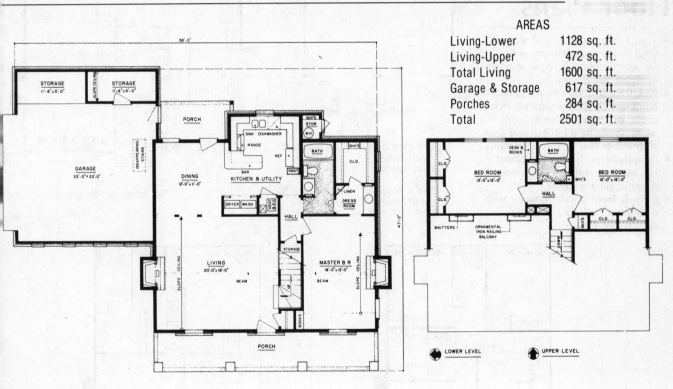

AREAS

Living-Lower	1128 sq. ft.
Living-Upper	472 sq. ft.
Total Living	1600 sq. ft.
Garage & Storage	617 sq. ft.
Porches	284 sq. ft.
Total	2501 sq. ft.

Exterior walls are 2x6 construction.
Specify basement, crawlspace or slab foundation.

An Energy Efficient Home
Blueprint Price Code B
Plan E-1609

TO ORDER THIS BLUEPRINT,
CALL TOLL-FREE 1-800-547-5570
(Prices and details on pp. 12-15.) **117**

Functional, Nostalgic Home Offers Choices in Floor Plans

- Your choice of first- and second-floor room arrangements and foundation plans is required when ordering this design.
- Pick from a family room/kitchen combination with a separate living room, or an expansive living/dining room adjoining a kitchen and nook with either two or three bedrooms.
- In both cases, front entry parlor has an open stairway brightened by a round glass window.
- 8' wide front porch connects with a covered walk to a detached double-car garage.

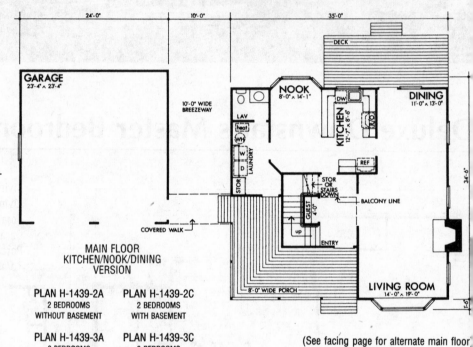

MAIN FLOOR
KITCHEN/NOOK/DINING VERSION

PLAN H-1439-2A
2 BEDROOMS
WITHOUT BASEMENT

PLAN H-1439-2C
2 BEDROOMS
WITH BASEMENT

PLAN H-1439-3A
3 BEDROOMS
WITHOUT BASEMENT

PLAN H-1439-3C
3 BEDROOMS
WITH BASEMENT

(See facing page for alternate main floor)

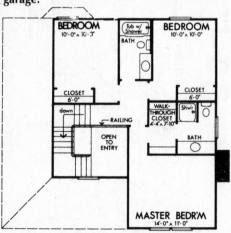

SECOND FLOOR - THREE BEDROOMS
678 SQUARE FEET

SECOND FLOOR - TWO BEDROOMS
678 SQUARE FEET

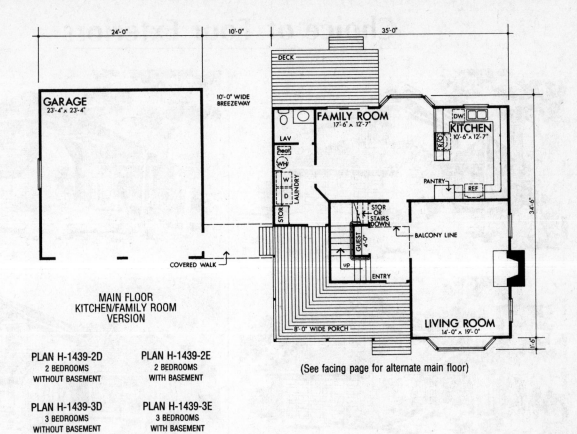

**MAIN FLOOR
KITCHEN/FAMILY ROOM
VERSION**

PLAN H-1439-2D
2 BEDROOMS
WITHOUT BASEMENT

PLAN H-1439-2E
2 BEDROOMS
WITH BASEMENT

PLAN H-1439-3D
3 BEDROOMS
WITHOUT BASEMENT

PLAN H-1439-3E
3 BEDROOMS
WITH BASEMENT

(See facing page for alternate main floor)

Plans H-1439-2A, -2C, -3A & -3C
Plans H-1439-2D, -2E, -3D & -3E

Bedrooms: 2-3	**Baths:** 2½

Space:
Upper floor: 678 sq. ft.
Main floor: 940 sq. ft.

Total living area: 1,618 sq. ft.
Basement: approx. 940 sq. ft.
Garage: 544 sq. ft.

Exterior Wall Framing: 2x6

Foundation options:
Standard basement (Plans H-1439-2C, -3C, -2E & -3E).
Crawlspace (Plans H-1439-2A, -3A, -2D & -3D).
(Foundation & framing conversion diagram available — see order form.)

Blueprint Price Code: B

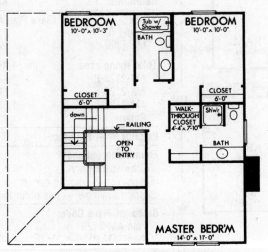

SECOND FLOOR — THREE BEDROOMS
678 SQUARE FEET

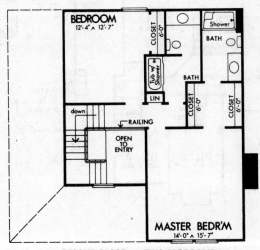

SECOND FLOOR — TWO BEDROOMS
678 SQUARE FEET

HomeStyles
SOURCE 1
DESIGNERS NETWORK

Plans H-1439-2D, -2E, -3D & -3E

TO ORDER THIS BLUEPRINT,
CALL TOLL-FREE 1-800-547-5570
(Prices and details on pp. 12-15.) **119**

Choice of Four Exteriors

PLAN 2126
1468 SQ. FT.

PLAN 2126
1636 SQ. FT.

PLAN 2126C
1663 SQ. FT.

PLAN 2126D
1686 SQ. FT.

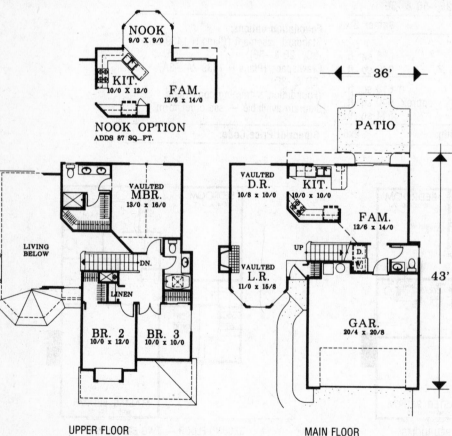

NOOK
9/0 X 9/0

KIT.
10/0 x 12/0

FAM.
12/6 x 14/0

NOOK OPTION
ADDS 87 SQ. FT.

← 36' →

PATIO

VAULTED
D.R.
10/8 x 10/0

KIT.
10/0 x 10/0

FAM.
12/6 x 14/0

UP

VAULTED
L.R.
11/0 x 15/8

GAR.
20/4 x 20/8

43'

VAULTED
MBR.
13/0 x 16/0

LIVING BELOW

DN.

LINEN

BR. 2
10/0 x 12/0

BR. 3
10/0 x 10/0

UPPER FLOOR

MAIN FLOOR

- Spacious living/dining area features vaulted ceilings.
- Living room fireplace included in all versions.
- Large family room adjoins kitchen, utility area and powder room.

Plans AM-2126, B, C, D

Bedrooms: 3		Baths: 2½
Space:	(Base Plan AM-2126)	
Upper floor:		720 sq. ft.
Main floor:		748 sq. ft.
Total living area:		1,468 sq. ft.
AM-2126-B		1,636 sq. ft.
AM-2126-C		1,663 sq. ft.
AM-2126-D		1,686 sq. ft.
Garage:		420 sq. ft.
Exterior Wall Framing:		2x4

Foundation options:
Crawlspace only.
(Foundation & framing conversion diagram available — see order form.)

Blueprint Price Code:

Plan AM-2126	A
Plans AM-2126-B, C, D	B

TO ORDER THIS BLUEPRINT, CALL TOLL-FREE 1-800-547-5570
(Prices and details on pp. 12-15.)

Plans AM-2126, B, C, D

HomeStyles
SOURCE 1
DESIGNERS NETWORK

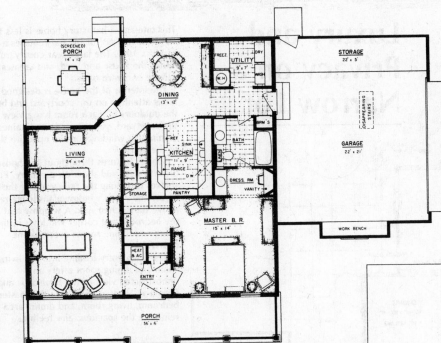

Specify basement, crawlspace or slab foundation.

LOWER LEVEL

Two-Story with Victorian Touch

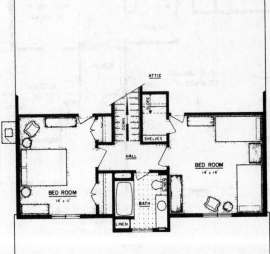

UPPER LEVEL

Living area:	1,686 sq. ft.
Porches:	393 sq. ft.
Garage & storage:	592 sq. ft.
Total area:	2,671 sq. ft.

An Energy Efficient Home

Blueprint Price Code B

Plan E-1631

Luxury and Privacy on a Narrow Lot

This one-and-a-half-story home is less than 39' wide and 63' deep, and requires a lot of 50' x 100'. The large rear courtyard unites the house and yard, and creates a private backyard oasis.

The interior of the house is designed to focus attention on the courtyard and bring the outdoors in. Each room has a view of the courtyard, yet privacy is maintained by eliminating windows on the opposite side of the house.

Special features throughout the house draw in light and show off greenery. Plant shelves run along the railing above the foyer, and a box window/plant ledge rests above the kitchen sink. A window seat in the bedroom and corner windows in the living and dining rooms overlook the courtyard.

The open entry leading into the living room and dining room offers an unobstructed view of the landscape and the fireplace. Vaulted ceilings in the master bedroom, living room, and dining area reinforce the spacious, airy feeling.

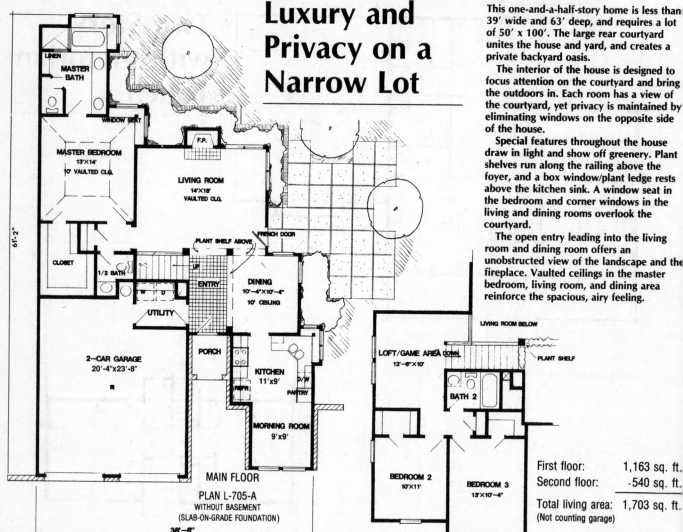

MAIN FLOOR

PLAN L-705-A
WITHOUT BASEMENT
(SLAB-ON-GRADE FOUNDATION)

First floor: 1,163 sq. ft.
Second floor: 540 sq. ft.
Total living area: 1,703 sq. ft.
(Not counting garage)

Blueprint Price Code B
Plan L-705-A

Stately and Comfortable

Plan AM-2132-A

Bedrooms: 3	Baths: 2½

Finished space:

Upper floor:	772 sq. ft.
Main floor:	935 sq. ft.
Total living area:	**1,707 sq. ft.**
Bonus area:	177 sq. ft.
Garage:	420 sq. ft.

Features:
Sunny breakfast nook.
Large family room with fireplace.
Deluxe master bedroom suite.
Bonus space over garage.

Exterior Wall Framing:	2x4

Foundation options:
Crawlspace only.
(Foundation & framing conversion
diagram available — see order form.)

Blueprint Price Code:	B

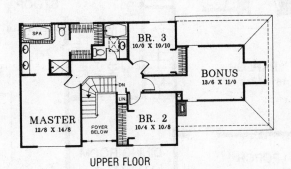

UPPER FLOOR

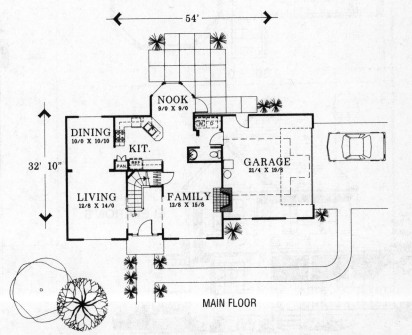

MAIN FLOOR

Plan AM-2132-A

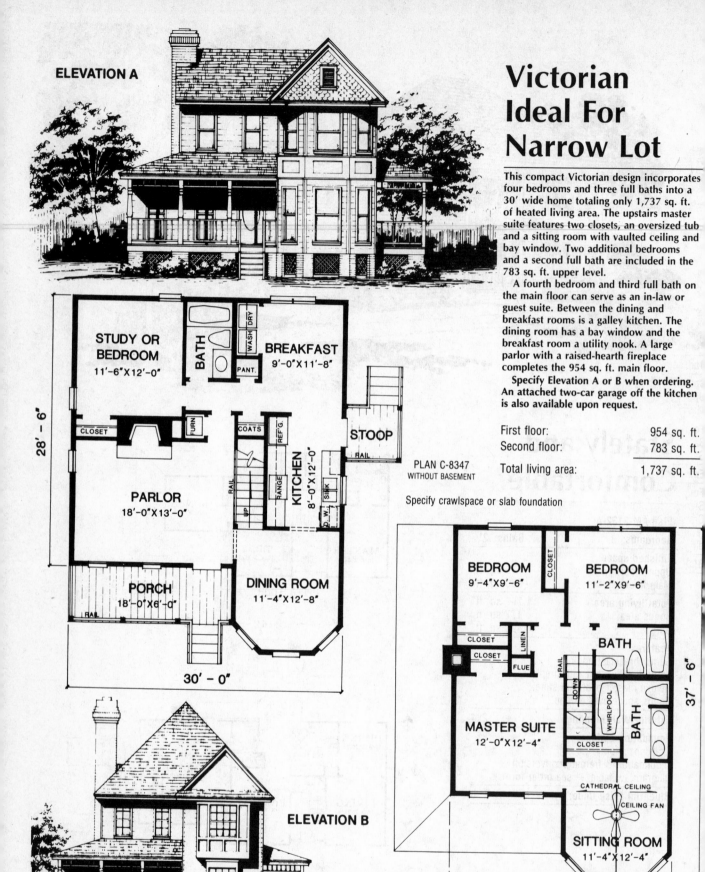

ELEVATION A

Victorian Ideal For Narrow Lot

This compact Victorian design incorporates four bedrooms and three full baths into a 30' wide home totaling only 1,737 sq. ft. of heated living area. The upstairs master suite features two closets, an oversized tub and a sitting room with vaulted ceiling and bay window. Two additional bedrooms and a second full bath are included in the 783 sq. ft. upper level.

A fourth bedroom and third full bath on the main floor can serve as an in-law or guest suite. Between the dining and breakfast rooms is a galley kitchen. The dining room has a bay window and the breakfast room a utility nook. A large parlor with a raised-hearth fireplace completes the 954 sq. ft. main floor.

Specify Elevation A or B when ordering. An attached two-car garage off the kitchen is also available upon request.

First floor: 954 sq. ft.
Second floor: 783 sq. ft.
Total living area: 1,737 sq. ft.

PLAN C-8347
WITHOUT BASEMENT

Specify crawlspace or slab foundation

STUDY OR BEDROOM 11'-6"X12'-0"
BATH
WASH DRY
BREAKFAST 9'-0"X11'-8"
PANT.
CLOSET
FURN
COATS
REF'G.
STOOP
RAIL
PARLOR 18'-0"X13'-0"
RAIL
UP
RANGE
KITCHEN 8'-0"X12'-0"
D.W. SINK
PLAN C-8347
28'-6"
PORCH 18'-0"X6'-0"
RAIL
DINING ROOM 11'-4"X12'-8"
30'-0"

ELEVATION B

BEDROOM 9'-4"X9'-6"
CLOSET
BEDROOM 11'-2"X9'-6"
CLOSET
CLOSET
LINEN
BATH
FLUE
RAIL
DOWN
WHIRLPOOL
BATH
MASTER SUITE 12'-0"X12'-4"
CLOSET
37'-6"
CATHEDRAL CEILING
CEILING FAN
SITTING ROOM 11'-4"X12'-4"
24'-0"

TO ORDER THIS BLUEPRINT, CALL TOLL-FREE 1-800-547-5570

Blueprint Price Code B
Plan C-8347

Elevation S-22189-B

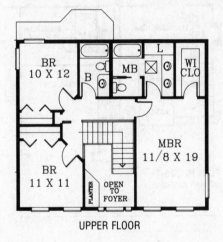

Elevation S-22189-A

Plans S-22189-A & -B

Bedrooms: 3	Baths: 2½

Space:

Upper floor:	774 sq. ft.
Main floor:	963 sq. ft.
Total living area:	**1,737 sq. ft.**
Basement:	963 sq. ft.
Garage:	462 sq. ft.

Exterior Wall Framing: 2x6

Foundation options:
Standard basement.
Crawlspace.
(Foundation & framing conversion
diagram available — see order form.)

Blueprint Price Code: B

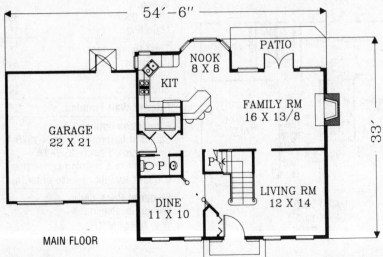

UPPER FLOOR

- BR 10 X 12
- MB
- L
- WI CLO
- B
- MBR 11/8 X 19
- BR 11 X 11
- PLANTER
- OPEN TO FOYER

MAIN FLOOR

54'-6"

33'

- GARAGE 22 X 21
- NOOK 8 X 8
- PATIO
- KIT
- FAMILY RM 16 X 13/8
- P
- DINE 11 X 10
- LIVING RM 12 X 14

Economical Traditional Offers Choice of Two Exteriors

- A compact and economical traditional, this plan will fit most smaller residential lots.
- Two elevations are available to fit your personal preference; the "A" version with its upper-level Palladian window, has a little more modern look, while the "B" version is more strictly traditional.
- A vaulted entry foyer leads to formal living and dining rooms.
- The family room, nook and kitchen are combined, but visually segregated for a more intimate look.
- The second floor master suite is roomy for a plan of this size, and includes a beautiful, skylighted bath and large closet.

HomeStyles
SOURCE 1
DESIGNERS NETWORK

Plans S-22189-A & -B

FRONT VIEW

Two-Level Home Features Dramatic Loft

- Clean, uncluttered lines give this basically traditional plan a modern look.
- Inside, the living room soars to a vaulted ceiling two stories above.
- The efficient U-shaped kitchen opens to a sunny nook in the front of the home.
- A formal dining room also features large front windows.
- Upstairs, two bedrooms share a connecting bath and open onto a balcony above the living room below.
- Also note the storage area over the garage.
- The plan version with a basement includes a lower level recreation room with a fireplace.

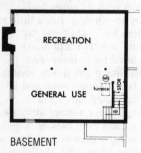

BASEMENT

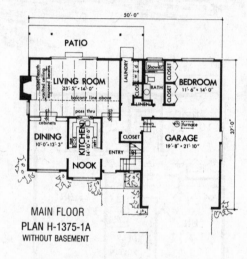

MAIN FLOOR
PLAN H-1375-1A
WITHOUT BASEMENT

MAIN FLOOR
PLAN H-1375-1
WITH BASEMENT

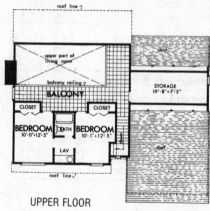

UPPER FLOOR

Plans H-1375-1 & H-1375-1A

Bedrooms: 3	Baths: 2

Space:	
Upper floor:	598 sq. ft.
Main floor:	1,153 sq. ft.

Total living area:	1,751 sq. ft.
Basement:	840 sq. ft.
Garage:	429 sq. ft.
Storage:	145 sq. ft.

Exterior Wall Framing:	2x4

Foundation options:
Standard basement, Plan H-1375-1.
Crawlspace, Plan H-1375-1A.
(Foundation & framing conversion diagram available — see order form.)

Blueprint Price Code:
Without basement: B
With basement: C

Plans H-1375-1 & -1A

Compact Design with Energy-Saving Features

- This stylish family home is wrapped in an attractive exterior of wood siding and brick veneer accents
- Covered entry leads into commodious living room with heat-circulating fireplace and sloped ceilings.
- Dining room opens to a patio via French doors and lies opposite an efficient U-shaped kitchen.
- Ample closet space, master bedroom, and two additional bedrooms comprise the second level.

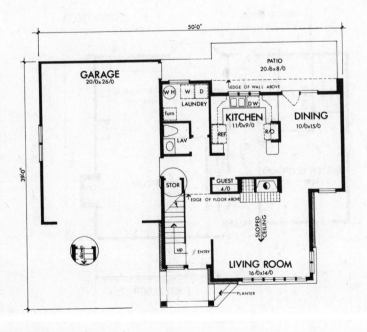

Plans H-3741-1 & -1A

Bedrooms: 3	Baths: 2½
Space:	
Upper floor:	900 sq. ft.
Main floor:	853 sq. ft.
Total living area:	1,753 sq. ft.
Basement:	approx. 853 sq. ft.
Garage:	520 sq. ft.
Exterior Wall Framing:	2x6

Foundation options:
Standard basement (Plans H-3741-1).
Crawlspace (Plans H-3741-1A).
(Foundation & framing conversion diagram available — see order form.)

Blueprint Price Code: B

Plans H-3741-1 & -1A

Rustic Home with Drive-Under Garage

This 1,760 sq. ft. rustic design includes a two-car garage as part of its full basement. All or part of the basement can be used to supplement the main living area. The master suite features a large walk-in closet and a double vanity in the master bath. An L-shaped kitchen with dining bay, a living room with raised-hearth fireplace and a centrally located utility room complete the 1,100 sq. ft. of heated living area on the main floor.

The open two-story foyer leads to an additional 660 sq. ft. of heated living area on the upper floor, consisting of two bedrooms with walk-in closets and a second full bath with two linen closets.

Front porch, multi-paned windows, shutters and horizontal wood siding combine for a rustic exterior. Basement version only.

First floor:	1,100 sq. ft.
Second floor:	660 sq. ft.
Total living area:	1,760 sq. ft.
(Not counting basement or garage)	

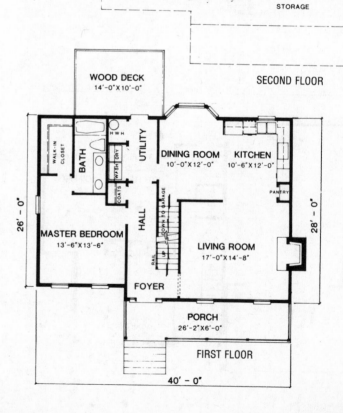

Blueprint Price Code B
Plan C-8339

Modern Country Cottage for Small Lot

This drive-under garage design is great for smaller lots. But even though the home is relatively compact, it's still loaded with modern features. The deluxe master bedroom has a large bath with garden tub and shower. The country kitchen/dining room combination has access to a deck out back. The large living room with fireplace is accessible from the two story foyer.

The upper floor has two large bedrooms and a full bath, and the large basement has room for two cars and expandable living areas.

This plan is available with basement foundation only.

Main floor:	1,100 sq. ft.
Second floor:	664 sq. ft.
Total living area:	1,764 sq. ft.
(Not counting basement or garage)	
Basement:	1,100 sq. ft.

PLAN C-8870
WITH BASEMENT

Compact and Luxurious

- The best from the past and present are bundled up in this compact design, reminiscent of a New England saltbox.
- Cozy kitchen has center island with breakfast counter and built-in range/oven; corner sink saves on counter space.
- Formal dining room, separated from the living room by a railing, affords a view to the sunken living room and the fireplace and deck beyond.
- Living room has vaulted ceiling and built-in shelves for entertainment center.
- Second-floor master suite features a hydro-spa, shower, and walk-in closet.

Plan H-1453-1A

Bedrooms: 3	Baths: 2

Space:	
Upper floor:	386 sq. ft.
Main floor:	1,385 sq. ft.

Total living area:	1,771 sq. ft.

Exterior Wall Framing:	2x6

Foundation options:
Crawlspace only.
(Foundation & framing conversion diagram available — see order form.)

Blueprint Price Code:	B

UPPER FLOOR

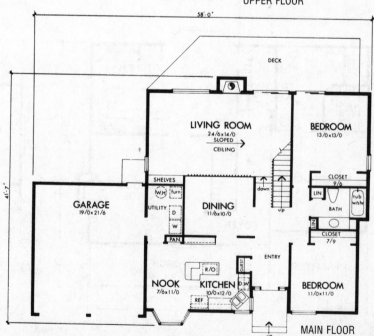

MAIN FLOOR

Plan H-1453-1A

FRONT VIEW

REAR VIEW

A Bungalow Style for Today

- Many of the features of the once popular bungalow are preserved and improved upon in this plan.
- A special touch is the pergola — the wooden trelliswork attached to the porch roof and supported by tapered columns.
- Spacious foyer has doors opening from porch and opposing garage.
- Sunken living room is separated from the dining room by a custom-designed handrail.
- French doors close off the den or third bedroom from the living room.
- Expansive kitchen features island work center, pantry, bay window with built-in desk, and access to rear deck.
- Master suite has numerous frills.

Plans H-1459-1 & -1A

Bedrooms: 2	Baths: 2
Space:	
Upper floor:	658 sq. ft.
Main floor:	1,137 sq. ft.
Total living area:	**1,795 sq. ft.**
Basement:	approx. 1,137 sq. ft.
Garage:	260 sq. ft.
Exterior Wall Framing:	2x6

Foundation options:
Standard basement.
Crawlspace.
(Foundation & framing conversion diagram available — see order form.)

Blueprint Price Code: B

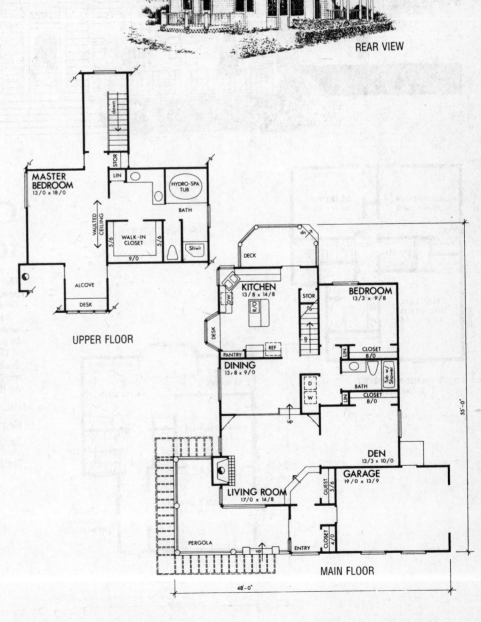

UPPER FLOOR

MAIN FLOOR

Plans H-1459-1 & -1A

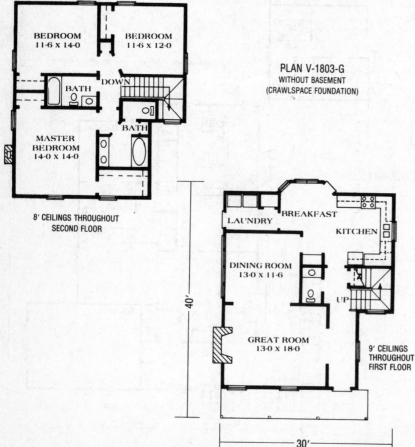

PLAN V-1803-G
WITHOUT BASEMENT
(CRAWLSPACE FOUNDATION)

BEDROOM
11-6 x 14-0

BEDROOM
11-6 x 12-0

DOWN

BATH

MASTER
BEDROOM
14-0 x 14-0

BATH

8' CEILINGS THROUGHOUT
SECOND FLOOR

LAUNDRY

BREAKFAST

KITCHEN

DINING ROOM
13-0 x 11-6

UP

GREAT ROOM
13-0 x 18-0

9' CEILINGS
THROUGHOUT
FIRST FLOOR

40'

30'

Classic Design for Small Lots

The quaint and restful appeal of this peaceful residence makes it appreciated in either urban or rural settings.

The openness of this plan gives those who enter the impression of a house much larger than its square footage indicates.

The stairs are dramatically lit by a double tier of windows. Please note the minimum of hall space when one arrives on the second floor.

First floor:	928 sq. ft.
Second floor:	875 sq. ft.
Total living area:	1,803 sq. ft.

Blueprint Price Code B

Plan V-1803-G

Modern Interior, Traditional Exterior

8' Ceilings Throughout
Unless Otherwise Noted

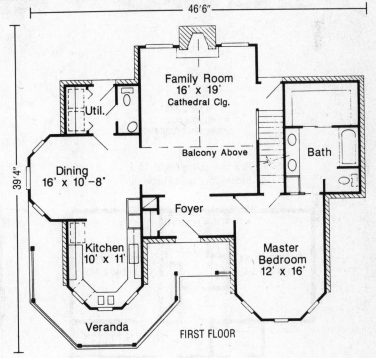

Util.

Family Room
16' x 19'
Cathedral Clg.

Balcony Above

Bath

Dining
16' x 10'-8"

Foyer

Master
Bedroom
12' x 16'

Kitchen
10' x 11'

Veranda

FIRST FLOOR

46'6"

39'4"

First floor: 1,201 sq. ft.
Second floor: 647 sq. ft.
Total living area: 1,848 sq. ft.

PLAN L-1848
WITHOUT BASEMENT
(SLAB FOUNDATION)

(Plans for a detached two-car garage
included with blueprint.)

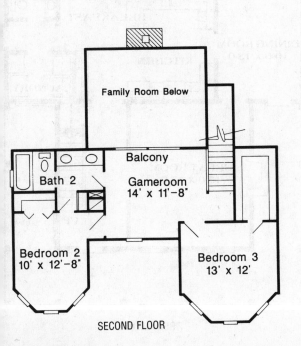

Family Room Below

Balcony

Bath 2

Gameroom
14' x 11'-8"

Bedroom 2
10' x 12'-8"

Bedroom 3
13' x 12'

SECOND FLOOR

HomeStyles
Source 1
DESIGNERS' NETWORK

Blueprint Price Code B
Plan L-1848

TO ORDER THIS BLUEPRINT,
CALL TOLL-FREE 1-800-547-5570
(Prices and details on pp. 12-15.) 133

Wrap Around Porch Adds Warmth

Undeniably appealing, the wrap-around porch of this engaging dwelling lends additional warmth to a very special house plan. Within, a graceful stairway is brightened by thoughtful window placement.

The formal dining room opens onto a sheltered porch; additional eating space is offered in the large breakfast bay. Nearby, a built-in cabinet provides shelves for cookbooks and cherished serving pieces; here, a desk could also be incorporated.

Upstairs space is particularly well-utilized; note the small amount of hallway. The master suite has a partitioned bath and separate tub and shower.

First floor:	1,005 sq. ft.
Second floor:	846 sq. ft.
Total living area:	1,851 sq. ft.

PLAN V-1851-C
WITHOUT BASEMENT
(CRAWLSPACE FOUNDATION)

First floor ceiling height: 10'
Second floor ceiling height: 9'

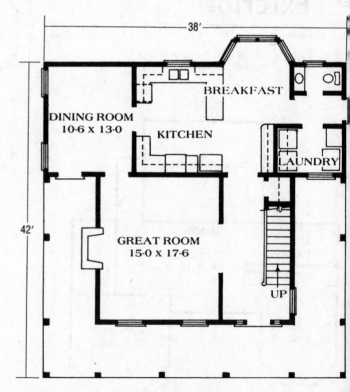

BATH

BEDROOM
10-6 x 13-0

BEDROOM
11-0 x 13-0

DOWN

MASTER
BEDROOM
13-0 x 14-0

BATH

SECOND FLOOR

38'

DINING ROOM
10-6 x 13-0

BREAKFAST

KITCHEN

LAUNDRY

42'

GREAT ROOM
15-0 x 17-6

UP

FIRST FLOOR

Blueprint Price Code B
Plan V-1851-C

Traditional Design With Open Floor Plan

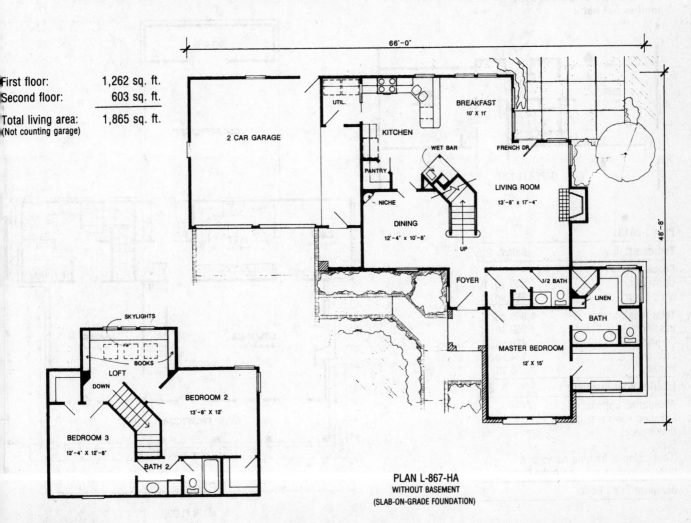

First floor: 1,262 sq. ft.
Second floor: 603 sq. ft.

Total living area: 1,865 sq. ft.
(Not counting garage)

66'-0"

2 CAR GARAGE

UTIL.

KITCHEN

BREAKFAST
10' X 11'

WET BAR

FRENCH DR

PANTRY

NICHE

DINING
12'-4" x 10'-8"

UP

LIVING ROOM
13'-8" x 17'-4"

48'-8"

FOYER

1/2 BATH

LINEN

BATH

MASTER BEDROOM
12' X 15'

SKYLIGHTS

BOOKS

LOFT

DOWN

BEDROOM 2
13'-8" X 12'

BEDROOM 3
12'-4" X 12'-8"

BATH 2

PLAN L-867-HA
WITHOUT BASEMENT
(SLAB-ON-GRADE FOUNDATION)

Blueprint Price Code B
Plan L-867-HA

TO ORDER THIS BLUEPRINT,
CALL TOLL-FREE 1-800-547-5570
(Prices and details on pp. 12-15.)

135

Cost-Efficient Cottage with Luxury Features

- This country cottage is easy to build, economical and attractive.
- The basic rectangular shape simplifies construction, and the steeply pitched roof accommodates upstairs bedrooms in space that would often otherwise be simply attic overhead.
- A huge living room with fireplace dominates the main floor.
- The dining room, kitchen, utility area and half bath make an efficient and livable area for casual family life.
- The main-floor master suite includes a spacious private bath with separate tub and shower, and a large closet.
- Upstairs, two bedrooms share another full bath.

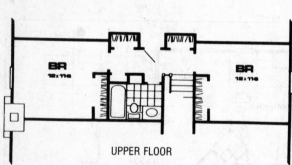

UPPER FLOOR

MAIN FLOOR

Plan J-86131

Bedrooms: 3	Baths: 2½

Space:	
Upper floor:	500 sq. ft.
Main floor:	1,369 sq. ft.

Total living area:	1,869 sq. ft.
Basement:	1,369 sq. ft.
Carport:	416 sq. ft.
Storage:	124 sq. ft.
Porch:	258 sq. ft.

Exterior Wall Framing:	2x4

Foundation options:
Standard basement.
Crawlspace.
Slab.
(Foundation & framing conversion diagram available — see order form.)

Blueprint Price Code:	B

Plan J-86131

Plan M-2214

Bedrooms: 4	**Baths: 2½**

Space:

Upper floor:	940 sq. ft.
Main floor:	964 sq. ft.
Total living area:	**1,904 sq. ft.**
Basement:	approx. 964 sq. ft.
Garage:	440 sq. ft.

Exterior Wall Framing: 2x4

Foundation options:
Standard basement only.
(Foundation & framing conversion
diagram available — see order form.)

Blueprint Price Code: B

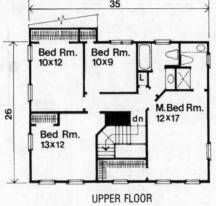

35

26

Bed Rm. 10x12

Bed Rm. 10x9

L

M.Bed Rm. 12x17

Bed Rm. 13x12

dn

UPPER FLOOR

Traditional Saltbox Roofline

- This classic saltbox exterior offers an open, flexible interior, with well-planned space for the large, busy family.
- The spacious living room includes an impressive fireplace and sliding doors to a screened porch at the rear of the home.
- The large, open-design kitchen blends in with the family room to create a delightful space for food preparation and family life.
- A formal dining room is found at the right as you enter the foyer.
- Upstairs, a deluxe master suite includes a private bath and large closet.
- Three secondary bedrooms share a second upstairs bath.
- Note the convenient washer/dryer area and half-bath off the kitchen.

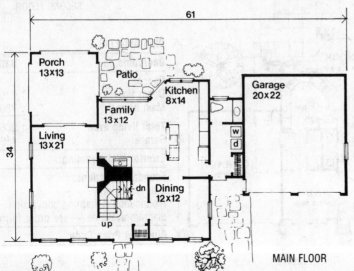

61

34

Porch 13x13

Patio

Kitchen 8x14

Garage 20x22

Family 13x12

Living 13x21

w
d

dn

Dining 12x12

up

MAIN FLOOR

Plan M-2214

Impressive Entry, Quality Design Throughout

- Towering brick archway attracts attention to this striking, impressive home.
- Interior design effectively blends formal and casual living.
- Living room includes a coffered, vaulted ceiling.
- Dining room displays imposing bay windows.
- Family room includes fireplace and joins a delightful all-glass nook.
- The convenient kitchen includes an angled breakfast bar and a pantry closet.
- Upstairs, the master suite features a magnificent bath with a spa tub in its own glass-enclosed bay overlook.
- The secondary bedrooms share a bath with double sinks, and both have large closets.

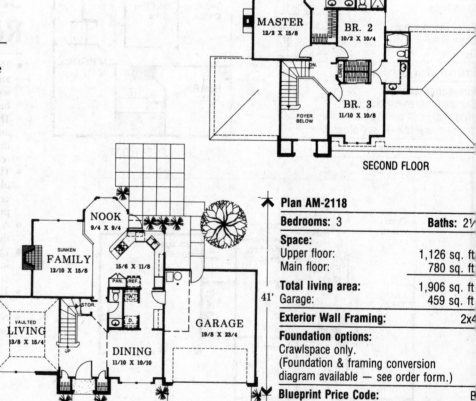

SECOND FLOOR

FIRST FLOOR

Plan AM-2118

Bedrooms: 3	Baths: 2½
Space:	
Upper floor:	1,126 sq. ft
Main floor:	780 sq. ft
Total living area:	1,906 sq. ft
Garage:	459 sq. ft
Exterior Wall Framing:	2x4

Foundation options:
Crawlspace only.
(Foundation & framing conversion diagram available — see order form.)

Blueprint Price Code: B

Plan AM-2118

Farm House for Today

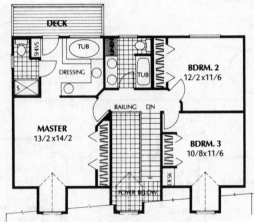

DECK

TUB

DRESSING

BDRM. 2
12/2 x 11/6

TUB

RAILING   DN

MASTER
13/2 x 14/2

BDRM. 3
10/8 x 11/6

FOYER BELOW

UPPER FLOOR

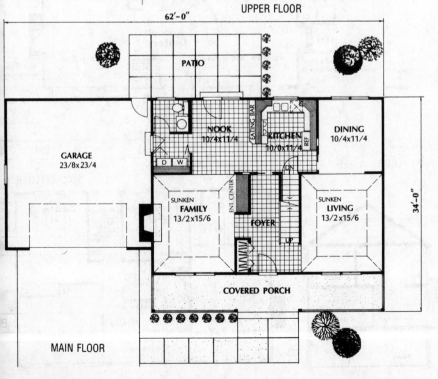

62'-0"

PATIO

GARAGE
23/8 x 23/4

NOOK
10/4 x 11/4

EATING BAR

KITCHEN
10/0 x 11/4

REF

DINING
10/4 x 11/4

D   W

34'-0"

**SUNKEN
FAMILY**
13/2 x 15/6

ENT. CENTER

FOYER

DN

**SUNKEN
LIVING**
13/2 x 15/6

UP

COVERED PORCH

MAIN FLOOR

- An inviting veranda and charming dormer windows lend traditional warmth to this attractive design.
- An up-to-date interior includes ample space for entertaining as well as for family life.
- An elegant foyer is flanked on one side by a formal, sunken living room and a sunken family room with fireplace on the other.
- A dining room joins the living room to increase the space available for parties.
- A roomy and efficient kitchen/nook/utility area combination with a half bath forms a spacious area for casual family life and domestic chores.
- Upstairs, a grand master suite includes a compartmentalized bath with separate tub and shower and a large closet.
- A second full bath serves the two secondary bedrooms.

Plan U-87-203

Bedrooms: 3	Baths: 2½
Space:	
Upper floor:	857 sq. ft.
Main floor:	1,064 sq. ft.
Total living area:	1,921 sq. ft.
Basement:	1,064 sq. ft.
Garage:	552 sq. ft.
Exterior Wall Framing:	2x4 & 2x6

Foundation options:
Standard basement.
Crawlspace.
Slab.
(Foundation & framing conversion diagram available — see order form.)

Blueprint Price Code:	B

HomeStyles
SOURCE
DESIGNERS NETWORK

Plan U-87-203

Classic Colonial Offers Open Floor Plan

The stately dignity of this two-story Colonial is immediately evident in its charming facade, accented by a columned, curved portico that provides an elegant and gracious welcome. Inside, the distinctive two-story reception gallery, with a classic curved staircase, efficiently channels household traffic. Formal living room and dining room share a wood-burning fireplace; sliding glass doors at the rear lead to a backyard terrace.

On the opposite side of the entry, a spacious family room and dinette are warmed by a second fireplace, creating a cozy ambience for casual informal living. The centrally located kitchen readily serves both the dinette and the dining room.

Above, four bedroons are planned around the light-filled upper gallery. The master bedroom features a large walk-in closet and a private bath, complete with a whirlpool tub. Total living area is 994 sq. ft. on the first floor and 944 sq. ft. on the second.

PLAN K-655-U
WITH BASEMENT

First floor:	994 sq. ft.
Second floor:	944 sq. ft.
Total living area:	1,938 sq. ft.
(Not counting basement or garage)	

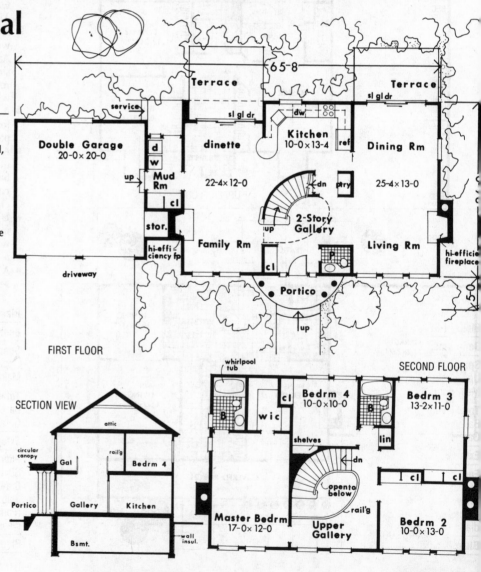

FIRST FLOOR

65-8

Terrace

Terrace

service

Double Garage
20-0 × 20-0

sl gl dr

dinette

Kitchen
10-0 × 13-4

ref

Dining Rm
25-4 × 13-0

sl gl dr

d
w

dw

up

Mud Rm

22-4 × 12-0

cl

stor.

2-Story Gallery

up

dn

hi-effi ciency fp

Family Rm

Living Rm

cl

hi-efficie fireplace

driveway

P

Portico

up

SECTION VIEW

attic

circular canopy

Gal

rail'g

Bedrm 4

Portico

Gallery

Kitchen

Bsmt.

wall insul.

SECOND FLOOR

whirlpool tub

Bedrm 4
10-0 × 10-0

cl

Bedrm 3
13-2 × 11-0

B

wic

B

lin

shelves

dn

Master Bedrm
17-0 × 12-0

open to below

rail'g

Upper Gallery

cl

cl

Bedrm 2
10-0 × 13-0

Blueprint Price Code B
Plan K-655-U

FRONT VIEW

MSLURE

Tradition with Modern Touch

- Dining room and master bedroom offer access to rear patio.
- Entryway approaches large living room with sloped ceilings and built-in fireplace, both exposed to second-level loft.
- Roomy kitchen has corner pantry and convenient nearby laundry facilities.
- First floor master bedroom includes generous walk-in closet and "his 'n hers" vanities.

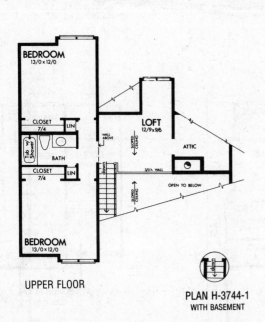

UPPER FLOOR

BEDROOM
13/0 × 12/0

CLOSET
7/4

LIN

BATH

CLOSET
7/4

LIN

LOFT
12/9 × 9/6

WALL ABOVE

SLOPED CEILING

ATTIC

3/0 h. WALL

SLOPED CEILING

OPEN TO BELOW

BEDROOM
13/0 × 12/0

down

PLAN H-3744-1
WITH BASEMENT

48'-0"

BEDROOM
13/0 × 15/0

PATIO

6/6

5/6

WALK-IN CLOSET

3/6

Shower

BATH

KITCHEN
11/0 × 11/3

DW

REF

R/O

DINING
12/0 × 13/3

LAUNDRY

W

D

PANTRY

WH heat

GARAGE
21/0 × 23/0

CLOSET
3/0

WOOD STORAGE

LAV

BUFFET

WALL ABOVE

SLOPED CEILING

up

WALL ABOVE

GUEST

ENTRY

LIVING ROOM
13/0 × 16/3

PLANTER

48'-0"

MAIN FLOOR

Plans H-3744-1 & -1A

Bedrooms: 3	Baths: 2½

Space:

Upper floor:	660 sq. ft.
Main floor:	1,300 sq. ft.

Total living area:	**1,960 sq. ft.**
Basement:	approx. 1,300 sq. ft.
Garage:	483 sq. ft.

Exterior Wall Framing:	2x6

Foundation options:
Standard basement (Plan H-3744-1).
Crawlspace (Plan H-3744-1A).
(Foundation & framing conversion diagram available — see order form.)

Blueprint Price Code:	B

REAR VIEW

Plans H-3744-1 & -1A

TO ORDER THIS BLUEPRINT,
CALL TOLL-FREE 1-800-547-5570
(Prices and details on pp. 12-15.) **141**

Contemporary Elegance

- This contemporary design includes elegant traditional overtones, and is finished in vertical cedar siding.
- An expansive space is devoted to the vaulted living room and adjoining family/dining room and kitchen.
- A convenient utility area is located between the kitchen and the garage, and includes a clothes sorting counter, deep sink and ironing space.
- The master suite is spacious for a home of this size, and includes a sumptuous master bath and large walk-in closet.
- A loft area can be used for an additional bedroom, playroom, exercise area or hobby space.
- An optional sunroom can be added to the rear at any time.

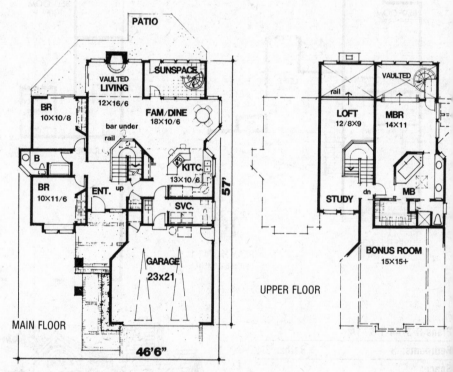

PATIO

VAULTED LIVING 12×16/6

SUNSPACE

BR 10×10/8

FAM/DINE 18×10/6

bar under rail

B

KITC 13×10/6

BR 10×11/6

ENT. up

SVC.

GARAGE 23x21

MAIN FLOOR

46'6"

57'

LOFT 12/8×9

VAULTED

MBR 14×11

rail

STUDY

dn

MB

BONUS ROOM 15×15+

UPPER FLOOR

Plan S-1971

Bedrooms: 3-4	Baths: 2

Space:

Upper floor:	723 sq. ft.
Main floor:	1,248 sq. ft.

Total living area:	**1,971 sq. ft.**
Bonus area:	225 sq. ft.
Basement:	approx. 1,248 sq. ft.
Garage:	483 sq. ft.

Exterior Wall Framing:	2x6

Foundation options:
Standard basement.
Crawlspace.
(Foundation & framing conversion diagram available — see order form.)

Blueprint Price Code:	B

TO ORDER THIS BLUEPRINT,
CALL TOLL-FREE 1-800-547-5570
142 (Prices and details on pp. 12-15.)

Plan S-1971

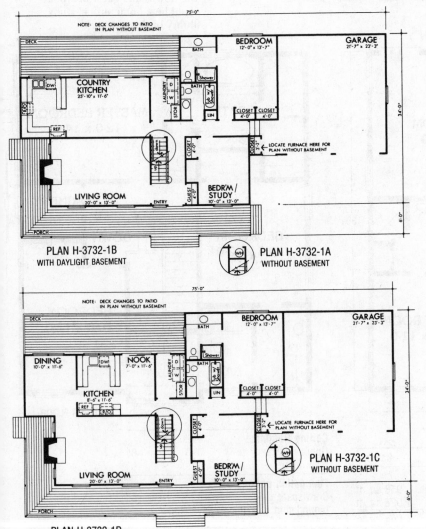

PLAN H-3732-1B
WITH DAYLIGHT BASEMENT

PLAN H-3732-1A
WITHOUT BASEMENT

PLAN H-3732-1D
WITH DAYLIGHT BASEMENT

PLAN H-3732-1C
WITHOUT BASEMENT

Old Homestead

Almost everyone has a soft place in his heart for a certain home in his childhood. A home like this one, with understated farmhouse styling and wrap-around porch, may be the image of "Home" that your children remember.

Two versions of the first floor plan provide a choice between a country kitchen and a more formal dining room.

All versions feature 2x6 exterior wall framing.

First floor:	1,359 sq. ft.
Second floor:	626 sq. ft.
Total living area:	1,985 sq. ft.

(Not counting basement or garage)
(Non-basement versions designed with crawlspace)

Garage:	528 sq. ft.

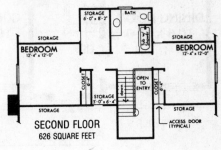

SECOND FLOOR
626 SQUARE FEET

Blueprint Price Code B

Plans H-3732-1A, H-3732-1B, H-3732-1C & H-3732-1D

143

A Stable Sign of Prosperous Times

- The timeless appeal of Georgian architecture is captured in this entrancing design.
- This plan maintains the flavor of the original Colonial dwellings on the exterior, while including modern features inside.
- A spacious kitchen opens to a sunny breakfast nook.
- A large Great Room with fireplace provides wonderful space for family living or entertaining.
- The master suite boasts a dazzling bath with whirlpool tub and double vanities, plus a large walk-in closet.
- Two secondary bedrooms share a connecting bath with separate vanity areas.
- The downstairs guest bedroom could be a home office, study, library or den.

BREAKFAST

GREAT ROOM
14-0 x 18-0

KITCHEN

BATH

DINING ROOM
10-6 x 12-0

UP

GUEST ROOM
10-6 x 11-0

36'

30'

MAIN FLOOR

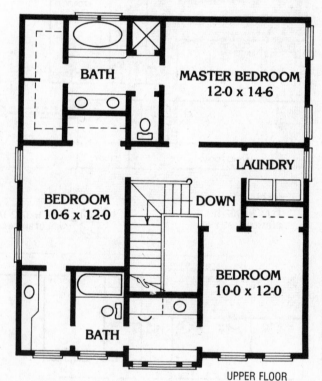

BATH

MASTER BEDROOM
12-0 x 14-6

LAUNDRY

BEDROOM
10-6 x 12-0

DOWN

BEDROOM
10-0 x 12-0

BATH

UPPER FLOOR

Plan V-1986

Bedrooms: 3-4	**Baths:** 3

Space:

Upper floor:	958 sq. ft.
Main floor:	1,028 sq. ft.
Total living area:	**1,926 sq. ft.**
Exterior Wall Framing:	2x6

Ceiling Heights:

Upper floor:	8'
Main floor:	9'

Foundation options:
Crawlspace only.
(Foundation & framing conversion diagram available — see order form.)

Blueprint Price Code:	B

TO ORDER THIS BLUEPRINT,
CALL TOLL-FREE 1-800-547-5570

Plan V-1986

HomeStyles SOURCE1 Designers Network

Designed for Family Living

First floor:	1,182 sq. ft.
Second floor:	882 sq. ft.
Total living area: (Not counting basement or garage)	2,064 sq. ft.

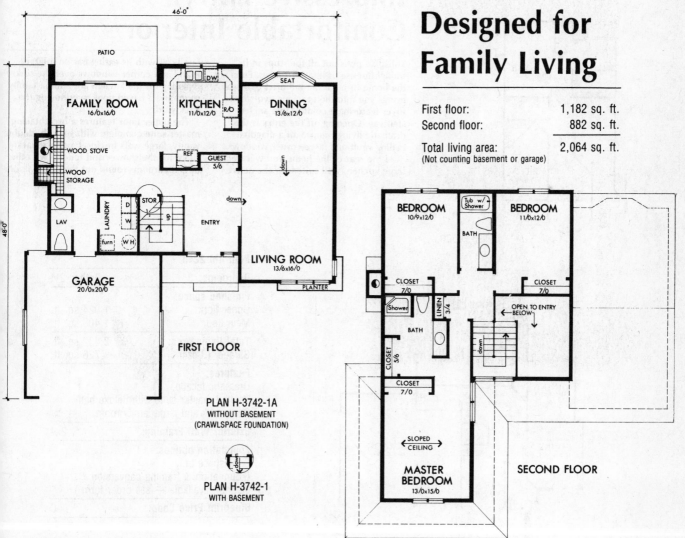

FIRST FLOOR

PATIO

FAMILY ROOM
16/0x16/0

KITCHEN
11/0x12/0

DINING
13/6x12/0

SEAT

DW

R/O

WOOD STOVE

WOOD STORAGE

REF

GUEST
5/6

down

LAV

LAUNDRY

D

W

STOR

furn

W H

up

ENTRY

down

LIVING ROOM
13/6x16/0

PLANTER

GARAGE
20/0x20/0

46'-0"

48'-0"

PLAN H-3742-1A
WITHOUT BASEMENT
(CRAWLSPACE FOUNDATION)

PLAN H-3742-1
WITH BASEMENT

SECOND FLOOR

BEDROOM
10/9x12/0

Tub w/ Shower

BEDROOM
11/0x12/0

BATH

CLOSET
7/0

CLOSET
7/0

Shower

LINEN

3/4

OPEN TO ENTRY BELOW

BATH

CLOSET
5/6

down

CLOSET
7/0

SLOPED CEILING

MASTER BEDROOM
13/0x15/0

Blueprint Price Code C

Plans H-3742-1 & H-3742-1A

TO ORDER THIS BLUEPRINT,
CALL TOLL-FREE 1-800-547-5570
(Prices and details on pp. 12-15.) **145**

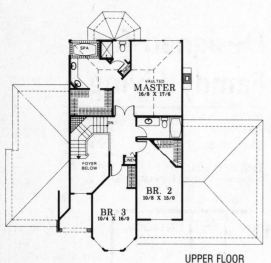

UPPER FLOOR

Impressive Entry, Comfortable Interior

This plan pulls out all the stops in its thoughtful use of interior spaces. Entering the home through the tall brick archway brings you into the spacious two-story foyer featuring a comfortable angled stairway. Opening off the entry is the dramatic living room with a diagonal ceiling vault and large corner windows.

At the rear of the home you will find a large kitchen, well suited for the active

family — with its eating bar on a large island and corner windows over the sink. Opening off the kitchen are a large family room and a bayed nook overlooking the back yard.

The upper floor features a breathtaking master suite complete with spa tub, double vanity, large walk-in closet and a separate room for the shower and toilet. Two other large bedrooms round out the upper floor.

MAIN FLOOR

Plan AM-2240	
Bedrooms: 3	**Baths:** 2½
Finished space:	
Upper floor:	1,024 sq. ft.
Main floor:	1,408 sq. ft.
Total living area:	2,432 sq. ft.
Garage: (3-car)	726 sq. ft.

Features:
Dramatic facade.
Vaulted master suite with deluxe bath.
Den, nook and large family room.

Exterior Wall Framing:	2x4

Foundation options:
Crawlspace only.
(Foundation & framing conversion
diagram available — see order form.)

Blueprint Price Code:	C

Plan AM-2240

Roomy Plan with Cozy Look

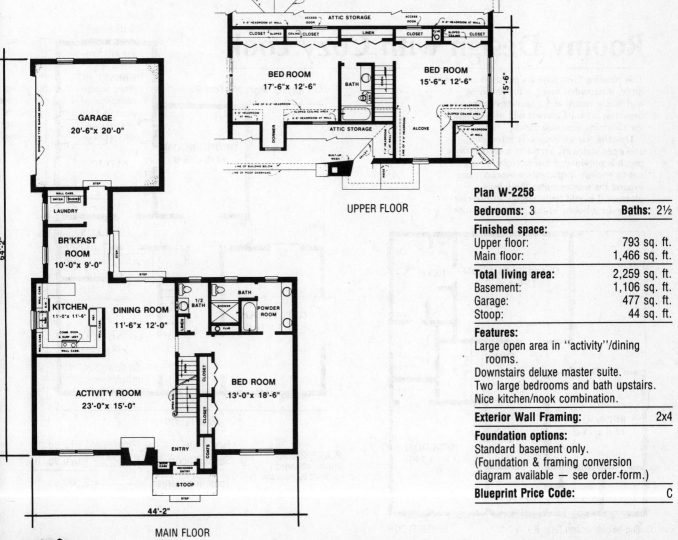

ATTIC STORAGE

ACCESS DOOR   ACCESS DOOR

8'-0" HEADROOM AT WALL   8'-0" HEADROOM AT WALL

CLOSET | SLOPED CEILING | CLOSET   LINEN   CLOSET | SLOPED CEILING | CLOSET

BED ROOM
17'-6" x 12'-6"

BATH

BED ROOM
15'-6" x 12'-6"

15'-6"

LINE OF 8'-0" HEADROOM

8'-0" HEADROOM AT WALL   SLOPED CEILING AREA   LINE OF 8'-0" HEADROOM   SLOPED CEILING AREA

8'-0" HEADROOM AT WALL

DORMER   **ATTIC STORAGE**   ALCOVE   8'-0" HEADROOM AT WALL

7'-6" HEADROOM AT WALL

BUILT-UP WASH

LINE OF BUILDING BELOW

LINE OF ROOF OVERHANG   VALLEY   VALLEY

UPPER FLOOR

GARAGE
20'-6" x 20'-0"

STEP

WALL CABS. | DRYER | WASHER

LAUNDRY

BR'KFAST ROOM
10'-0" x 9'-0"

STEP

STEP

KITCHEN
11'-0" x 11'-6"

COMB. OVEN & SURF. UNIT

WALL CABS.

DINING ROOM
11'-6" x 12'-0"

1/2 BATH   **BATH**   SHOWER   LINEN   **POWDER ROOM**   FLUE

64'-2"

ACTIVITY ROOM
23'-0" x 15'-0"

CLOSET

CLOSET

BED ROOM
13'-0" x 18'-6"

ENTRY

COATS

BOOK CASE | RECESSED ENTRY

STOOP

STEP

44'-2"

MAIN FLOOR

Plan W-2258

Bedrooms: 3	**Baths:** 2½

Finished space:

Upper floor:	793 sq. ft.
Main floor:	1,466 sq. ft.

Total living area:	2,259 sq. ft.
Basement:	1,106 sq. ft.
Garage:	477 sq. ft.
Stoop:	44 sq. ft.

Features:
Large open area in ''activity''/dining rooms.
Downstairs deluxe master suite.
Two large bedrooms and bath upstairs.
Nice kitchen/nook combination.

Exterior Wall Framing:	2x4

Foundation options:
Standard basement only.
(Foundation & framing conversion diagram available — see order form.)

Blueprint Price Code:	C

HomeStyles Source 1
DESIGNERS' NETWORK

Plan W-2258

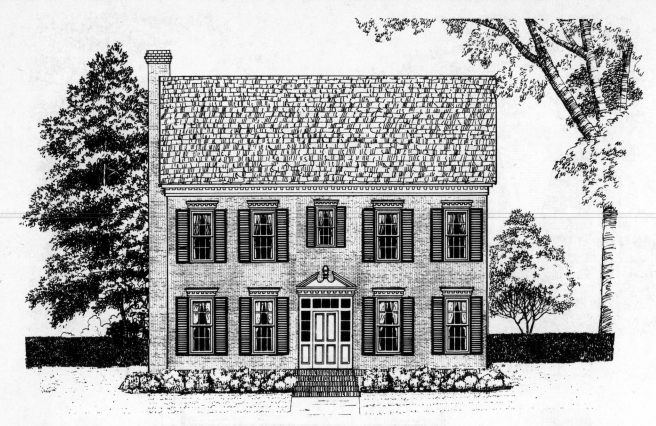

Roomy Design with Cozy Look

This pleasing Georgian design has it all — a large, uncrowded foyer, a formal living and dining room, and a spacious sunny breakfast area. Its owners will also delight in the charming rear side porch.

Upstairs, via an especially interesting and open stairway, access to a second-floor porch is provided. Some occupants may opt to enclose it to create a sunroom and expand the master suite. Think how pleasant it would be to engage in exercise or pursue a hobby in this pleasant location!

Ceiling height first floor 9'

BREAKFAST

DINING ROOM
12-0 x 13-6

KITCHEN

LAUN

GREAT ROOM
13-0 x 18-0

UP

LIVING ROOM
13-0 x 14-0

38'

45'

MAIN FLOOR

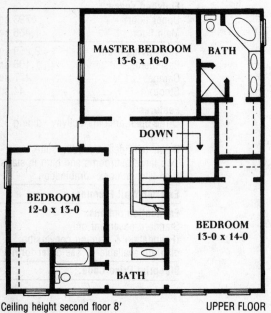

MASTER BEDROOM
13-6 x 16-0

BATH

DOWN

BEDROOM
12-0 x 13-0

BEDROOM
13-0 x 14-0

BATH

Ceiling height second floor 8'

UPPER FLOOR

PLAN V-2330-C
WITHOUT BASEMENT
(CRAWLSPACE FOUNDATION)

First floor: 1,260 sq. ft.
Second floor: 1,070 sq. ft.
Total living area: 2,330 sq. ft.

Blueprint Price Code C
Plan V-2330-C

HomeStyles
SOURCE 1
DESIGNERS NETWORK

Classic Charm

- Exterior features massive brick fireplace.
- Living room has corner window seat.
- Large gameroom on 2nd floor features skylights.
- 9′ ceilings in kitchen, breakfast area and master bedroom. 8′ throughout balance of home.

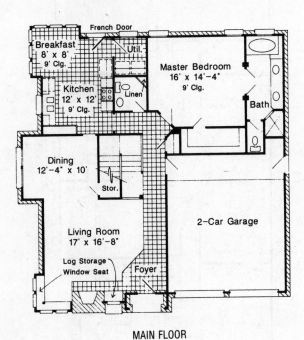

MAIN FLOOR

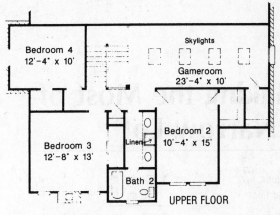

UPPER FLOOR

Plan L-400-CB

Bedrooms: 4	**Baths:** 2½

Finished space:
Upper floor:	999 sq. ft.
Main floor:	1,401 sq. ft.

Total living area:	2,400 sq. ft.

Ceiling height:
Main floor: 8′ unless otherwise noted on floor plan.
Upper floor: 8′

Exterior Wall Framing:	2x4

Dimensions:
Width:	45′0″
Depth:	46′8″

Foundation options:
Slab only.
(Foundation & framing conversion diagram available — see order form.)

Blueprint Price Code:	C

HomeStyles
SOURCE 1
DESIGNERS' NETWORK

Plan L-400-CB

Making the Most of a Narrow Lot

First floor:	1,734 sq. ft.
Second floor:	756 sq. ft.
Total living area:	2,490 sq. ft.
(Not counting garage)	

PLAN L-492-6B
WITHOUT BASEMENT
(SLAB-ON-GRADE FOUNDATION)

SECOND FLOOR
9'-0" CEILINGS THROUGHOUT

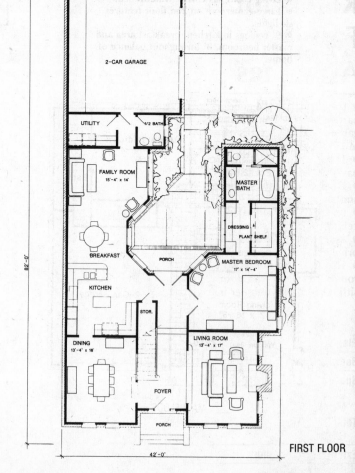

FIRST FLOOR

Blueprint Price Code C
Plan L-492-6B

Sunny Garden Room for Family Activities

- Designed to make good use of a narrow lot, this home features a garden room with walls of windows to brighten any day.
- The large island kitchen adjoins a bay-windowed breakfast area.
- Dining room offers a unique shape, and an 11′ ceiling.
- Living room also has an 11′ vaulted ceiling, plus a fireplace.
- Master suite includes a deluxe private bath and a large walk-in closet.
- Upstairs, you'll find two more roomy bedrooms with dormered sitting areas, and another bath.

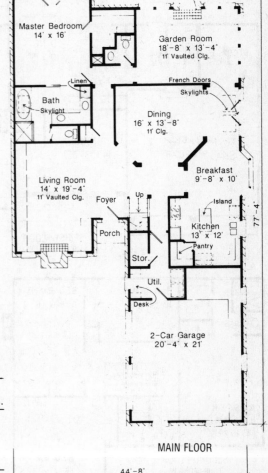

UPPER FLOOR

MAIN FLOOR

Plan L-667-7B

Bedrooms: 3	Baths: 2½

Space:	
Upper floor:	601 sq. ft.
Main floor:	2,066 sq. ft.
Total living area:	**2,667 sq. ft.**
Garage:	427 sq. ft.
Exterior Wall Framing:	2x4

Ceiling Heights: 9′ unless otherwise noted.

Foundation options:
Slab.
(Foundation & framing conversion diagram available — see order form.)

Blueprint Price Code: D

Plan L-667-7B

TO ORDER THIS BLUEPRINT,
CALL TOLL-FREE 1-800-547-5570
(Prices and details on pp. 12-15.) **151**

Four- or Five-Bedroom Option

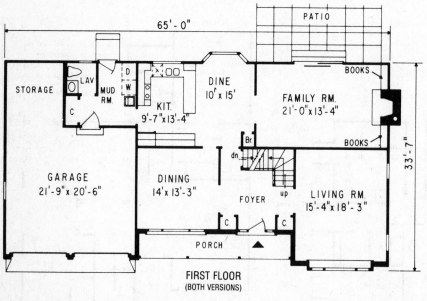

PATIO

65'-0"

STORAGE

LAV

MUD RM.

C

D W
D W

KIT.
9'-7"x13'-4"

DINE
10'x 15'

FAMILY RM.
21'-0"x13'-4"

BOOKS

BOOKS

Br.

dn

GARAGE
21'-9"x 20'-6"

DINING
14'x 13'-3"

FOYER

up

LIVING RM.
15'-4"x18'-3"

33'-7"

C

C

PORCH

▲

FIRST FLOOR
(BOTH VERSIONS)

B

C

BED RM -2
13'-4" x 10'

C

BED RM -3
11'-9" x 16'-4"

DRESS

C

L

MASTER
BED RM
14' x 17'-6"

dn
OPEN

C

BATH -2

C

BED RM -4
15'-4" x 13'-9"

SECOND FLOOR
FOUR-BEDROOM

BED RM. - 4
12'x13'-3"

C

BED RM. - 3
13'-3"x10'

c BED RM. - 2
11'-9"x14'-4"

C

L

C.

dn
OPEN

C.

C.

BED RM. - 5
12'x11'

L

B.

MASTER
BED RM.
15'-4"x 15'-10"

BATH

SECOND FLOOR
FIVE-BEDROOM

First floor: 1,392 sq. ft.
Second floor: 1,282 sq. ft.

Total living area: 2,674 sq. ft.
(Not counting basement or garage)

PLAN N-1066
WITH BASEMENT

Blueprints
include both four-
and five-bedroom
plans. PLAN AVAILABLE
ONLY WITH BASEMENT

Blueprint Price Code D
Plan N-1066

HomeStyles
Source 1
DESIGNERS NETWORK

A Tudor Home for a Contemporary Lifestyle

Timbered walls, multi-paned windows, an arched entry alcove and wrought iron strap hinges lend strong Tudor styling to the exterior, but this 2,741 sq. ft. open plan home flows over two floors for a contemporary family's full enjoyment. It's also up to date in its concern for energy efficiency.

This Tudor for the Nineties has a double-door entry hall that divides traffic throughout the 1,609 sq. ft. main floor. An open stairway leads from the high-ceiling entry hall to the 1,132 sq. ft. upper floor, and stairs replace a hall storage closet in the daylight basement version of the plan.

The living room is to the left of the entry hall, and the adjacent dining area opens into one of the patios. The U-shaped kitchen has a large island and a corner window wall. The nook and family room, with a log-sized fireplace, offer a separate area for family activities or entertaining.

The master bedroom suite, occupying half of the upper floor, has a walk-in closet and dressing area, spa tub and separate bathroom with shower, and opens onto an elevated, covered wood deck.

The other two bedrooms also have walk-in wardrobes and share a bathroom. An adjacent unfinished area can be used for storage or finished for other uses.

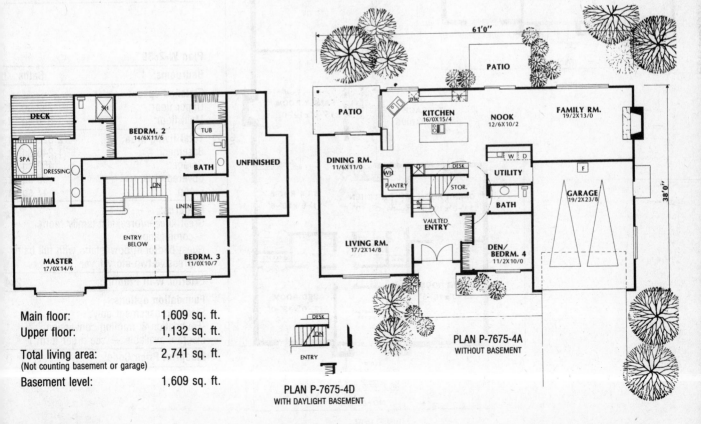

Main floor:	1,609 sq. ft.
Upper floor:	1,132 sq. ft.
Total living area: (Not counting basement or garage)	2,741 sq. ft.
Basement level:	1,609 sq. ft.

PLAN P-7675-4D
WITH DAYLIGHT BASEMENT

PLAN P-7675-4A
WITHOUT BASEMENT

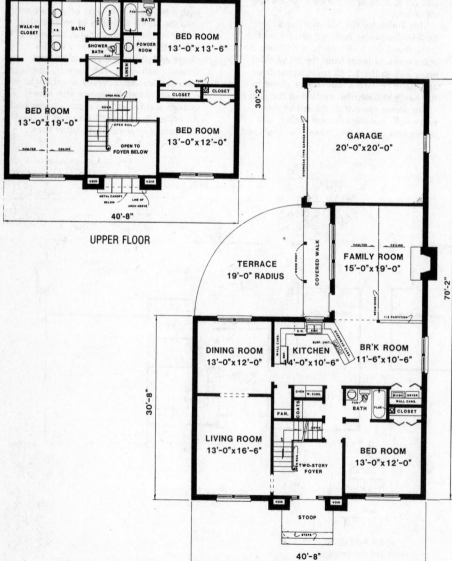

UPPER FLOOR

- WALK-IN CLOSET
- BATH
- BATH
- BED ROOM 13'-0" x 13'-6"
- SHOWER BATH
- POWDER ROOM
- CLOSET / CLOSET
- BED ROOM 13'-0" x 19'-0"
- OPEN RAIL / DOWN
- OPEN RAIL
- OPEN TO FOYER BELOW
- BED ROOM 13'-0" x 12'-0"
- VAULTED CEILING
- VOID
- METAL CANOPY BELOW / LINE OF ARCH ABOVE
- 30'-2"
- 40'-8"

MAIN FLOOR

- GARAGE 20'-0" x 20'-0"
- OVERHEAD TYPE GARAGE DOOR
- TERRACE 19'-0" RADIUS
- COVERED WALK
- WOOD POST
- FAMILY ROOM 15'-0" x 19'-0"
- VAULTED CEILING
- 1/2 PARTITION
- DINING ROOM 13'-0" x 12'-0"
- KITCHEN 14'-0" x 10'-6"
- WALL CABS.
- D.W. / SINK
- SURF. UNIT
- BR'K ROOM 11'-6" x 10'-6"
- OVEN W. CABS.
- PAN.
- COATS
- WASH / DRYER
- BATH
- WALL CABS.
- FLUE
- CLOSET
- LIVING ROOM 13'-0" x 16'-6"
- TWO-STORY FOYER
- BED ROOM 13'-0" x 12'-0"
- VOID
- STOOP
- STEPS
- 30'-8"
- 70'-2"
- 40'-8"

The Solid, Substantial Look of Brick

Plan W-2839

Bedrooms: 4	Baths: 3

Finished space:

Upper floor:	1,252 sq. ft.
Main floor:	1,570 sq. ft.

Total living area:	**2,822 sq. ft.**
Basement:	1,246 sq. ft.
Garage:	452 sq. ft.
Covered walk:	95 sq. ft.
Stoop:	47 sq. ft.

Features:
Great kitchen/breakfast/family room combination.
Guest bedroom downstairs with full bath.
Impressive two-story foyer.

Exterior Wall Framing: 2x4

Foundation options:
Standard basement only.
(Foundation & framing conversion diagram available — see order form.)

Blueprint Price Code: D

TO ORDER THIS BLUEPRINT, CALL TOLL-FREE 1-800-547-5570
154 (Prices and details on pp. 12-15.)

Plan W-2839

HomeStyles SOURCE 1 DESIGNERS NETWORK

Luxury Home for the Nineties and Beyond

- This plan will impress family and visitors alike with its elegant and impressive exterior and interior design.
- The main floor is well zoned into formal, casual and utility areas, so it lends itself well to both active family life and formal entertaining on a regular basis.
- All bedrooms are upstairs, and the master suite consists of an incredible bath, huge closet and large sleeping area with a bright bay window.
- Alternate Plan AM-2317-A offers a 3-car garage, a larger laundry area and bigger bonus space over the garage.

Plans AM-2317 & AM-2317-A

Bedrooms: 3	Baths: 2½
Space:	
Upper floor:	1,295 sq. ft.
Main floor:	1,661 sq. ft.
Total living area:	2,956 sq. ft.
Bonus area:	272 sq. ft.
Garage (Double):	614 sq. ft.
Exterior Wall Framing:	2x4

Foundation options:
Crawlspace only.
(Foundation & framing conversion diagram available — see order form.)

Blueprint Price Code:	D

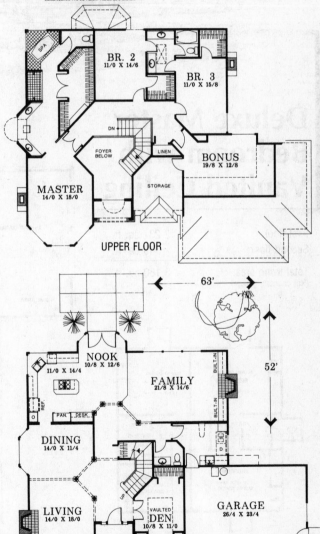

UPPER FLOOR

MAIN FLOOR

Deluxe Master Bedroom with Vaulted Ceiling

First floor: 2,237 sq. ft.
Second floor: 943 sq. ft.

Total living area: 3,180 sq. ft.
(Not counting garage)

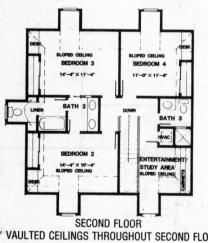

SECOND FLOOR
9' VAULTED CEILINGS THROUGHOUT SECOND FLOOR

PLAN L-182-FCC
WITHOUT BASEMENT
(SLAB-ON-GRADE FOUNDATION)

9' CEILINGS THROUGHOUT FIRST FLOOR
UNLESS OTHERWISE NOTED

TO ORDER THIS BLUEPRINT,
CALL TOLL-FREE 1-800-547-5570
156 (Prices and details on pp. 12-15.)

Blueprint Price Code E
Plan L-182-FCC

Two Stories High in Back

This magnificent home has the look of one story but the convenience and space of two, and is ideal for entertaining, both formally and informally, with its two living and dining areas.

The unique kitchen features a circular sink-bar. A den/workroom is located off the family room with French doors providing privacy. The walk-through utility is a pleasant work area with plentiful counter space, fold-down ironing board, and additional storage.

Vaulted ceilings and abundant windows lend a feeling of spaciousness to the living room. A generous master suite features a large walk-in closet and custom master bath.

For the health-conscious person, an exercise room is located on the upper level.

Square footage on this residence is 3,415. Dimensions are 79' wide and 73' deep.

First floor:	2,595 sq. ft.
Second floor:	820 sq. ft.
Total living area:	**3,415 sq. ft.**
(Not counting garage)	

MAIN FLOOR

SECOND FLOOR

Exterior walls are 2x6 construction.

PLAN S-2187
WITHOUT BASEMENT
(CRAWLSPACE FOUNDATION)

Blueprint Price Code E
Plan S-2187

***TO ORDER THIS BLUEPRINT,
CALL TOLL-FREE 1-800-547-5570***
(Prices and details on pp. 12-15.)

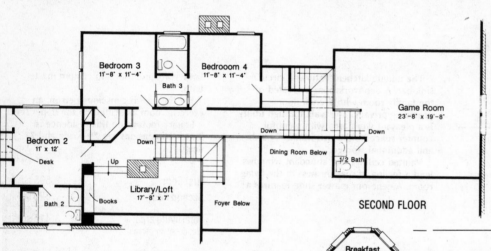

Exquisite Design For Active Famil Living

SECOND FLOOR

Bedroom 3
11'-8" x 11'-4"

Bath 3

Bedrooom 4
11'-8" x 11'-4"

Game Room
23'-8" x 19'-8"

Bedroom 2
11' x 12'
Desk

Down

Down

Dining Room Below

1/2 Bath

Up

Library/Loft
17'-8" x 7'

Foyer Below

Bath 2

Books

First floor:	2,272 sq. ft.
Second floor:	988 sq. ft.
Game Room:	465 sq. ft.
Total living area: (Not counting garage)	**3,725 sq. ft.**

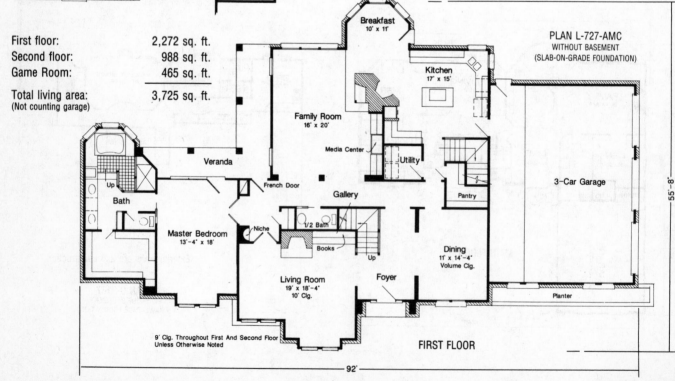

FIRST FLOOR

PLAN L-727-AMC
WITHOUT BASEMENT
(SLAB-ON-GRADE FOUNDATION)

Breakfast
10' x 11'

Kitchen
17' x 15'

Family Room
16' x 20'

Media Center

Utility

3-Car Garage

Pantry

Veranda

French Door

Gallery

Bath

Up

Master Bedroom
13'-4" x 18'

Niche

1/2 Bath

Books

Up

Dining
11' x 14'-4"
Volume Clg.

Living Room
19' x 18'-4"
10' Clg.

Foyer

Planter

9' Clg. Throughout First And Second Floor
Unless Otherwise Noted

92'

55'-8"

Blueprint Price Code F
Plan L-727-AMC

Separate Guest Quarters

PLAN L-191-PBD
WITHOUT BASEMENT
(SLAB-ON-GRADE FOUNDATION)

First floor: 2,381 sq. ft.
Second floor: 1,202 sq. ft.
Guest quarters: 606 sq. ft.

Total living area: 4,189 sq. ft.
(Not counting garage)

Spacious, Splendid Design

Breathtaking is only one of many appropriate adjectives that can be applied to this splendid house. An intriguing floor plan delivers its owners every inch of excitement and convenience they could possibly imagine. The kitchen is open to a cozy keeping area and contains its own set of stairs to the second floor. The walk-in bar could double as a butler's pantry.

Above, the master suite deserves special attention. The sunny sitting area will provide a well-deserved parent retreat; and the completely separate "his and hers" baths are the answer to a petition we frequently receive.

BATH

BEDROOM
13-0 x 13-6

BEDROOM
13-6 x 15-0

BEDROOM
13-6 x 15-0

BEDROOM
13-6 x 15-0

BATH

MASTER BEDROOM
15-0 x 17-6

SITTING ROOM
11-6 x 12-0

BATH

PLAN V-4302-C
WITHOUT BASEMENT
(CRAWLSPACE FOUNDATION)

First floor: 2,212 sq. ft.
Second floor: 2,090 sq. ft.
Total living area: 4,302 sq. ft.

Ceiling height first floor 10'

Ceiling height second floor 9'

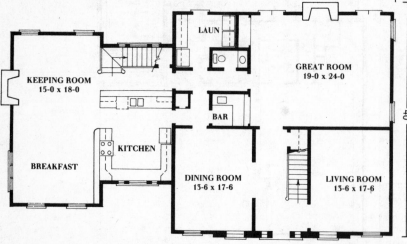

68'

40'

LAUN

GREAT ROOM
19-0 x 24-0

KEEPING ROOM
15-0 x 18-0

BAR

KITCHEN

BREAKFAST

DINING ROOM
13-6 x 17-6

LIVING ROOM
13-6 x 17-6

TO ORDER THIS BLUEPRINT,
CALL TOLL-FREE 1-800-547-5570
160 (Prices and details on pp. 12-15.)

Blueprint Price Code G
Plan V-4302-C

Ever-Popular Early American Style

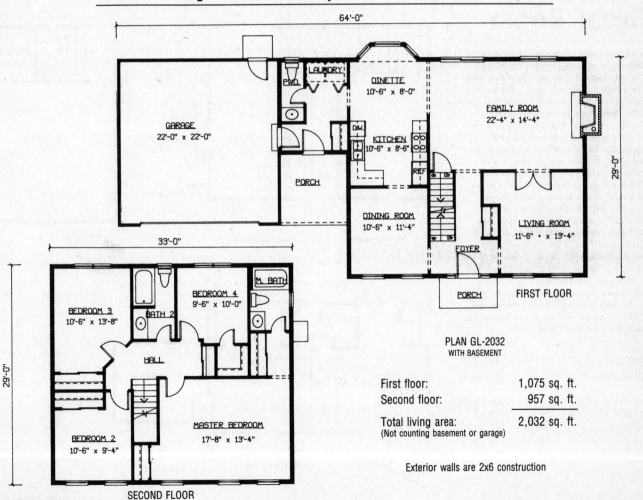

64'-0"

GARAGE
22'-0" x 22'-0"

PWD.

LAUNDRY

DINETTE
10'-6" x 8'-0"

FAMILY ROOM
22'-4" x 14'-4"

KITCHEN
10'-6" x 8'-6"

D.W.

REF.

PORCH

29'-0"

DINING ROOM
10'-6" x 11'-4"

LIVING ROOM
11'-6" + x 13'-4"

FOYER

PORCH

FIRST FLOOR

33'-0"

BEDROOM 3
10'-6" x 13'-8"

BATH 2

BEDROOM 4
9'-6" x 10'-0"

M. BATH

HALL

29'-0"

BEDROOM 2
10'-6" x 9'-4"

MASTER BEDROOM
17'-8" x 13'-4"

SECOND FLOOR

PLAN GL-2032
WITH BASEMENT

First floor:	1,075 sq. ft.
Second floor:	957 sq. ft.
Total living area:	2,032 sq. ft.

(Not counting basement or garage)

Exterior walls are 2x6 construction

HomeStyles
SOURCE 1
DESIGNERS' NETWORK

Blueprint Price Code C
Plan GL-2032

TO ORDER THIS BLUEPRINT,
CALL TOLL-FREE 1-800-547-5570
(Prices and details on pp. 12-15.)
161

Country Kitchen and Great Room

Cozy front porch, dormers, shutters and multi-paned windows on the exterior of this Cape Code design are complemented by an informal interior. The 1,318 sq. ft. of heated living area on the main floor is divided into three sections. In the first section is an eat-in country kitchen with island counter and bay window and a large utility room which can be entered from either the kitchen or garage. The second section is the Great Room with inside fireplace, an informal dining nook and double doors opening onto the rear deck. The third section consists of a master suite, which features a walk-in closet and compartmentalized bath with linen closet.

An additional 718 sq. ft. of heated living area on the upper floor includes a second full bath and two bedrooms with ample closet space and window seats. A large storage area is provided over the garage. All or part of the basement can be used to supplement the main living area.

First floor:	1,318 sq. ft.
Second floor:	718 sq. ft.
Total living area:	2,036 sq. ft.
(Not counting basement or garage)	
Basement:	1,221 sq. ft.
Garage:	436 sq. ft.

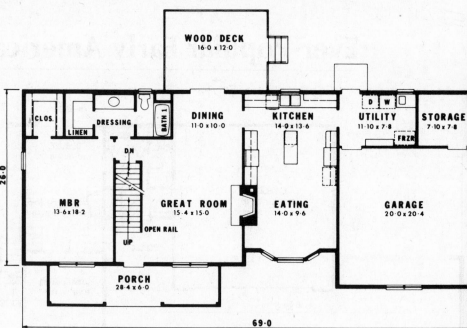

Specify basement, crawlspace or slab foundation when ordering.

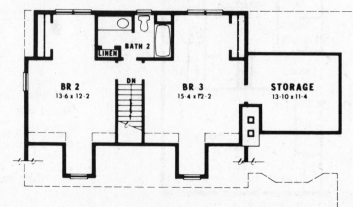

Blueprint Price Code C
Plan C-8040

Impressive Foyer, Deluxe Master Suite

- A dignified design and brick exterior lend an air of permanence and stability to this design.
- Inside, the impressive foyer leads to a sunken family room with fireplace on one side or a formal, sunken living room on the other.
- The formal dining room adjoins the living room to create a large space for entertaining.
- The kitchen and nook combine to make space for family living, and the utility area and half-bath are also conveniently located.
- A first-rate master suite upstairs includes a compartmentalized bath and large walk-in closet.
- Bedrooms 2 & 3 share a second full bath and each has a large closet.

UPPER FLOOR

U-87-205

Bedrooms: 3	Baths: 2½
Space:	
Upper floor:	966 sq. ft.
Main floor:	1,086 sq. ft.
Total living area:	**2,052 sq. ft.**
Basement:	1,086 sq. ft.
Garage:	552 sq. ft.
Exterior Wall Framing:	2x4 & 2x6

Foundation options:
Standard basement.
Crawlspace.
Slab.
(Foundation & framing conversion diagram available — see order form.)

Blueprint Price Code:	C

MAIN FLOOR

Plan U-87-205

TO ORDER THIS BLUEPRINT, CALL TOLL-FREE 1-800-547-5570
(Prices and details on pp. 12-15.) **163**

Sunken Great Room Opens to Inviting Veranda

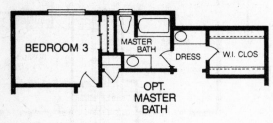

BEDROOM 3

MASTER BATH

DRESS

W.I. CLOS

OPT. MASTER BATH

PLAN GL-4161
WITH BASEMENT

First floor:	1,074 sq. ft.
Second floor:	978 sq. ft.
Total living area:	2,052 sq. ft.

(Not counting basement or garage)

Second Floor

38'-0"

28'-0"

BEDROOM 3
11'-2" x 10'-4"

BATH 1

DRESSING   W.I. CLOS.

HALL

BATH 2

MASTER BEDROOM
14'-4" x 17'-0"

BEDROOM 2
13'-10" x 10'-4"

LOFT/LIBRARY

SECOND FLOOR

First Floor

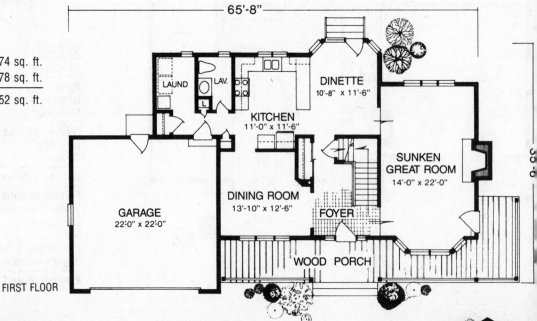

65'-8"

35'-6"

LAUND   LAV.

DINETTE
10'-8" x 11'-6"

KITCHEN
11'-0" x 11'-6"

GARAGE
22'-0" x 22'-0"

DINING ROOM
13'-10" x 12'-6"

SUNKEN GREAT ROOM
14'-0" x 22'-0"

FOYER

WOOD PORCH

FIRST FLOOR

TO ORDER THIS BLUEPRINT, CALL TOLL-FREE 1-800-547-5570
164 (Prices and details on pp. 12-15.)

Blueprint Price Code C
Plan GL-4161

HomeStyles **SOURCE 1** DESIGNERS NETWORK

Quality Four-Bedroom Design

- Here's another fine example of a traditional plan that has faithfully stood the test of time.
- While not huge, the interior provides plenty of space for a busy family.
- The large family room includes a fireplace and adjoins the casual dinette area.
- A big kitchen includes a handy work island and is open to the dinette area.
- The living and dining rooms flow together when big space is needed for formal entertaining or large family gatherings.
- Upstairs, you'll find four roomy bedrooms and two full baths, one of which is private to the master bedroom.
- Also note the balcony overlooking the foyer below.

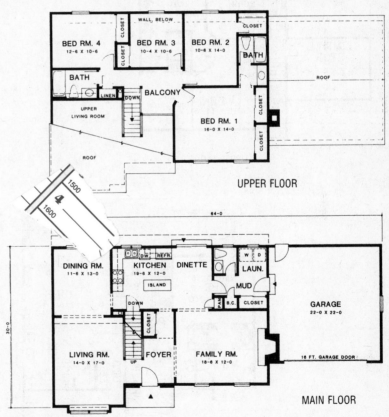

UPPER FLOOR

BED RM. 4
12-6 X 10-6

BED RM. 3
10-4 X 10-6

BED RM. 2
10-6 X 14-0

BATH

CLOSET

WALL BELOW

BATH

LINEN

DOWN

BALCONY

UPPER LIVING ROOM

BED RM. 1
16-0 X 14-0

ROOF

ROOF

CLOSET

1500

1600

MAIN FLOOR

DINING RM.
11-6 X 13-0

KITCHEN
19-6 X 12-0

DINETTE

LAUN.

ISLAND

MUD

W D

DOWN

PAN.

B.C.

CLOSET

GARAGE
22-0 X 22-0

LIVING RM.
14-0 X 17-0

FOYER

UP

FAMILY RM.
18-6 X 12-0

16 FT. GARAGE DOOR

64-0

30-0

Plan A-2109-DS

Bedrooms: 4		**Baths:** 2½	

Space:

Upper floor: 942 sq. ft.
Main floor: 1,148 sq. ft.

Total living area: 2,090 sq. ft.
Basement: 1,148 sq. ft.
Garage: 484 sq. ft.

Exterior Wall Framing: 2x4

Foundation options:
Standard basement only.
(Foundation & framing conversion diagram available — see order form.)

Blueprint Price Code: C

Plan A-2109-DS

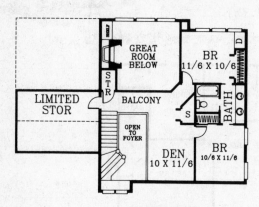

UPPER FLOOR

GREAT ROOM BELOW

BR 11/6 X 10/6

D

STR

LIMITED STOR

BALCONY

BATH

S

OPEN TO FOYER

DEN 10 X 11/6

BR 10/6 X 11/6

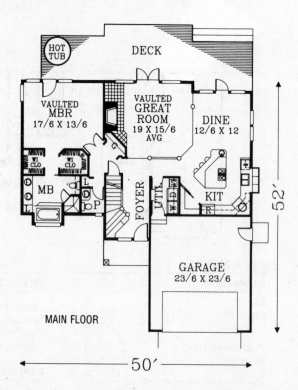

HOT TUB

DECK

VAULTED MBR 17/6 X 13/6

VAULTED GREAT ROOM 19 X 15/6 AVG

DINE 12/6 X 12

WI CLO

WI CLO

MB

L

FOYER

UTIL

W D

KIT

R

52'

GARAGE 23/6 X 23/6

MAIN FLOOR

50'

Traditional Overtones in Modern Design

- An exciting contemporary home with traditional overtones.
- The vaulted Great Room with adjacent kitchen and dining room give the home an open and spacious feeling.
- The master suite is located on the first floor away from the other bedrooms and features his and her walk-in closets.
- The custom master bath has a jacuzzi tub and double vanities plus an additional linen closet.
- A hot tub is located on the patio and can be reached from the Great Room or directly from the master bedroom.
- Upstairs are the two bedrooms with a continental bath between them.
- The den views down into the vaulted foyer.

Plan S-81189

Bedrooms: 3	Baths: 2½
Finished space:	
Upper floor:	660 sq. ft.
Main floor:	1,440 sq. ft.
Total living area:	2,100 sq. ft.
Bonus area:	220 sq. ft.
Garage:	552 sq. ft.
Exterior Wall Framing:	2x6

Foundation options:
Basement.
Crawlspace.
(Foundation & framing conversion diagram available — see order form.)

Blueprint Price Code: C

TO ORDER THIS BLUEPRINT,
CALL TOLL-FREE 1-800-547-5570
166 (Prices and details on pp. 12-15.)

Plan S-81189

Dramatic Interior Angles

- Beautifully Spanish on the outside, this home is thoroughly modern American on the inside.
- An angled stairway, corner fireplace, bay windows and five-sided rooms make this an exciting home to visit as well as to occupy year-round.
- The expansive living room features a vaulted ceiling and flows into the bay-windowed dining room.

- If not needed for a fourth bedroom, the bay-windowed study would make a spectacular home office.
- The master suite on the main floor is highlighted by a stunning five-sided bath with spa tub and shower, and a huge walk-in closet.
- A second main floor bath includes a shower and is handily off the foyer for the convenience of party guests.

- Two large upstairs bedrooms each have large closets and share a full bath.
- Note the balcony "bridge" upstairs.

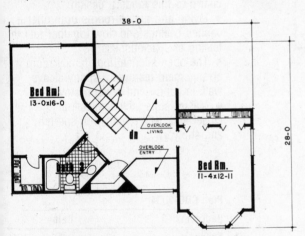

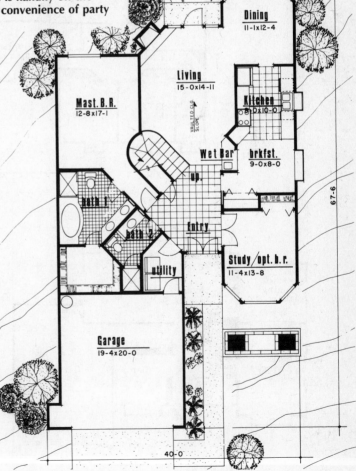

Plan Q-2107-1A

Bedrooms: 3-4	Baths: 3

Space:

Upper floor:	600 sq. ft.
Main floor:	1,507 sq. ft.
Total living area:	**2,107 sq. ft.**
Garage:	387 sq. ft.

Exterior Wall Framing:	2x4

Foundation options:
Slab only.
(Foundation & framing conversion diagram available — see order form.)

Blueprint Price Code:	C

Old-Fashioned Charm

- A trio of dormers add old-fashioned charm to this modern design.
- Living and dining rooms both offer vaulted ceilings and flow together for feeling of spaciousness.
- The open kitchen/nook/family room arrangement features a sunny alcove, walk-in pantry and a wood stove.
- Master suite includes walk-in closet and deluxe bath with spa tub and shower.

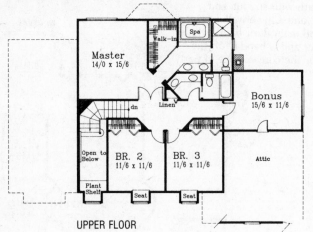

UPPER FLOOR

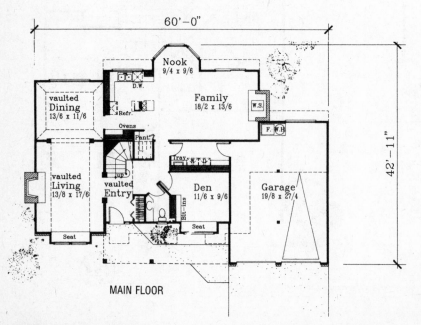

MAIN FLOOR

Plan CDG-2004	
Bedrooms: 3	**Baths:** 2½

Space:

Upper floor:	928 sq. ft.
Main floor:	1,317 sq. ft.

Total living area:	**2,245 sq. ft.**
Bonus area:	192 sq. ft.
Basement:	882 sq. ft.
Garage:	537 sq. ft.

Exterior Wall Framing:	2x4

Foundation options:
Daylight basement.
Crawlspace.
(Foundation & framing conversion diagram available — see order form.)

Blueprint Price Code:	C

Plan CDG-2004

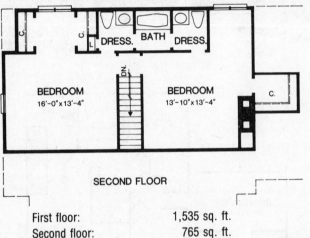

SECOND FLOOR

BEDROOM
16'-0"x13'-4"

BEDROOM
13'-10"x13'-4"

DRESS. BATH DRESS.

First floor: 1,535 sq. ft.
Second floor: 765 sq. ft.

Total living area: 2,300 sq. ft.
(Not counting basement or garage)

PLAN C-8535
WITH BASEMENT

Traditional Touches Dress Up a Country Cottage

Multipaned windows, shutters and a covered porch embellish the traditional exterior of this country cottage. The floor plan incorporates a central Great Room. A raised-hearth stone fireplace forms part of a wall separating the Great Room from the kitchen.

The large country kitchen features an island and abundant counter space. The breakfast room includes a bay window. A large dining room faces the front.

First-level master bedroom has its own super bath with separate shower, garden tub, twin vanities and walk in closets. Two large bedrooms, separate dressing areas and compartment tub occupy the second level.

MASTER BATH

LIN.

BATH

MASTER B. R.
16'-0"x17'-0"

GREAT ROOM
15'-10"x25'-4"

SCR. PORCH
15'-8"x12'-0"

KITCHEN
13'-8"x12'-2"

BREAKFAST
10'-6"x9'-4"

W. D.

STOR.

DINING ROOM
13'-8"x11'-2"

GARAGE
20'-6"x20'-8"

PORCH
30'-0"x6'-0"

39'-0"

71'-4"

FIRST FLOOR

Blueprint Price Code C

Plan C-8535

TO ORDER THIS BLUEPRINT, CALL TOLL-FREE 1-800-547-5570
(Prices and details on pp. 12-15.) **169**

Gracious, Timeless Styling

- This gracious home integrates timeless traditional styling with a functional, cost-effective plan.
- The dramatic foyer, with its angled stairway and double doors opening to the main floor den, sets the stage for the elegance through the rest of the home.
- A large family room includes a fireplace and flows into the striking two-story-high nook.
- The living and dining rooms merge together to provide a large space for entertaining groups of family or friends.
- Upstairs, the deluxe master suite includes an unusual bath arrangement, a large closet and a private "retreat."
- The large bonus area over the garage can be used for an exercise room, play room, office, sewing room or whatever else you prefer.

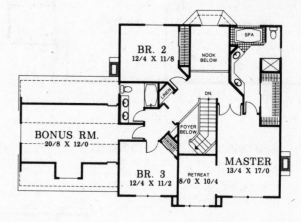

UPPER FLOOR

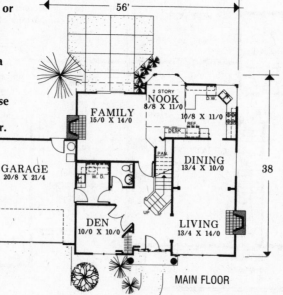

MAIN FLOOR

Plan AM-2228-A

Bedrooms: 3	Baths: 2½
Space:	
Upper floor:	1,120 sq. ft.
Main floor:	1,236 sq. ft.
Total living area:	2,356 sq. ft.
Bonus area:	270 sq. ft.
Garage:	440 sq. ft.
Exterior Wall Framing:	2x4

Foundation options:
Crawlspace only.
(Foundation & framing conversion diagram available — see order form.)

Blueprint Price Code:	C

Plan AM-2228-A

Main Floor Master Suite

- A traditional design with a contemporary interior, this home offers plenty of space and features for today's family.
- A large living room is brightened by a beautiful bay window.

- A spacious family room features an impressive fireplace.
- The kitchen/nook combination is roomy and efficient, with a pantry and adjoining laundry and half-bath.

- The downstairs master suite is luxurious, with a private, skylighted bath and large walk-in closet.
- Upstairs, three bedrooms share another full bath.

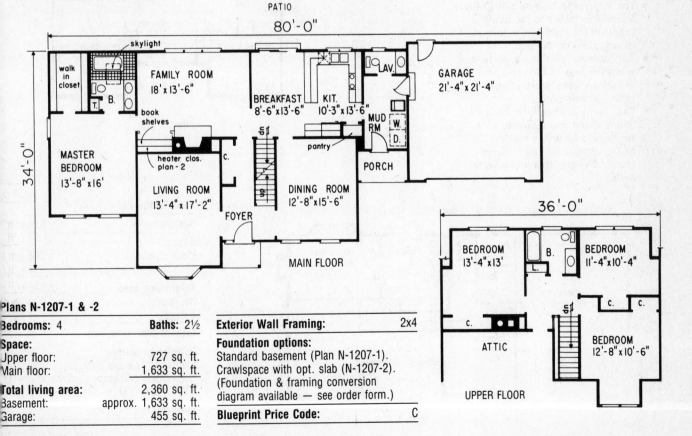

Plans N-1207-1 & -2

Bedrooms: 4	Baths: 2½

Space:

Upper floor:	727 sq. ft.
Main floor:	1,633 sq. ft.
Total living area:	**2,360 sq. ft.**
Basement:	approx. 1,633 sq. ft.
Garage:	455 sq. ft.

Exterior Wall Framing: 2x4

Foundation options:
Standard basement (Plan N-1207-1).
Crawlspace with opt. slab (N-1207-2).
(Foundation & framing conversion diagram available — see order form.)

Blueprint Price Code: C

Luxurious Master Bedroom Suite

- Stately, dignified symmetry, the solid look of brick and the French quoins on the corners identify this home as something extra special.
- The impressive two-story-high foyer introduces guests to the living room on the right or the formal dining room on the left.
- The informal portion of the home spans the rear of the plan, and includes a large sunken family room with fireplace.
- The roomy kitchen includes a handy island and a dinette area.
- Upstairs, a luxurious master bedroom suite includes a large closet, dressing area and private bath.

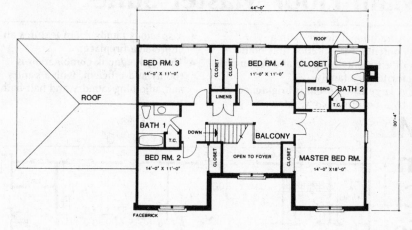

UPPER FLOOR

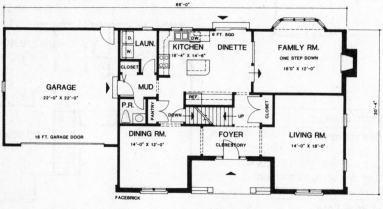

MAIN FLOOR

Plan A-2166-DS

Bedrooms: 4	Baths: 2

Space:

Upper floor:	1,156 sq. ft.
Main floor:	1,224 sq. ft.
Total living area:	2,380 sq. ft.
Basement:	1,224 sq. ft.
Garage:	484 sq. ft.

Exterior Wall Framing:	2x

Foundation options:
Standard basement only.
(Foundation & framing conversion diagram available — see order form.)

Blueprint Price Code:

Plan A-2166-DS

Modern Interior in Classic Federal Design

Two of the primary characteristics of the Federal (late Georgian) era are splayed keystone lintels and intricate fanlights. Our version carefully maintains the flavor of the original dwelling on the exterior, yet such a modern amenity as the spacious kitchen is a radical departure from the original floor plan!

A first-floor guest room can double as a study. Upstairs, a particularly spacious master suite offers separate walk-in closets. The laundry room is conveniently located near the bedrooms.

First floor: 1,224 sq. ft.

Second floor: 1,175 sq. ft.

Total living area: 2,399 sq. ft.

(Not counting garage)

9' CEILINGS THROUGHOUT BOTH FLOORS

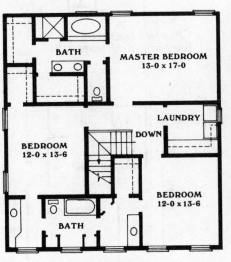

SECOND FLOOR

BATH

MASTER BEDROOM
13-0 x 17-0

LAUNDRY

DOWN

BEDROOM
12-0 x 13-6

BEDROOM
12-0 x 13-6

BATH

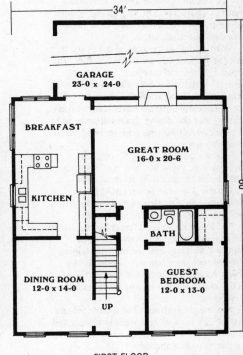

FIRST FLOOR

GARAGE
23-0 x 24-0

BREAKFAST

GREAT ROOM
16-0 x 20-6

KITCHEN

BATH

DINING ROOM
12-0 x 14-0

GUEST BEDROOM
12-0 x 13-0

UP

PLAN V-2399-C
WITHOUT BASEMENT
(CRAWLSPACE FOUNDATION)

Blueprint Price Code C

Plan V-2399-C

TO ORDER THIS BLUEPRINT,
CALL TOLL-FREE 1-800-547-5570
(Prices and details on pp. 12-15.) **173**

Country Home with Wrap-Around Porch

This country-style home is popular for its stylish yet casual look. The dormer windows and wrap-around porch give the exterior its country charm. The bay window in the morning room and the clean, simple roofline further define the house's character. The overall dimensions of 60 ft. x 45 ft. are tailored to fit the average suburban lot.

With a total living area of 2,449 sq. ft., it's the perfect size for today's family. The open kitchen and morning room have plenty of space for everyday meals, leaving the formal dining room for special occasions. The kitchen has a pantry/broom closet near the dining room entrance and a snack bar or serving counter near the morning room.

To cut down on traffic through the living room, there are two rear entrances. One leads to the utility room and the half-bath. The rear porch could be converted to a mudroom to keep dirt from being tracked into the utility room.

The living room, or "Great Room," with its vaulted ceiling is suitable for both family gatherings and formal entertaining. The second-story balcony overlooks the living room. A door at the base of the stairs closes off the second level from the first level.

The master bedroom has a large private bath, with his and hers walk-in closets and a double vanity. The linen closet could be replaced with a shower.

The upstairs game room can be made into a fourth bedroom by adding a wall to create a hallway in the balcony area. The dormer windows in the bedrooms can be finished with either a built-in desk or a window seat.

First floor: 1,669 sq. ft.
Second floor: 780 sq. ft.
Total living area: 2,449 sq. ft.

PLAN L-2449
WITHOUT BASEMENT
(SLAB FOUNDATION)

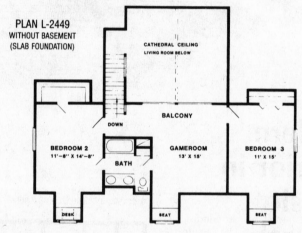

(Plans for a detached two-car garage included with blueprints.)

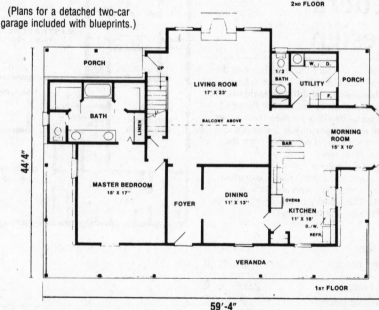

Blueprint Price Code C
Plan L-2449

Elegant Post-Modern Design

- Here's a design that is highly fashionable today and that will undoubtedly stay in style for decades.
- A wagon roof porch with paired columns lends sophistication to an elegant design.
- Half-round transom windows and gable vents unify the facade.
- Inside, a diagonal stairway forms the keystone of an exciting, angular design.
- The foyer leads visitors past the den into the sunken living room with vaulted ceiling and fireplace.
- Square columned arcades separate the living room from the dining room.
- A sunny bay window defines the breakfast area, which includes a sliding glass door to the deck.
- The thoroughly modern kitchen includes an islet cooktop and pantry.
- The generously sized family room also sports a vaulted ceiling and offers easy access to the outdoor deck.
- Upstairs, a stylish master suite features a private bath and large closet.

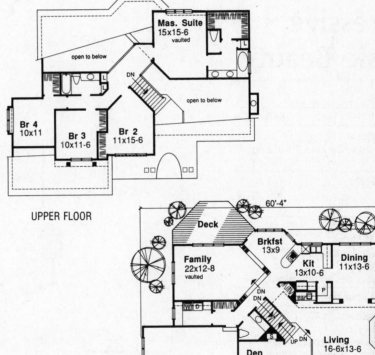

UPPER FLOOR

MAIN FLOOR

Plan B-89005

Bedrooms: 4	Baths: 2½
Space:	
Upper floor:	1,083 sq. ft.
Main floor:	1,380 sq. ft.
Total living area:	2,463 sq. ft.
Basement:	1,380 sq. ft.
Garage:	483 sq. ft.

Exterior Wall Framing: 2x4

Foundation options:
Standard basement only.
(Foundation & framing conversion diagram available — see order form.)

Blueprint Price Code: C

Plan B-89005

Impressive Classic Beauty

Plan AM-2257

Bedrooms: 4	Baths: 2½

Finished space:
| Upper floor: | 1,013 sq. ft. |
| Main floor: | 1,462 sq. ft. |

Total living area:	2,475 sq. ft.
Bonus area:	180 sq. ft.
Garage:	469 sq. ft.

Features:
Luxurious master suite.
Guest bedroom downstairs could
  be home office.
Quality executive design throughout.

| **Exterior Wall Framing:** | 2x4 |

Foundation options:
Crawlspace only.
(Foundation & framing conversion
diagram available — see order form.)

| **Blueprint Price Code:** | C |

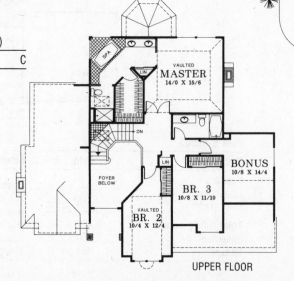

MAIN FLOOR

UPPER FLOOR

Plan AM-2257

Glorious Blend of New and Old

A three-bedroom, two and one-half-bath home is a glorious blend of contemporary and traditional lines. Inside, its 2,035 sq. ft. are wisely distributed among amply proportioned, practically appointed rooms. A vaulted entry gives way to a second reception area bordering on a broad, vaulted living room nearly 20' long. With its walls of windows overlooking the back yard, this grand room's centerpiece is a massive woodstove, whose central location contributes extra energy efficiency to the home — upstairs as well as down. The dining room offers quiet separation from the living room, while still enjoying the warmth from its woodstove. A sliding door accesses a large wraparound covered patio to create a cool, shady refuge.

For sun-seeking, another wraparound patio at the front is fenced but uncovered, and elegantly accessed by double doors from a well-lighted, vaulted nook.

Placed conveniently between the two living areas is a kitchen with all the trimmings: pantry, large sink window, and expansive breakfast bar.

A stylish upstairs landing overlooks the living room on one side and the entry on the other, and leads to a master suite that ables over fully half of the second floor.

Adjacent to the huge bedroom area is a spacious dressing area bordered by an abundance of closet space and a double-sink bath area. Unusual extras include walk-in wardrobe in the third bedroom and the long double-sink counter in the second upstairs bath.

Note also the exceptional abundance of closet space on both floors, and the separate utility room that also serves as a clean-up room connecting with the garage.

Main floor:	950 sq. ft.
Upper floor:	1,085 sq. ft.
Total living area: (Not counting basement or garage)	2,035 sq. ft.

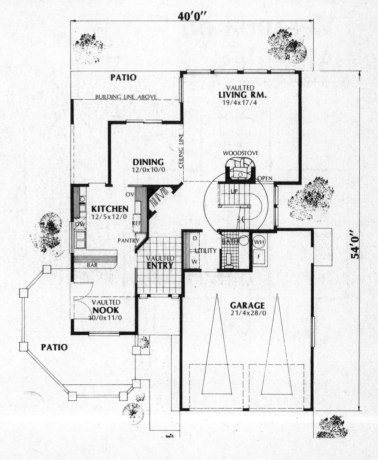

UPPER FLOOR

MASTER SUITE 17/8x15/8

OPEN TO LIVING BELOW

RAILING

DRESSING

SHWR

BATH

RAILING

OPEN TO ENTRY BELOW

DN

LIN

BATH

TUB

LIN

LIN

BEDRM. 3 10/6x12/8

BEDRM. 2 10/6x13/2

LIVING RM.

DN UP

PLAN P-6597-2A
WITHOUT BASEMENT
(CRAWLSPACE FOUNDATION)

PLAN P-6597-2D
(WITH DAYLIGHT BASEMENT)

40'0"

PATIO

BUILDING LINE ABOVE

VAULTED LIVING RM. 19/4x17/4

CEILING LINE

DINING 12/0x10/0

WOODSTOVE

OPEN

UP

KITCHEN 12/5x12/0

OV

DW

REF

PANTRY

BAR

VAULTED ENTRY

D W

UTILITY

BATH

WH

F

VAULTED NOOK 10/0x11/0

PATIO

GARAGE 21/4x28/0

54'0"

Blueprint Price Code C

Plans P-6597-2A & P-6597-2D

TO ORDER THIS BLUEPRINT, CALL TOLL-FREE 1-800-547-5570
(Prices and details on pp. 12-15.) **177**

Shady Veranda on All Sides

SITTING AREA
10' x 11'-8"

DOWN

BEDROOM 2
11'-4" x 15'-8"

BATH 2

BEDROOM 3
11'-8" x 14'-4"

SLOPE

SLOPE

SECOND FLOOR

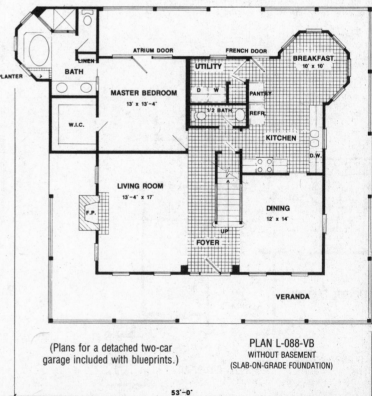

PLANTER

LINEN

BATH

ATRIUM DOOR

FRENCH DOOR

UTILITY

D   W

PANTRY

BREAKFAST
10' x 10'

MASTER BEDROOM
13' x 13'-4"

1/2 BATH

REFR.

KITCHEN

W.I.C.

D.W.

LIVING ROOM
13'-4" x 17'

DINING
12' x 14'

F.P.

UP

FOYER

VERANDA

(Plans for a detached two-car garage included with blueprints.)

PLAN L-088-VB
WITHOUT BASEMENT
(SLAB-ON-GRADE FOUNDATION)

53'-0"

First floor:	1,326 sq. ft.
Second floor:	760 sq. ft.
Total living area:	2,086 sq. ft.

**TO ORDER THIS BLUEPRINT,
CALL TOLL-FREE 1-800-547-5570**
178 (Prices and details on pp. 12-15.)

Blueprint Price Code C
Plan L-088-VB

Energy-Conscious Early American

Many energy-saving details have been incorporated into this traditional home. Window treatment, horizontal siding and a dignified entryway give an impressive Colonial look. A central gallery provides direct access to all areas of the house. The family room, complete with brick fireplace and sliding glass doors to the back terrace and side porch, is designed for times of privacy, or to join with dinette-kitchen and/or living room by use of folding doors.

Upstairs are four bedrooms with a master suite featuring a private bath, dressing area, and optional wood-burning fireplace. First floor is 998 sq. ft.; second floor is 1,108 sq. ft., for a total of 2,106. Optional basement is 998; garage, etc., is 568.

First floor:	998 sq. ft.
Second floor:	1,108 sq. ft.
Total living area:	2,106 sq. ft.
Garage, etc.:	568 sq. ft.
Basement (opt.):	998 sq. ft.

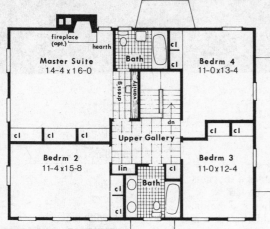

SECOND FLOOR

Master Suite 14-4 x 16-0
Bath
Bedrm 4 11-0 x 13-4
fireplace (opt.)
hearth
dress'g
vanity
Upper Gallery
dn
cl
lin
Bath
Bedrm 2 11-4 x 15-8
Bedrm 3 11-0 x 12-4

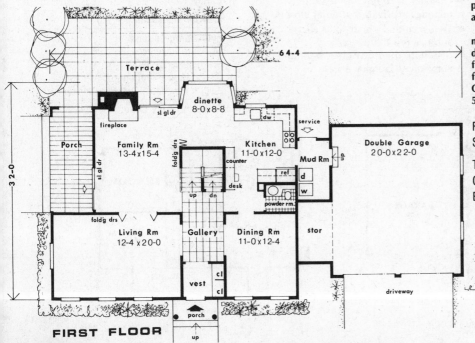

FIRST FLOOR

Terrace
64-4
32-0
dinette 8-0 x 8-8
sl gl dr
service
fireplace
Porch
Family Rm 13-4 x 15-4
foldg drs
Kitchen 11-0 x 12-0
Mud Rm
Double Garage 20-0 x 22-0
sl gl dr
counter
desk
ref
d
w
powder rm.
foldg drs
Living Rm 12-4 x 20-0
Gallery
Dining Rm 11-0 x 12-4
stor
vest
cl
cl
driveway
porch
up
up

Blueprint Price Code C

Plan K-168-S

TO ORDER THIS BLUEPRINT, CALL TOLL-FREE 1-800-547-5570
(Prices and details on pp. 12-15.) **179**

Early American
Includes Solar Elements

- Classic Colonial styling creates a warm, inviting home with plenty of space for a busy family.
- The construction, however, is anything but Colonial, with energy-efficient features throughout.
- This plan also includes optional solar heating features, with provisions for solar heat collectors on a rear shed roof to supplement a conventional heating system.

- The main floor includes a spacious dining/living area, large family room, efficient kitchen and optional bedroom which could also serve as an office, den or study room.
- Upstairs, a roomy master suite includes a private bath and closets.
- Two secondary bedrooms share another full bath.
- Also note the downstairs bath and convenient laundry area.

Plans H-3704-1 & -1A

Bedrooms: 3-4	Baths: 3

Space:

Upper floor:	943 sq. ft.
Main floor:	1,200 sq. ft.

Total living area:	2,143 sq. ft.
Basement:	1,200 sq. ft.
Garage:	461 sq. ft.

Exterior Wall Framing:	2x6

Foundation options:
Standard basement (H-3704-1).
Crawlspace (H-3704-1A).
(Foundation & framing conversion diagram available — see order form.)

Blueprint Price Code:	C

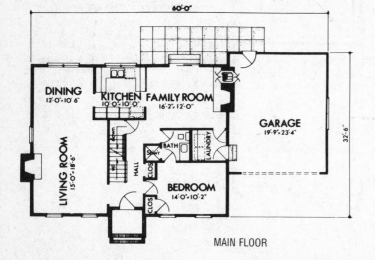

MAIN FLOOR

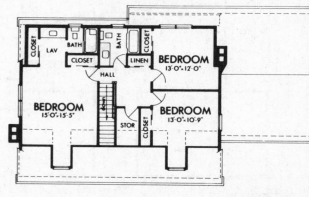

UPPER FLOOR

Plans H-3704-1 & -1A

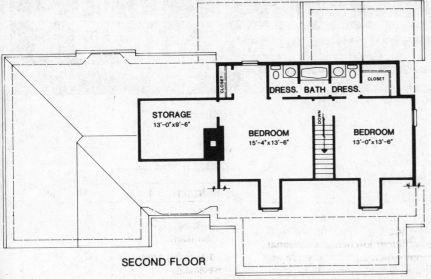

SECOND FLOOR

STORAGE
13'-0"x9'-6"

DRESS. BATH DRESS.
CLOSET   CLOSET

BEDROOM
15'-4"x13'-6"

DOWN

BEDROOM
13'-0"x13'-6"

Country Kitchen and Deluxe Master Bath

Front porch, dormers and shutters on the exterior of this country design are complemented by an informal modern interior. The 1,477 sq. ft. of heated living area on the main floor is divided into three sections. In the first section is a country kitchen with connecting breakfast area and utility space. The second section is a Great Room, half-bath, fireplace and double doors opening onto the rear deck.

The master suite section features a deluxe compartmentalized bath with garden tub, double vanities, shower and two walk-in closets.

An additional 704 sq. ft. of heated living area on the upper floor consists of a second full bath and two bedrooms with ample closets. A large storage area is provided over the kitchen. Specify basement, crawlspace or slab foundation when ordering.

First floor:	1,477 sq. ft.
Second floor:	704 sq. ft.
Total living area:	2,181 sq. ft.
(Not counting basement or garage)	

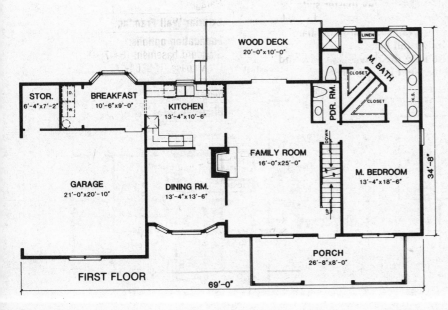

WOOD DECK
20'-0"x10'-0"

LINEN

M. BATH

STOR.
6'-4"x7'-2"

BREAKFAST
10'-6"x9'-0"

KITCHEN
13'-4"x10'-6"

CLOSET

PDR. RM.

CLOSET

W.K.S.

FAMILY ROOM
16'-0"x25'-0"

DOWN

GARAGE
21'-0"x20'-10"

DINING RM.
13'-4"x13'-6"

M. BEDROOM
13'-4"x18'-6"

34'-8"

FIRST FLOOR

69'-0"

PORCH
26'-8"x8'-0"

HomeStyles
SOURCE
DESIGNERS' NETWORK

Blueprint Price Code C
Plan C-8645

*TO ORDER THIS BLUEPRINT,
CALL TOLL-FREE 1-800-547-5570*
(Prices and details on pp. 12-15.) **181**

Open Interior in Victorian Home

- Victorian exterior with fish-scale shingles on gable.
- Wide wrap-around veranda with optional piazza at the left side.
- Open foyer with staircase.
- Dining room features 13' ceiling.
- Master bedroom includes luxurious bath and French doors opening to porch.
- Second floor includes three large bedrooms.

First floor: 1,351 sq. ft.
Second floor: 862 sq. ft.

Total living area: 2,213 sq. ft.
(Not counting garage)

PLAN L-215-VSB
WITHOUT BASEMENT
(SLAB-ON-GRADE FOUNDATION)

9' CEILINGS THROUGHOUT FIRST AND SECOND FLOORS UNLESS OTHERWISE NOTED

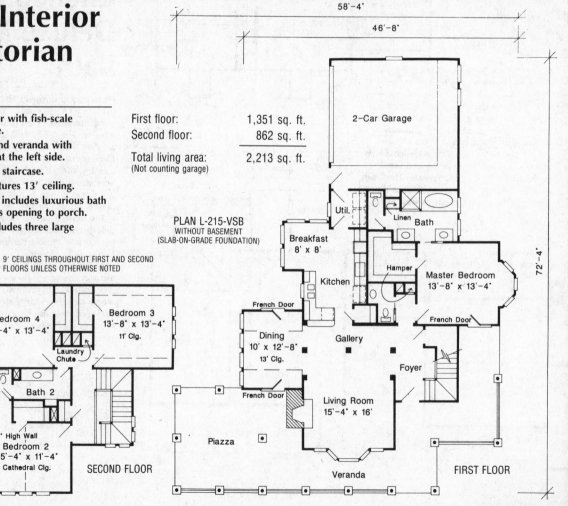

SECOND FLOOR

Bedroom 4
12'-4" x 13'-4"

Bedroom 3
13'-8" x 13'-4"
11' Clg.

Laundry Chute

Bath 2

42" High Wall

Bedroom 2
15'-4" x 11'-4"
Cathedral Clg.

FIRST FLOOR

58'-4"

46'-8"

72'-4"

2-Car Garage

Util.

Linen Bath

Breakfast
8' x 8'

Hamper

Kitchen

Master Bedroom
13'-8" x 13'-4"

French Door

French Door

Dining
10' x 12'-8"
13' Clg.

Gallery

French Door

Foyer

Living Room
15'-4" x 16'

Piazza

Veranda

TO ORDER THIS BLUEPRINT, CALL TOLL-FREE 1-800-547-5570
182 (Prices and details on pp. 12-15.)

Blueprint Price Code C

Plan L-215-VSB

A Touch Of Elegance

The interplay between rooflines and horizontal siding give the exterior of this two-story design an aura of gracious repose. Open planning makes for an exciting spatial relationship served by an entrance gallery. The living and family rooms can be joined for greater flexibility in entertaining. A spacious kitchen-dinette opens to the dining room as well as the

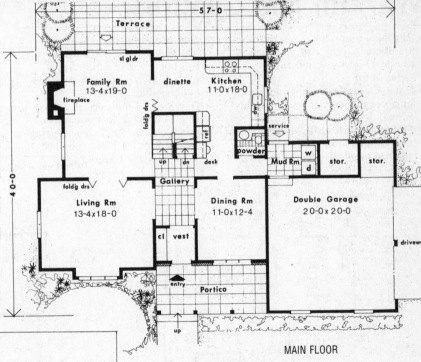

MAIN FLOOR

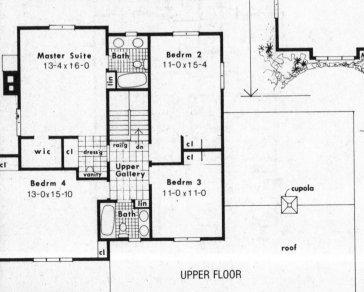

UPPER FLOOR

informal family room. Four bedrooms and two baths are on the second level, vertically isolated from the active area. Energy-saving details are part of the blueprints. Living area is 1,092 sq. ft. on the first floor and 1,123 sq. ft. on the second, for a total of 2,215. Optional basement is 1,092 sq. ft.; garage, mud room, etc., 538 sq. ft.

Design Exudes Warmth and Comfort

- This plan represents a return to traditional styling with the open concept interior so much in demand today.
- Vaulted entry and living room with adjacent dining room make up the formal design of this plan.
- Spacious hall leads the large informal entertaining area composed of the kitchen, nook and family rooms.

- The second floor offers a large master suite and two additional bedrooms with a future bonus space that can be left unfinished until needed.
- Exterior roof lines are all gabled for ease of construction and lower framing costs. Brick veneer garage face echoes the brick columns supporting the covered entry.

Plan S-8389	
Bedrooms: 3-4	Baths: 2½

Space:

Upper floor:	932 sq. ft.
Main floor:	1,290 sq. ft.

Total living area:	**2,222 sq. ft.**
Basement:	Approx. 1,290 sq. ft.
Bonus area:	228 sq. ft.
Garage:	429 sq. ft.

Exterior Wall Framing:	2x6

Foundation options:
Crawlspace.
Standard basement.
(Foundation & framing conversion diagram available — see order form.)

Blueprint Price Code: C

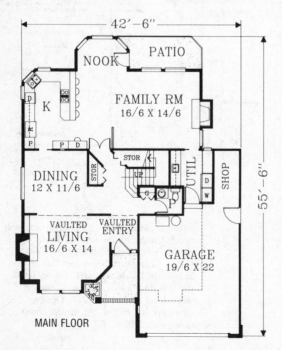

MAIN FLOOR

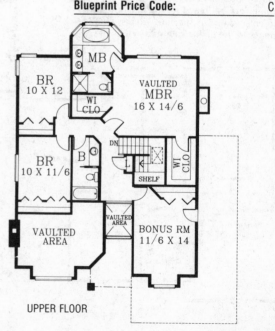

UPPER FLOOR

Plan S-8389

Space and Luxury

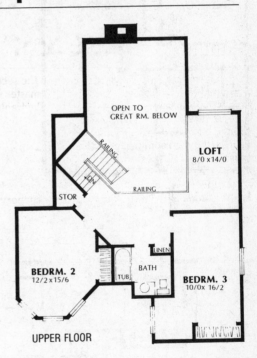

OPEN TO
GREAT RM. BELOW

RAILING

LOFT
8/0 x14/0

STOR

RAILING

DN

LINEN

BEDRM. 2
12/2 x15/6

TUB

BATH

BEDRM. 3
10/0x 16/2

UPPER FLOOR

PLAN P-6593-3D
WITH DAYLIGHT BASEMENT

Basement level: 1,427 sq. ft.

Main Floor plan labels:

DECK

40'0"

PATIO

SUNKEN
TUB

BATH

VAULTED
GREAT RM.
15/4 x21/0

PWR

RAILING

DINING
10/0x14/0

SKYLIGHTS

MASTER
12/0x16/0

ENTRY

BATH

KITCHEN
11/6 x11/0

DW

NOOK
13/0x 8/0

REF

PANTRY

72'0"

STORAGE

PATIO

COURTYARD

UTILITY

D   W

FENCE

F

WH

GARAGE
21/4 x20/6

MAIN FLOOR
PLAN P-6593-3A
WITHOUT BASEMENT
(CRAWLSPACE FOUNDATION)

Main floor: 1,427 sq. ft.

Upper floor: 707 sq. ft.

Total living area: 2,134 sq. ft.
(Not counting garage)

UPPER FLOOR

Modern Traditional-Style Home

- Covered porch and decorative double doors offer an invitation into this three or four bedroom home.
- Main floor bedroom may be used as a den, home office, or guest room, with convenient bath facilities.

- Adjoining dining room makes living room seem even more spacious; breakfast nook enlarges the look of the attached kitchen.
- Brick-size concrete block veneer and masonry tile roof give the exterior a look of durability.

PLAN H-1351-M1A
WITHOUT BASEMENT

MAIN FLOOR

DINING 10/0 x 11/6
KITCHEN 10/3 x 11/0
NOOK 10/0 x 8/9
FAMILY ROOM 17/6 x 13/6
STORAGE
LIVING ROOM 19/3 x 14/6
LAUNDRY
GARAGE 20/0 x 20/8
PATIO
ENTRY
STUDY/BEDROOM 13/6 x 11/8

Plans H-1351-M1 & -M1A	
Bedrooms: 3-4	**Baths: 3**
Space:	
Upper floor:	862 sq. ft.
Main floor:	1,383 sq. ft.
Total living area:	2,245 sq. ft.
Basement:	1,383 sq. ft.
Garage:	413 sq. ft.
Exterior Wall Framing:	2x6
Foundation options:	
Standard basement (Plan H-1351-M1). Crawlspace (Plan H-1351-M1A). (Foundation & framing conversion diagram available — see order form.)	
Blueprint Price Code:	C

Plans H-1351-M1 & -M1A

Deluxe Master Bedroom, Spacious Kitchen

Time-tested traditional design combines brick and wood for an attractive facade.

- A vast kitchen/breakfast area provides abundant space for a large, busy family.
- The generously sized living room includes a fireplace, vaulted ceiling and wet bar.
- A formal dining room is located right off the foyer.
- The magnificent master suite includes bay window at the front, a 10' ceiling, a large walk-in closet and a superb master bath with separate tub and shower plus twin vanities.
- Upstairs, the spaciousness continues, with two bedrooms sharing a connecting bath.
- Note the versatile loft area, available for many different purposes.
- Plans for a detached two-car garage are included with blueprints.

Plan L-2247-C

Bedrooms: 3	**Baths:** 2½

Space:
Upper floor:	735 sq. ft.
Main floor:	1,512 sq. ft.

Total living area: 2,247 sq. ft.
Garage: (Plans for a detached two-car, 505 sq. ft. garage are included with blueprints.)

Exterior Wall Framing: 2x4

Foundation options:
Slab only.
(Foundation & framing conversion diagram available — see order form.)

Blueprint Price Code: C

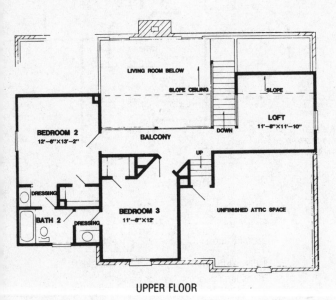

UPPER FLOOR

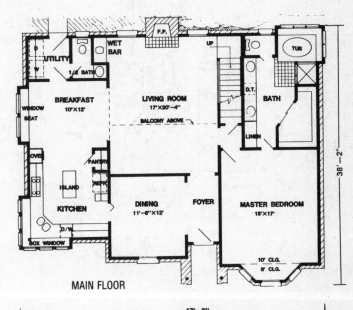

MAIN FLOOR

Plan L-2247-C

Tomorrow's Interior in Classic Exterior Design

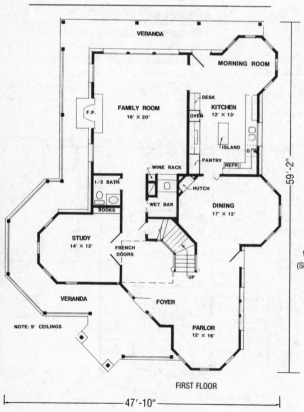

VERANDA

MORNING ROOM

FAMILY ROOM
16' × 20'

F.P.

DESK

OVEN

KITCHEN
12' × 13'

ISLAND

D/W

REFR

PANTRY

WINE RACK

1/2 BATH

BOOKS

WET BAR

HUTCH

DINING
17' × 12'

STUDY
14' × 12'

FRENCH DOORS

UP

VERANDA

FOYER

PARLOR
12' × 16'

NOTE: 9' CEILINGS

FIRST FLOOR

59'-2"

47'-10"

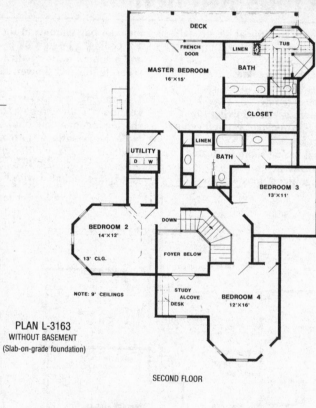

DECK

FRENCH DOOR

LINEN

TUB

MASTER BEDROOM
16' × 15'

BATH

CLOSET

LINEN

UTILITY
D   W

BATH

BEDROOM 3
13' × 11'

BEDROOM 2
14' × 12'

13' CLG.

DOWN

FOYER BELOW

NOTE: 9' CEILINGS

STUDY ALCOVE DESK

BEDROOM 4
12' × 16'

SECOND FLOOR

PLAN L-3163
WITHOUT BASEMENT
(Slab-on-grade foundation)

First floor:	1,565 sq. ft.
Second floor:	1,598 sq. ft.
Total living area:	3,163 sq. ft.

(Plans for a detached two-car garage
are included with blueprints)

Blueprint Price Code E
Plan L-3163

Gracious Traditional

- Traditional style ranch is perfect for a corner building lot. Long windows and dormers add distinctive elegance.
- Floor plan has popular "split-bedroom" design. Master bedroom is secluded away from other bedrooms.
- Large Great Room has vaulted ceiling and stairs leading up to a loft.

- Upstairs loft is perfect for recreation area, and also has a full bath.
- Master bedroom bath has large corner tub and his-n-her vanities. Large walk-in closet provides plenty of storage.
- Two other bedrooms have large walk-in closets, desks, and share a full bath.
- Kitchen and private breakfast nook are located conveniently near the utility/garage area.

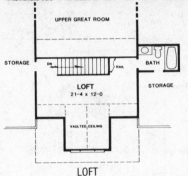

LOFT

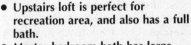

MAIN FLOOR

Plan C-8920

Bedrooms: 3	Baths: 3

Space:

Upper floor:	305 sq. ft.
Main floor:	1,996 sq. ft.

Total living area:	**2,301 sq. ft.**
Basement:	1,996 sq. ft.
Garage:	469 sq. ft.

Exterior Wall Framing:	2x4

Foundation options:
Daylight basement.
Standard basement.
Crawlspace.
(Foundation & framing conversion diagram available — see order form.)

Blueprint Price Code:	C

TO ORDER THIS BLUEPRINT, CALL TOLL-FREE 1-800-547-5570
(Prices and details on pp. 12-15.)

Classic Lines, Elegant Flair

- The rich brick arches and classic lines of this home lend an elegant air which will never be outdated.
- Inside, graceful archways lead from the vaulted entry to the living and dining rooms, which both feature heightened ceilings.
- The kitchen offers abundant counter space, an expansive window over the kitchen sink, large island, desk and pantry.
- The kitchen also is open to the nook and family room, which combine to make a great space for family living.
- The master suite is a pure delight, with a luxurious whirlpool tub and his-and-hers walk-in closets.
- The room marked for storage could also be an exercise or hobby room.

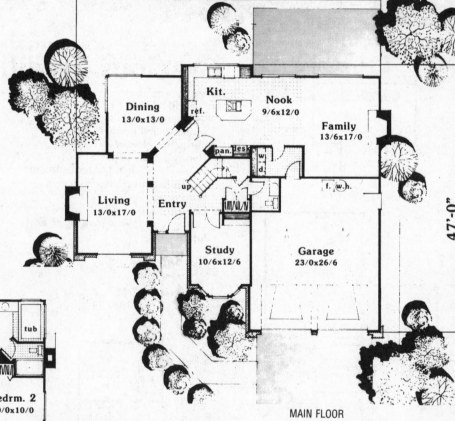

MAIN FLOOR

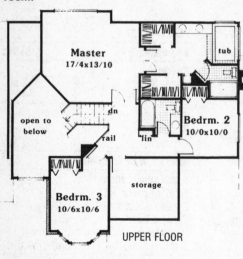

UPPER FLOOR

Plan R-2083

Bedrooms: 3	Baths: 2½

Space:		**Exterior Wall Framing:**	2x
Upper floor:	926 sq. ft.		
Main floor:	1,447 sq. ft.	**Foundation options:**	
Total living area:	2,373 sq. ft.	Crawlspace only.	
Garage:	609 sq. ft.	(Foundation & framing conversion diagram available — see order form.)	
Storage:	138 sq. ft.		
		Blueprint Price Code:	

TO ORDER THIS BLUEPRINT,
CALL TOLL-FREE 1-800-547-5570
190 (Prices and details on pp. 12-15.)

Plan R-2083

Simple, Economical, Comfortable Space

First floor:	1,740 sq. ft.
Second floor:	658 sq. ft.
Total living area:	2,398 sq. ft.
Carport:	440 sq. ft.
Porch:	324 sq. ft.

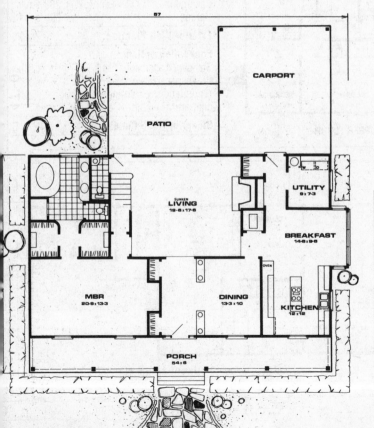

CARPORT

PATIO

UTILITY
9 x 7-3

SUNKEN
LIVING
19-6 x 17-6

BREAKFAST
14-8 x 9-8

MBR
20-9 x 13-3

DINING
13-3 x 10

KITCHEN
12 x 12

OVEN

PORCH
54 x 6

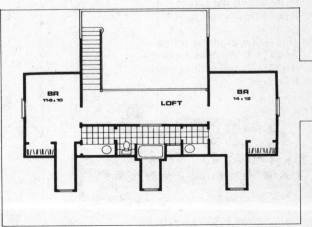

BR
11-6 x 10

LOFT

BR
14 x 12

Specify basement, crawlspace or slab foundation.

PLANS H-3711-1 & H-3711-1A
(WITH GARAGE)

All-American Country Home

- Romantic, old-fashioned and spacious living areas combine to create this modern home.
- Off the entryway is the generous living room with fireplace and French doors which open onto the traditional rear porch.
- Country kitchen features an island table for informal occasions, while the adjoining family room is ideal for family gatherings.
- Practically placed, a laundry/mud room lies off the garage for immediate disposal of soiled garments.
- This plan is available with garage (H-3711-1) or without garage (H-3711-2) and with or without basement.

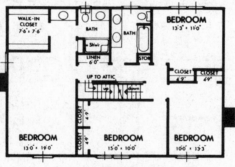

UPPER FLOOR

Plans H-3711-1/1A & -2/2A	
Bedrooms: 4	Baths: 2½
Space:	
Upper floor:	1,176 sq. ft.
Main floor:	1,288 sq. ft.
Total living area:	2,464 sq. ft.
Basement:	approx. 1,288 sq. ft.
Garage:	505 sq. ft.
Exterior Wall Framing:	2x6

Foundation options:
Standard basement (Plans H-3711-1 & -2).
Crawlspace (Plans H-3711-1A & -2A).
(Foundation & framing conversion diagram available — see order form.)

Blueprint Price Code: C

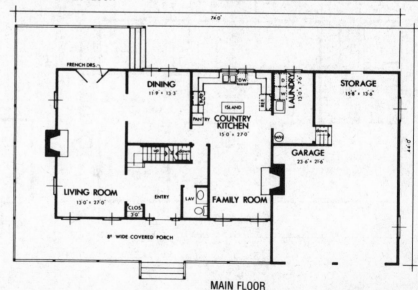

MAIN FLOOR

PLANS H-3711-2 & H-3711-2A
(WITHOUT GARAGE)

Plans H-3711-1/1A & -2/2A

Open, Fresh and Modern Interior

Stucco is used for the subtle finish of the porch walls and columns. Brick is used for the balance of the exterior.

- The interior is open, fresh and modern, featuring minimal division between the main living areas. The foyer contains an elegant circular stairwell.
- The master suite has an adjoining sitting area complete with TV space. The master bath is spacious.
- The country kitchen offers a large butler's pantry, adjoining eating area and utility room.

- Two upstairs bedrooms have a bath and a balcony which overlooks the lower level.
- This home is energy efficient.
- The living room and foyer have 17' ceilings. The sitting area and eating area feature sloped ceilings of varied heights. Typical ceiling heights are 8'.

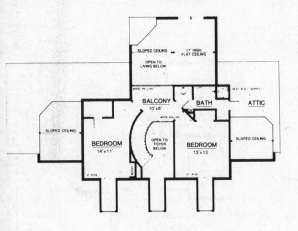

UPPER LEVEL

Exterior walls are 2x6 construction.
Specify basement, crawlspace or slab foundation.

LOWER LEVEL

Heated area:	2,330 sq. ft.
Unheated area:	1,035 sq. ft.
Total area:	3,365 sq. ft.
(Not counting basement)	

Blueprint Price Code C

Plan E-2305

For A Strong First Impression

This home is designed for those who like to make a strong first impression. The front entryway soars, with skylights providing the first glimpse of even more open, light-filled space to come.

This home has a convenient lower level master bedroom with its own private bath and large walk-in closet. A centrally located family room has a bar counter and fireplace. Also downstairs is a sizable kitchen and dining room with French doors and a double-bow window enhancing its charm. A spacious utility room connected to the garage is a necessary convenience.

A second floor with dramatic views of the downstairs on almost every step of the upstairs passage bridge will delight you. Also upstairs is something every modern family should have — its own computer room complete with built-in desk. One bedroom has a deck off the side and both have more than enough storage space.

This two-story contemporary has 2,508 sq. ft. of living area, and an optional side- or front-entry double-car garage. Exterior walls feature 2x6 construction for energy efficiency.

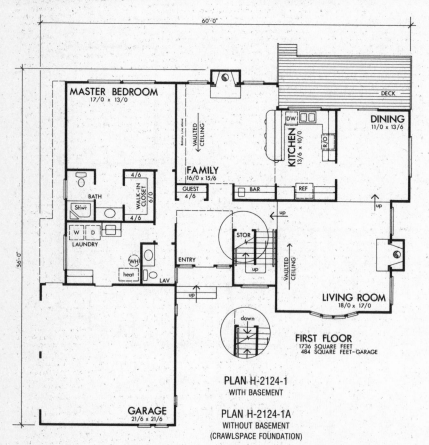

PLAN H-2124-1
WITH BASEMENT

PLAN H-2124-1A
WITHOUT BASEMENT
(CRAWLSPACE FOUNDATION)

FIRST FLOOR
1736 SQUARE FEET
484 SQUARE FEET-GARAGE

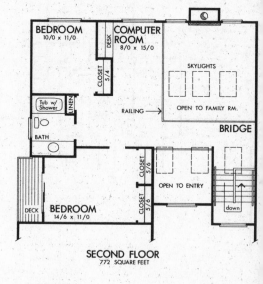

SECOND FLOOR
772 SQUARE FEET

First floor:	1,736 sq. ft.
Second floor:	772 sq. ft.
Total living area: (Not counting basement or garage)	2,508 sq. ft.

Blueprint Price Code D

Plans H-2124-1 & H-2124-1A

European Elegance

PLAN L-564-HB
WITHOUT BASEMENT
(SLAB-ON-GRADE FOUNDATION)

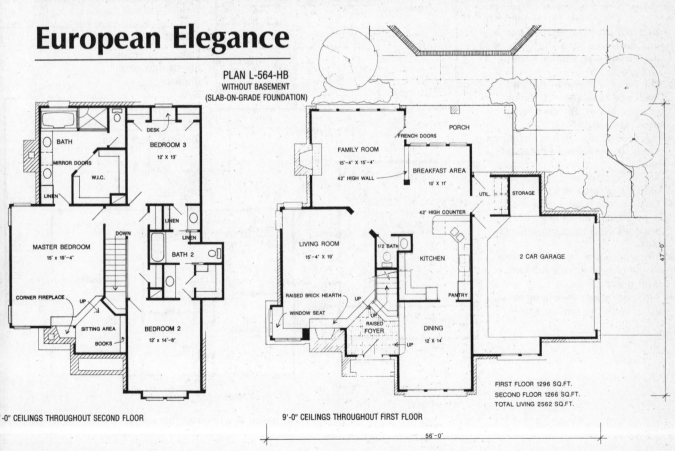

BATH

DESK

BEDROOM 3
12' X 13'

MIRROR DOORS

W.I.C.

LINEN

MASTER BEDROOM
15' X 19'-4"

DOWN

LINEN

LINEN

BATH 2

CORNER FIREPLACE

UP

SITTING AREA

BOOKS

UP

BEDROOM 2
12' X 14'-8"

-0" CEILINGS THROUGHOUT SECOND FLOOR

FAMILY ROOM
15'-4" X 15'-4"

FRENCH DOORS

PORCH

BREAKFAST AREA
10' X 11'

42' HIGH WALL

UTIL.

STORAGE

42' HIGH COUNTER

LIVING ROOM
15'-4" X 19'

1/2 BATH

KITCHEN

2 CAR GARAGE

RAISED BRICK HEARTH

UP

PANTRY

WINDOW SEAT

UP

RAISED FOYER

DINING
12' X 14'

UP

FIRST FLOOR 1296 SQ.FT.
SECOND FLOOR 1266 SQ.FT.
TOTAL LIVING 2562 SQ.FT.

9'-0" CEILINGS THROUGHOUT FIRST FLOOR

56'-0"

47'-0"

Blueprint Price Code D
Plan L-564-HB

TO ORDER THIS BLUEPRINT,
CALL TOLL-FREE 1-800-547-5570
(Prices and details on pp. 12-15.) **195**

Classic Country-Style Home

- Almost completely surrounded by an expansive wrap-around porch that measures almost 1,200 sq. ft., this classic plan exudes warmth and grace.
- The foyer is liberal in size and leads guests to a formal dining room at left or the large living room at right.
- A large country kitchen includes a sunny, bay-windowed breakfast nook.
- The main floor also includes a utility area and full bath.
- Upstairs, the master suite is impressive, with its large sleeping area, big closet and magnificent bath.
- Three secondary bedrooms with ample closets share a full bath with double sinks.
- Also note stairs leading up to an attic, useful for storage space.

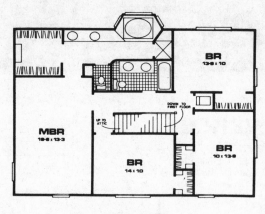

UPPER FLOOR

Plan J-86134

Bedrooms: 4	Baths: 3

Space:

Upper floor:	1,195 sq. ft.
Main floor:	1,370 sq. ft

Total living area: 2,565 sq. ft.

Basement:	1,370 sq. ft.
Garage:	576 sq. ft.
Storage:	144 sq. ft.
Porch:	1,181 sq. ft.

Exterior Wall Framing: 2x4

Foundation options:
Standard basement.
Crawlspace.
Slab.
(Foundation & framing conversion diagram available — see order form.)

Blueprint Price Code: D

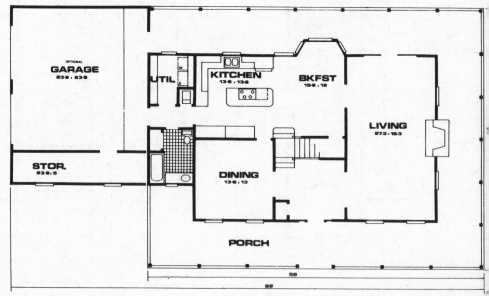

MAIN FLOOR

Plan J-86134

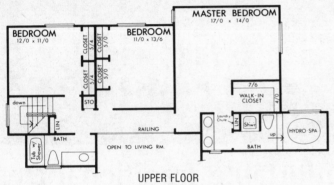

BEDROOM
12/0 x 11/0

BEDROOM
11/0 x 13/6

MASTER BEDROOM
17/0 x 14/0

CLOSET 1
5/4

CLOSET
5/4

CLOSET
5/0

CLOSET
5/0

down

STO

LIN

BATH

Tub w/ Shower

RAILING

OPEN TO LIVING RM.

7/6

WALK-IN CLOSET

4/0

Laundry Chute

LIN

Shwr

up

HYDRO-SPA

BATH

UPPER FLOOR

Grace and Prestige

- Dormer and bay windows and a hipped roof give this home a modern, yet traditional look.
- Tri-level room arrangement features a sunken living room, step-up U-shaped kitchen with island work center, and a second floor sleeping section with hallway balcony overlooking the living room.
- Living room boasts an entrance bordered by 3-ft. railings, corner fireplace, and vaulted ceilings.
- Master suite includes a convenient laundry chute, double-sink vanity, and a relaxing hydro-spa.

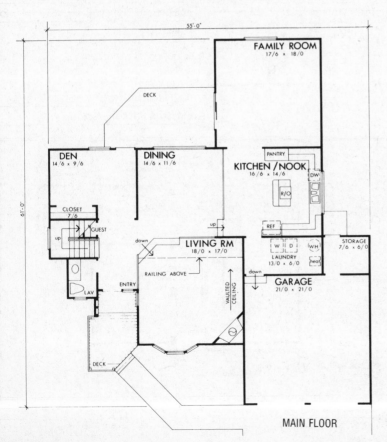

55'-0"

FAMILY ROOM
17/6 x 18/0

DECK

61'-0"

DEN
14/6 x 9/6

DINING
14/6 x 11/6

PANTRY

KITCHEN / NOOK
16/6 x 14/6

DW

R/O

REF

CLOSET
7/6

GUEST

up

down

up

LIVING RM
18/0 x 17/0

RAILING ABOVE

W D

WH

LAUNDRY
13/6 x 6/0

heat

STORAGE
7/6 x 6/0

LAV

ENTRY

VAULTED CEILING

down

GARAGE
21/0 x 21/0

DECK

MAIN FLOOR

Plan H-2123-1A	
Bedrooms: 3	**Baths:** 2½

Space:	
Upper floor:	989 sq. ft.
Main floor:	1,597 sq. ft.

Total living area:	2,586 sq. ft.
Garage:	441 sq. ft.
Storage:	45 sq. ft.

Exterior Wall Framing:	2x6

Foundation options:
Crawlspace only.
(Foundation & framing conversion diagram available — see order form.)

Blueprint Price Code:	C

HomeStyles
SOURCE 1
DESIGNERS' NETWORK

Plan H-2123-1A

Comfortable Traditional Design

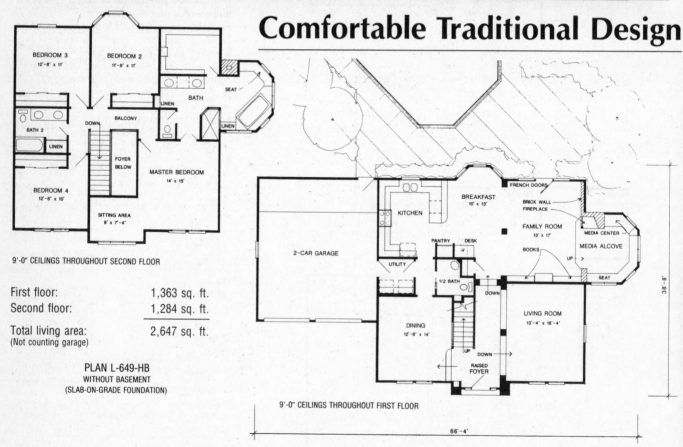

9'-0" CEILINGS THROUGHOUT SECOND FLOOR

Second floor plan:
- BEDROOM 3 — 12'-8" x 11'
- BEDROOM 2 — 11'-8" x 11'
- BATH
- SEAT
- LINEN
- BALCONY
- BATH 2
- LINEN
- DOWN
- FOYER BELOW
- MASTER BEDROOM — 14' x 15'
- BEDROOM 4 — 12'-8" x 10'
- SITTING AREA — 9' x 7'-4"
- LINEN

First floor plan:
- 2-CAR GARAGE
- UTILITY
- KITCHEN
- PANTRY
- DESK
- BREAKFAST — 10' x 13'
- FRENCH DOORS
- BRICK WALL FIREPLACE
- FAMILY ROOM — 13' x 17'
- MEDIA CENTER
- MEDIA ALCOVE
- BOOKS
- UP
- SEAT
- 1/2 BATH
- DOWN
- DINING — 12'-8" x 14'
- LIVING ROOM — 13'-4" x 16'-4"
- UP
- DOWN
- RAISED FOYER

9'-0" CEILINGS THROUGHOUT FIRST FLOOR

66'-4"

38'-8"

First floor: 1,363 sq. ft.
Second floor: 1,284 sq. ft.

Total living area: 2,647 sq. ft.
(Not counting garage)

PLAN L-649-HB
WITHOUT BASEMENT
(SLAB-ON-GRADE FOUNDATION)

Blueprint Price Code D

Plan L-649-HB

HomeStyles
Source
DESIGNERS NETWORK

Upper Floor

OPEN TO LIVING

Railing

READING AREA

CLOSET 9/6

down

LIN | BATH

HYDRO-SPA

Laundry Chute

Shr | BATH

HYDRO-SPA

LIN

6/0
4/6
9/6

WALK-IN CLOSET

BEDROOM 11/0×11/4

OPEN TO ENTRY

CLOSET 8/0

BEDROOM 13/0×10/10

BEDROOM 15/0×14/0

UPPER FLOOR

62'-0"

47'-0"

DECK

GREAT ROOM 19/6×19/0

VAULTED CEILING

NOOK 10/0×10/0

down

VAULTED CEILING

OVEN | DW

KITCHEN 10/0×15/6

RANGE

PANTRY

REF

PLAN H-2125-1 WITH BASEMENT

down

Balcony Line

LAUNDRY

D
W

Railing

LOG BIN

down

up

LINEN

STORAGE

LAV

GUEST

Laundry Chute

WH

CHINA CLOSET

heat

GARAGE 21/6×22/0

Built-in Bookcases

DESK

LIBRARY 13/0×13/0

ENTRY

Balcony Line

DINING 13/6×13/0

PORCH

MAIN FLOOR

Delightful Blend of Old and New

- A contemporary floor plan is hidden in a traditional farmhouse exterior.
- Vaulted entrance is open to the upper level; adjacent open stairwell is lit by a semi-circular window.
- French doors open into a library with built-in bookcase and deck.
- Sunken Great Room features a fireplace, vaulted ceiling open to the upstairs balcony, and French doors leading to a backyard deck.
- Roomy kitchen has center cooking island, eating bar, and attached nook with corner fireplace.
- Upper level has reading area and exciting master suite with hydro-spa.

Plans H-2125-1 & -1A

Bedrooms: 3	Baths: 2½

Space:

Upper floor:	1,105 sq. ft.
Main floor:	1,554 sq. ft.

Total living area:	**2,659 sq. ft.**
Basement:	approx. 1,554 sq. ft.
Garage:	475 sq. ft.

Exterior Wall Framing:	2x6

Foundation options:
Standard basement (Plan H-2125-1).
Crawlspace (Plan H-2125-1A).
(Foundation & framing conversion diagram available — see order form.)

Blueprint Price Code:	C

Plans H-2125-1 & -1A

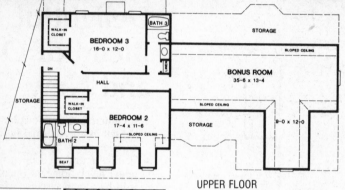

UPPER FLOOR

MAIN FLOOR

Deluxe Main Floor Master Suite

- Traditional style exterior with modern floor plan. Dormers and stone add curb appeal to this home.
- Formal entry with staircase leads to formal living or large family room.
- Large kitchen is conveniently located between formal dining room and secluded breakfast nook with bay window.
- Private master suite has trey ceiling and walk-in closet. Master bath has corner tub, shower, and dual vanities.
- Large screened porch off family room is perfect for outdoor living.
- Large utility room with pantry and toilet are conveniently located off the garage.
- Second floor features two large bedrooms with walk-in closets and two full baths.
- Optional bonus room (624 sq. ft.) can be finished as a large game room, bedroom, office, etc.

Plan C-8915

Bedrooms: 3	Baths: 3½

Space:

Upper floor:	832 sq. ft.
Main floor:	1,927 sq. ft.
Total living area:	**2,759 sq. ft.**
Bonus area:	624 sq. ft.
Basement:	1,674 sq. ft.
Garage:	484 sq. ft.

Exterior Wall Framing:	2x4

Ceiling Heights:

First floor:	9'
Second floor:	8'

Foundation options:
Daylight basement.
Standard basement.
Crawlspace.
(Foundation & framing conversion diagram available — see order form.)

Blueprint Price Code:	D

**TO ORDER THIS BLUEPRINT,
CALL TOLL-FREE 1-800-547-5570**
200 (Prices and details on pp. 12-15.)

Plan C-8915

First floor: 2,042 sq. ft.
Second floor: 900 sq. ft.

Total living area: 2,942 sq. ft.

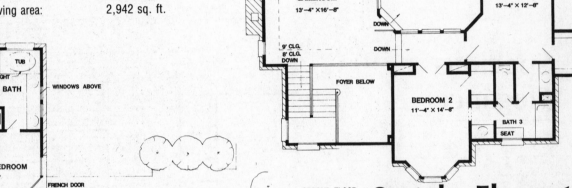

SECOND FLOOR

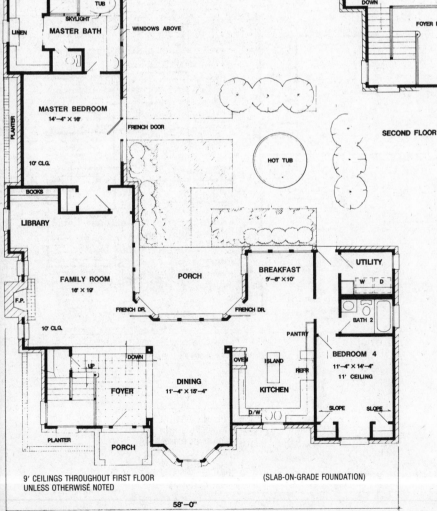

9' CEILINGS THROUGHOUT FIRST FLOOR
UNLESS OTHERWISE NOTED

(SLAB-ON-GRADE FOUNDATION)

58'—0"

(Plans for a detached
two-car garage are
included with blueprints)

Stately, Elegant And Luxurious

The front and left side elevations of this 2,942 sq. ft. home are equally impressive, with the finely detailed chimney, corner glass at the staircase, and a two-story bay window. A raised foyer steps down to a formal dining room and the family room. A U-shaped staircase leads to a balcony game area upstairs. The family room features an interior brick wall at the fireplace and a library alcove with built-in bookcase.

The master bedroom features a 10' ceiling and French doors leading to the rear yard. The master bath has an oval tub with a skylight above, a glass enclosed shower, mirrored closet doors, and a private commode area.

The kitchen has a center island, brick enclosed oven, and an efficient pantry wall. The fourth bedroom, located downstairs, is an excellent guest room or hobby room.

Upstairs, the large game room has a wet bar for entertaining, a half-bath and access to an outdoor deck. Two bedrooms have walk-in closets and private dressing areas while sharing a common bath.

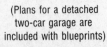
Blueprint Price Code D

Plan L-2942-C

***TO ORDER THIS BLUEPRINT,
CALL TOLL-FREE 1-800-547-5570***
(Prices and details on pp. 12-15.) **201**

Spacious
Elegance

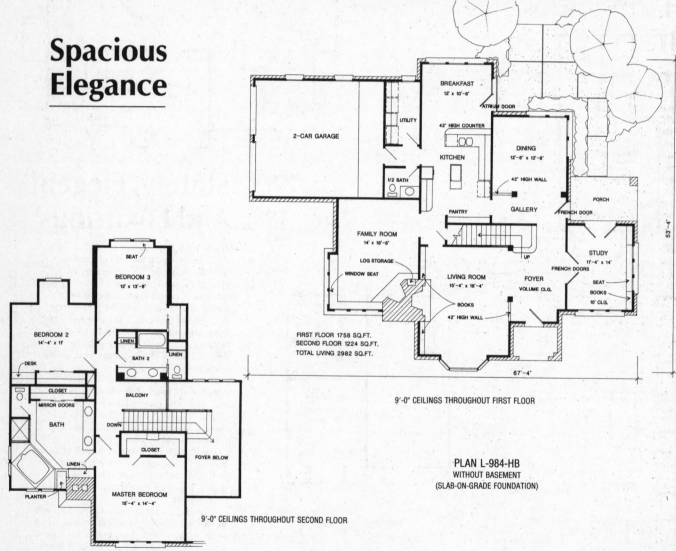

SEAT

BEDROOM 3
12' x 13'-8"

BEDROOM 2
14'-4" x 11'

DESK

CLOSET

MIRROR DOORS

BATH

LINEN

PLANTER

LINEN

LINEN

BATH 2

BALCONY

DOWN

CLOSET

FOYER BELOW

MASTER BEDROOM
15'-4" x 14'-4"

9'-0" CEILINGS THROUGHOUT SECOND FLOOR

BREAKFAST
12' x 10'-8"

ATRIUM DOOR

2-CAR GARAGE

UTILITY

42" HIGH COUNTER

DINING
12'-8" x 12'-8"

KITCHEN

1/2 BATH

42" HIGH WALL

PANTRY

GALLERY

PORCH

FRENCH DOOR

FAMILY ROOM
14' x 18'-8"

LOG STORAGE

WINDOW SEAT

UP

STUDY
11'-4" x 14'

FRENCH DOORS

LIVING ROOM
15'-4" x 18'-4"

FOYER
VOLUME CLG.

SEAT

BOOKS

10' CLG.

BOOKS

42" HIGH WALL

FIRST FLOOR 1758 SQ.FT.
SECOND FLOOR 1224 SQ.FT.
TOTAL LIVING 2982 SQ.FT.

53'-4"

67'-4"

9'-0" CEILINGS THROUGHOUT FIRST FLOOR

PLAN L-984-HB
WITHOUT BASEMENT
(SLAB-ON-GRADE FOUNDATION)

Blueprint Price Code D
Plan L-984-HB

Harmonious Blend of Old and New

A gracious wrap-around front porch with finely detailed columns and railing, and a garden room with leaded glass transom windows will appeal to the homebuyer looking for a luxury home with a harmonious blend of old and new. A two-way fireplace separates the living room with its built-in T.V. and stereo area from the garden room with its French doors and leaded transoms. The kitchen overlooks both the breakfast and the family room with its fireplace and flanking bookcases. The master bedroom has a sitting area and French doors opening to a side porch. The master bath has his and hers lavatories, an oval tub, glass enclosed shower, and a large walk-in closet.

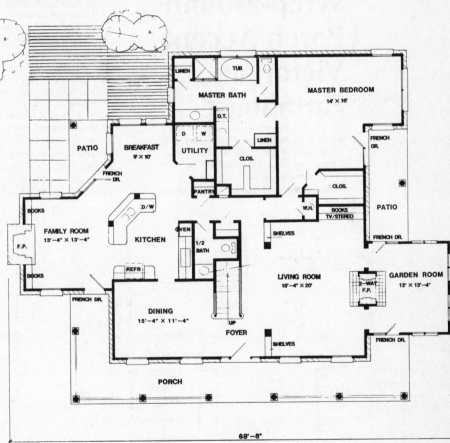

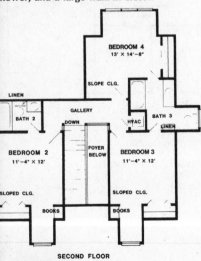

SECOND FLOOR

Main floor:	2,263 sq. ft.
Upper floor:	787 sq. ft.
Total living area:	3,050 sq. ft.

(Plans for a two-car detached garage included with blueprints)

Blueprint Price Code E

Plan L-3050-C

TO ORDER THIS BLUEPRINT, CALL TOLL-FREE 1-800-547-5570 (Prices and details on pp. 12-15.)

Wrap-around Porch Accents Victorian Farmhouse

- Fish-scale shingles and horizontal siding team with the detailed front porch to create this look of yesterday. The sides and rear are brick.
- The main level features a center section of informal family room and formal living and dining rooms. They can all be connected via French doors.
- A separate workshop is located on the main level and connected to the main house by a covered breezeway.
- The master bath ceiling is sloped and has built-in skylights. The kitchen and eating area have high sloped ceilings also. Typical ceiling heights are 8' on the basement and upper level and 10' on the main level.
- This home is energy efficient.
- This home is designed on a full daylight basement. The two-car garage is located on the basement level.

UPPER LEVEL

PLAN E-3103
WITH DAYLIGHT BASEMENT

Exterior walls are 2x6 construction.

Heated area:	3,153 sq. ft.
Unheated area	2,066 sq. ft.
Total area: (Not counting basement)	5,219 sq. ft.

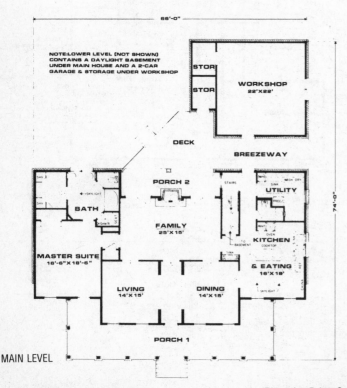

MAIN LEVEL

TO ORDER THIS BLUEPRINT, CALL TOLL-FREE 1-800-547-5570

Blueprint Price Code E
Plan E-3103

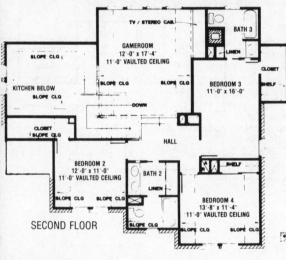

TV / STEREO CAB.

BATH 3

GAMEROOM
12'-0" x 17'-4"
11'-0" VAULTED CEILING

LINEN

SLOPE CLG

SLOPE CLG

SLOPE CLG

SLOPE CLG

CLOSET

SHELF

KITCHEN BELOW
SLOPE CLG

BEDROOM 3
11'-0" x 16'-0"

DOWN

CLOSET
SLOPE CLG

HALL

SHELF

BEDROOM 2
12'-0" x 11'-0"
11'-0" VAULTED CEILING

BATH 2

LINEN

BEDROOM 4
13'-8" x 11'-4"
11'-0" VAULTED CEILING

SLOPE CLG

SLOPE CLG

SLOPE CLG

SLOPE CLG

SECOND FLOOR

First floor:	2,114 sq. ft.
Second floor:	1,116 sq. ft.
Total living area: (Slab-on-grade foundation)	3,230 sq. ft.

(Plans for a detached two-car garage
are included with blueprints)

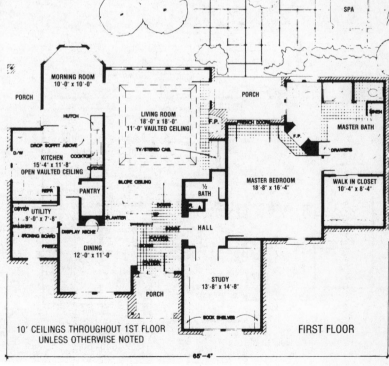

SPA

MORNING ROOM
10'-0" x 10'-0"

PORCH

PORCH

LINEN

HUTCH

LIVING ROOM
18'-0" x 18'-0"
11'-0" VAULTED CEILING

MASTER BATH

F.P.

FRENCH DOORS

F.P.

DROP SOFFIT ABOVE

D/W

KITCHEN
15'-4" x 11'-8"
OPEN VAULTED CEILING

COOKTOP

TV / STEREO CAB.

DRAWERS

OVENS

SLOPE CEILING

MASTER BEDROOM
18'-8" x 16'-4"

WALK IN CLOSET
10'-4" x 8'-4"

REFR.

PANTRY

½
BATH

DRYER
WASHER

UTILITY
9'-0" x 7'-8"

PLANTER

HALL

IRONING BOARD

DISPLAY NICHE

FOYER

FREEZER

DINING
12'-0" x 11'-0"

STUDY
13'-8" x 14'-8"

PORCH

BOOK SHELVES

10' CEILINGS THROUGHOUT 1ST FLOOR
UNLESS OTHERWISE NOTED

FIRST FLOOR

65'-4"

Dream Kitchen Adds Extra Elegance

his elegant home features arched
windows, paned glass, elaborate brickwork,
nd many other luxury touches. The raised
oyer leads into the living room, with an
ll-glass wall at the rear. The living room
eiling slopes up to 11 ft.

Other ceilings throughout the first floor
re 10 ft. high, except in the kitchen. The
itchen ceiling is 1½ stories high in the
enter, and takes up what is usually attic
pace. This deluxe kitchen also boasts a
uilt-in hutch, a serving counter near the
norning room, and a walk-in pantry.

HomeStyles
SOURCE 1
DESIGNERS NETWORK

Blueprint Price Code E

Plan L-232-TC

Deluxe Master Bedroom Suite on Main Floor

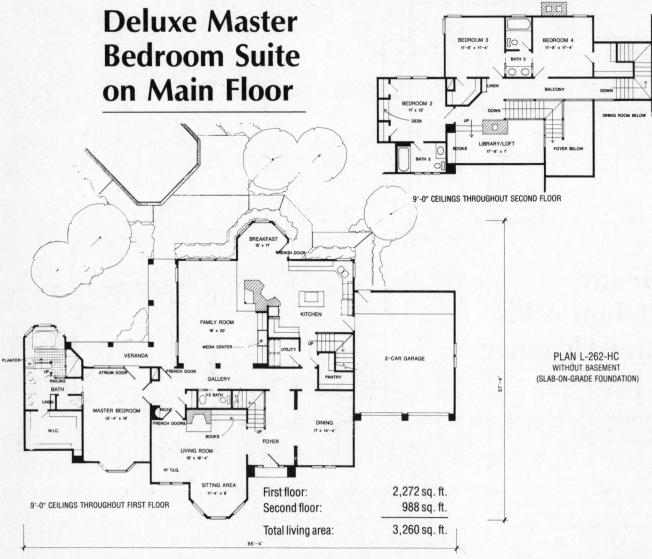

BREAKFAST
10' x 11'
FRENCH DOOR

BEDROOM 3
11'-8" x 11'-4"

BEDROOM 4
11'-8" x 11'-4"

BATH 3

LINEN

BALCONY

DOWN

BEDROOM 2
11' x 12'

DESK

DOWN

UP

DINING ROOM BELOW

LIBRARY/LOFT
17'-8" x 7'

BOOKS

BATH 2

FOYER BELOW

9'-0" CEILINGS THROUGHOUT SECOND FLOOR

FAMILY ROOM
16' x 20'

KITCHEN

MEDIA CENTER

UTILITY

UP

2-CAR GARAGE

PLANTER

VERANDA

FRENCH DOOR

GALLERY

PANTRY

ATRIUM DOOR

RAILING

UP

BATH

LINEN

1/2 BATH

MASTER BEDROOM
13'-4" x 16'

NICHE

FRENCH DOORS

BOOKS

UP

DINING
11' x 14'-4"

W.I.C.

LIVING ROOM
19' x 16'-4"

FOYER

10' CLG.

SITTING AREA
11'-4" x 6'

9'-0" CEILINGS THROUGHOUT FIRST FLOOR

PLAN L-262-HC
WITHOUT BASEMENT
(SLAB-ON-GRADE FOUNDATION)

57'-4"

86'-4"

First floor:	2,272 sq. ft.
Second floor:	988 sq. ft.
Total living area:	3,260 sq. ft.

Blueprint Price Code E

Plan L-262-HC

Elegance and Practicality

Elegant in styling, practical in livability — those words describe this 3,454 sq. ft. traditional home. An excellent family home, it has five bedrooms and three full baths.

The entry, with double front doors, leads directly to the large vaulted living room. An enormous kitchen features an island bar with a cutting board for meal preparation. The beamed dining room and adjacent family room are efficiently heated by a wood stove.

The upper level again reflects the spaciousness of the home with a balcony overlooking the vaulted living area below. The loft room can be used as a hobby or study room. Parents can relax in the luxurious master suite which features a walk-in closet and private bath. The master bedroom measures 25'6" x 14'. The master bath is also large, with double vanities, separate shower and tub, and an area for plants or seating.

Upper floor:	1,578 sq. ft.
Main floor:	1,876 sq. ft.
Total living area:	3,454 sq. ft.

(Not counting basement or garage)

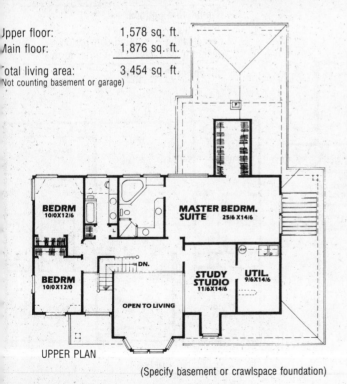

UPPER PLAN

(Specify basement or crawlspace foundation)

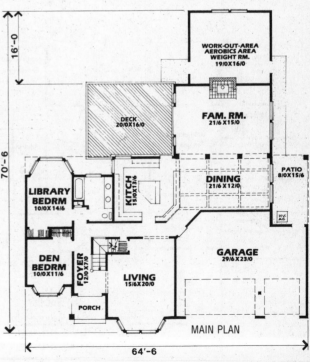

MAIN PLAN

Stately Charm

- This home exudes a stately charm that suggests gracious living on a grand style. Its 3,503 square feet provide plenty of space for family living as well as formal entertaining.
- The main floor presents a large formal dining room, spacious living room, big family room, pleasant morning room and a study with built-in bookshelves and a desk.
- The large kitchen includes a cooktop island, pantry and abundant cabinet and counter space.
- The downstairs master suite includes an ample sleeping area plus a majestic master bath with a huge walk-in closet and built-in plant shelves.
- Upstairs, you will find four more bedrooms, two more baths and a large game room with a vaulted ceiling.

Plan L-505-CG

Bedrooms: 5	Baths: 3½

Space:

Upper floor:	1,346 sq. ft.
Main floor:	2,157 sq. ft.

Total living area: 3,503 sq. ft.

Garage: (Plans for a 505 sq. ft. detached two-car garage are included with blueprints.)

Exterior Wall Framing:	2x4

Ceiling Heights: (Unless noted otherwise):

Upper floor:	8'
Main floor:	9'

Foundation options:
Slab only.
(Foundation & framing conversion diagram available — see order form.)

Blueprint Price Code:	F

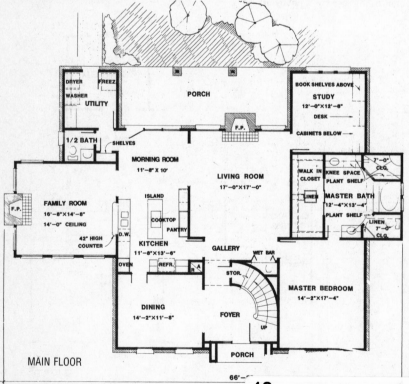

MAIN FLOOR

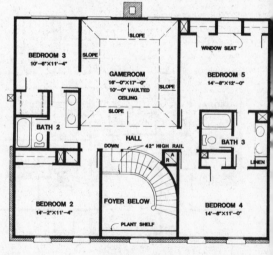

UPPER FLOOR

Plan L-505-CG